Library of
Davidson College

Innerworldly Individualism

Innerworldly Individualism

Charismatic Community and its Institutionalization

Adam B. Seligman

Transaction Publishers
New Brunswick (U.S.A.) and London (U.K.)

Copyright © 1994 by Transaction Publishers,
New Brunswick, New Jersey 08903

All rights reserved under International and Pan-American Copyright Conventions. No part of this book may be reproduced or transmitted in any form or by any means, electronic or mechanical, including photocopy, recording, or any information storage and retrieval system, without prior permission in writing from the publisher. All inquiries should be addressed to Transaction Publishers, Rutgers—The State University, New Brunswick, New Jersey 08903.

Library of Congress Catalog Number: 93–21107
ISBN: 1–56000–128–3
Printed in the United States of America

Library of Congress Cataloging-in-Publication Data

Seligman, A.
   Innerworldly individualism : charismatic community and its institutionalization / Adam B. Seligman.
      p.   cm.
   Includes bibliographical references and index.
   ISBN 1–56000–128–3 (cloth) : $34.95
   1. New England—Social conditions. 2. New England—History—Colonial period, ca. 1600–1775. 3. Civil society—New England—History—17th century. 4. Group identity—New England—History—17th century. 5. Individualism—New England—History—17th century. 6. Puritans—New England—History—17th century. 7. Church and social problems—New England—History—17th century. 8. Sociology, Christian—New England—History—17th century.   I. Title.
HN79.A11S45   1994
306' .0974—dc20   93–21107
                                                                                                       CIP

Contents

Preface and Acknowledgments   vii

Introduction   1

1. Charisma, the Church, and the Reformation   11
2. The Origins of Settlement   47
3. Protest and Collective Boundaries   73
4. The Emergent Tensions of Institutionalization   101
5. The Half Way Covenant and the Jeremiad Sermon   127
6. The Institutionalization of Charisma in Society   159
7. Conclusion   199

Bibliography   225

Index   251

Preface and Acknowledgments

Whatever else may characterize the civilization of modernity one thing is clear. Central to the modern worldview is the idea of the autonomous individual, imbued with moral agency as standing at the foundation of the social and cultural orders. From this view of the individual stems our contemporary ideas of justice and equity, our concerns with rights and entitlements, and, in fact, our conception of the proper or ideal models of the social order. It is this that sets off the civilization that developed in the Western European and North Atlantic communities at the end of the seventeenth and beginning of the eighteenth centuries from other social formations and indeed, to a large extent from their own premodern or traditional pasts.

This later statement needs some qualification. For as the work of scholars such as Ernst Troeltsch, Max Weber, Marcell Mauss, Benjamin Nelson, and, most recently, Luis Dumont have shown, it is impossible to understand the development of the idea of the individual without an appreciation of its roots in Christian civilization and the idea of, in Ernst Troeltsch's terms, the individual-in-relation-to-God. Moreover, and in terms of the thesis associated most popularly with the work of Max Weber (but central to the writings of Troeltsch, Nelson, and Dumont as well), it was only in the period of the Protestant Reformation and the transformation that ascetic-Protestantism engendered in the overall cultural assumptions of Western Christendom that the idea of the modern individual emerged.

This thesis is well known and does not warrant repeating here except to point out that it is still hotly debated. Today, ninety years have passed since Weber's *The Protestant Ethic and the Spirit of Capitalism* was first published, and while we have accumulated a good-sized library of works dealing with Weber's "Protestant Ethic Thesis," we still have little sense of the concrete historical and sociological processes through which the modern idea of the individual (whose status was enshrined in the revolutions of the eighteenth century) emerged from the religious doctrines of seventeenth-century ascetic-Protestant sects. Equally problematic is the fact that most of the diverse groups of religious virtuosi who gathered in England, France, the Netherlands, Germany, New England, and elsewhere in the late sixteenth and early seventeenth centuries, to further the work of reforming the social and spiritual orders of the world, were tied together by intense bonds of spiritual brotherhood. Their venture was a communal one and they were, in every sense of the word, religious sects. What characterized them was less the individual-in-the-world and more a charismatic community of spiritual elect imbued with the Holy Light. This fact just exacerbates the problem of the emergence of modern individualism from the communities of seventeenth-century religious virtuosi. (As does the fact that those sectarian and Pietistic groups who did articulate a doctrine of "free grace" and individual "election"–such as Quakers and Anabaptists–did not, on the whole, succeed in institutionalizing their religious doctrine beyond the boundaries of their own confession. This point is especially pertinent in the case of New England–and later the United States–which provided for Weber, as it does for us, the model for modern individualism in general.)

Indeed, what I would like to argue is that this matter of institutionalization, as idea and practice, stands as the central challenge to any attempt to understand the development of modern identities from the religious convictions of ascetic- Protestantism. The challenge then is twofold. On the historical level it involves analyzing the concrete social practices through which the religious doctrines of ascetic-Puritanism became, over the course of the seventeenth century, fundamental principles of modern social and political practice. On the theoretical level it involves explaining a seemingly intractable contradiction. For to become components of modern consciousness and sensibility, the religious doctrines of ascetic-Protestantism had to be, in some way, institutionalized within the collective. Yet, the very sectarian character of a virtuosi religion would seem, by definition, to preclude any such process of institutionalization. Weber himself, it may be noted, did not–in his analysis of Puritanism in New England–manage to overcome this contradiction. Thus, his *Protestant Ethic and the Spirit of Capitalism* analyzed the continuing importance of Puritan New England in the making of the American national identity, while in sections of *Economy and Society* he clearly sees New England Congregational Puritanism as losing its sectarian character at mid-century.

The very posing of this contradiction takes us, however, to the heart of our analysis and to the intensely communal nature of individual identities in the early modern period. Indeed, what is argued here is that any appreciation of the emergence of modern individual identities (in the eighteenth century) must be prefaced by an analysis of the changing terms of collective identities in the preceding century, which is our task here. Consequently, as we shall see, certain problems, of the institutionalization of ascetic-Protestantism and of the relations of religious virtuosi or sectarian religion to the world at large are thus central to our understanding of the modern world, however rooted they may seem to be in the problems and perspectives of a premodern and religious culture. They will, indeed, find a place of no little importance in the following analysis. For what I have attempted in this study is precisely to analyze the emergence of modern ideas of individual and collective identity in and through the concrete process of institutionalization that characterized ascetic-Protestantism in one seventeenth-century community—that of New England Congregational Puritanism.

The reasons for choosing this case are, I believe, clear. The United States provides today (as it did for Max Weber) that social formation where the idea of the autonomous, rights-bearing individual endowed with almost transcendental attributes stands most securely at the matrix of the social order. The idea of the individual was already, in 1789, enshrined within the political order and has provided for many, from that time until today, a model of modernity, as idea and ideal. However, seventeenth-century Congregational Puritanism was, as is now recognized by all historians working in the field, an intensely communal religion, where the covenant bond, uniting the "visible saints" in pursuit of the "Holy Commonwealth," was a defining feature of their religious vision. Here then, in precisely that society where individualism is (and was already in the eighteenth century) the most developed, the case for its emergence from seventeenth-century religion is most difficult to explain.

The following attempts such an explanation, which, while concentrating on the religious doctrines of the Puritan emigrants to the American Strand, seeks to isolate the processes of their institutionalization (and transformation) over the course of the seventeenth century. The title of this study thus reverses the course of historical development. The "innerworldly individualism" to which it refers is but the result of a process that began with a "charismatic community" of elect who, in the process of institutionalizing their religious vision, transformed the premises of their social existence. In this transformation a tightly bound, almost totalistic community of religious virtuosi standing in a highly ambivalent relation to the surrounding world was transformed into one of morally responsible individuals participating with a high degree of commitment in the making of a new cultural and political order. And if more time is spent on the origins and process of this transformation than on its result that is because it is these developments that have, in this context, been hitherto least explored.

The following study cannot presume to offer more than an interpretive framework for understanding this transformation. It is moreover a framework of a specific nature. For while it seeks to understand how the concrete action of social groups affected the course of historical development, it nevertheless sees these actions as structured by the overriding symbolic assumptions shared by the social actors involved. To a great extent the model of analysis adopted here sees the development (and even transformation) of seventeenth-century Congregationalism as profoundly influenced by the overriding logic of its original convictions and the attempt to implement them as principles of world mastery and social construction.

Any such entry into the world of seventeenth-century historiography can only be undertaken with great trepidation. The contemporary historical work on seventeenth-century New England is vast and can hardly be mastered in its entirety. In the following I have built on the work of many historians, providing (I can only hope) that broader and more analytic perspective allowed by the interdisciplinary approach.

There are, undoubtedly certain dangers incurred in this mode of analysis. For one, it is sure to incur the wrath of historians (always suspicious of "theory") as well as the impatience of sociologists (who will wonder just why they are being treated to esoteric debates on the relation of "sanctification," "justification," and "regeneration" in the process of salvation in order to understand the development of modern individualism). Here I can only hope that, in the end, sociologists will appreciate the relevance of these debates (or at least certain aspects of them) and that historians—however suspicious they may remain of the theoretical construct—will at least be set to thinking of the intrinsic connection between certain developments of seventeenth-century New England history (such as that between the development of protest and legal codification in the early years of settlement or between the Jeremiad and the Half Way Covenant after mid-century for example) that have not previously been explicated.

Moreover, and as I am aware, the type of analysis developed here is somewhat out of fashion these days. For while history is written from the "top down," or the "bottom up" (depending on current fashion) and anthropology from the "inside out" (or at least so it presumes) it is precisely this mode of writing that can be seen as imposed from the "outside in." And while I have attempted to refrain from blindly imposing any set of "etic" meaning on the actions and writings of seventeenth century men and women, there is little doubt that the interpretive framework employed—of charisma and its institutionalization—stems from our own contemporary categories and not those of the past.

This is however in line with the purpose of my project, which is less to draw us "nearer" the past and more to understand our debt to it. How shallow after all would our understanding of ourselves be without Ernst Troeltsch's magisterial study (and interpretation) of *The Social Teachings of the Christian Churches*. Indeed, in many ways, the following work is but an attempt to explicate the unique social consequences of the fact that, as Troeltsch indicated, "Congregationalism stands mid-way between the Calvinist church-type and the sect-type." In this cryptic statement and its implications for the developing relations between the world and the Church, between the orders of nature and those of grace, lies the seeds of any understanding of that nascent (and secular) modern consciousness that has become our own.

If, as Max Weber has claimed, "world images" often "act as switchmen determin[ing] the tracks upon which action has been pushed by interest" the image of the workings of grace in the orders of the world will remain a potent one in understanding the emergence of modern modalities of action and the type of interest that has motivated them.

In my own attempts to understand the source of modern action and interest in "world images" seemingly long since gone I am indebted to many people. S. N. Eisenstadt, Avihu Zakai, Don Handelman, Erik Cohen, and Shlomo Fischer were all critical partners in a long-standing conversation on the meaning of modern civilization that took place in Jerusalem during the 1980s in a period where the force of tradition and premodern arguments were especially salient. Part of this conversation took place within the framework of the seminar on "Utopias in Axial Age Civilizations" conducted between 1985 and 1987 at The Hebrew University of Jerusalem. Together with the other participants of this seminar I will always remain grateful (and somewhat nostalgic) for that intense intellectual experience with its own otherworldly elements and of a time now seemingly gone.

Over the years and the engagement with other themes this work has been sustained and encouraged by numerous colleagues. I would like especially to thank Craig Calhoun, Terence Evens, John Reed, Arthur Vidich, Krishan Kumar, John Hall, and Irving Louis Horowitz for their continuing support of this project and their belief in its worth.

The Jerusalem Center for Anthropological Research and the Rothchild Foundation both provided generous funding for research and study in the early years of my work on seventeenth-century New England. Many of the ideas presented here first saw the light of day in other forms. Chapter 1 is a development and reworking of themes originally published as "Christian Utopias and Christian Salvation: A General Introduction" and "The Eucharist Sacrifice and the Changing Utopian Moment in Post Reformation Christianity," in *Order and Transcendence: The Role of Utopias and the Dynamics of Civilizations*, ed. A. Seligman (Leiden: E.J. Brill, 1989), 13–43. Much of chapter 2 appeared as "Moral Authority and Reformation Religion," *International Journal of Politics, Culture and Society* 14 (Winter 1990): 159–79. Chapters 3 and 4 are developments of arguments first presented in "Protest and Institution Building in Seventeenth Century New England," *Comparative Social Research* 13 (1991): 75–103. Chapter 5 appeared as "Collective Boundaries and Social Reconstruction in Seventeenth Century New England," *The Journal of Religious History* 16 (June 1991): 260–79. Chapter 6 expands on arguments first made in "Innerworldly Individualism and the Institutionalization of Puritanism in Late Seventeenth Century New England," *British Journal of Sociology* 14 (December 1990): 537–57. Chapter 7 is based on material that appeared as "Charisma and the Transformation of Grace in the Early Modern Era," *Social Research* 58 (Fall 1991): 591–620. I am grateful to these publishers and publications for permission to use this previously published material.

Introduction

This study examines the charismatic roots of nation formation in one of the world's prototypical modern societies. Concentrating on the case of seventeenth-century New England, it makes use of a Weberian paradigm of sociological inquiry to elucidate the cosmological premises and structural preconditions for the development of "modern" conceptions of social authority and collective identity among New England communities of "covenanted saints." These, in turn, are viewed as central to our comprehension of modern nation building generally, of how it came to be that we are as we are in today's world.

More concretely, this study seeks to analyze how a particular set of cultural assumptions on the nature of collective identity and sources of social authority emerged out of the religious beliefs of the first generation of settlers in New England and crystallized three generations later into perduring patterns of normative order. These are seen to turn, most significantly, on the emergence of the individual social actor as an autonomous moral entity, on a politics based on the premises of reason and equality, and on a cultural order devoid of any transcendent matrix. The origin as well as development of these assumptions are viewed as part of a process that can usefully be conceived as the symbolization, routinization, and, in fact, institutionalization of charisma within society.

To understand this dynamic (of the institutionalization of charisma), analysis first seeks to posit the sources of charisma within Christian civilization, as well as their transformation in the period of the Protestant Reformation, especially within English Puritanism. This provides the necessary context within which to analyze the attempt of Puritan emigrants to build a "Godly Commonwealth" on the American Strand.

Thus, the emergence of new charismatic forms of social organization in the Protestant Reformation is analyzed in terms of the break engendered by the Reformation with existing definitions of the sacred as well as with dominant models of community and authority. The process of its reroutinization among Puritan communities in the New World is then studied in depth.

This more concrete analysis of seventeenth- and early eighteenth-century social developments focuses on the interaction and mutual impingement of forces of authority and frameworks of community in the first decades of settlement. Analysis suggests that the very attempt to implement the religious premises of the emigrants as the symbolic basis for social ordering led to far-reaching changes in both symbolic and organizational spheres of social life. Indeed, my analysis concerns itself with how the very dynamics of institutionalization drove a wedge—as it were—between community and authority in the first—decades of settlement. The resolution of this developing contraction between structures of authority and models of the ideal community was, as is shown, incumbent on a fundamental reworking, not only of the organizational structures of social life, but of the original religious visions themselves. It is moreover argued that precisely this reworking of the symbolic and organizational referents of Congregational Puritanism provided the necessary "preconditions" for the latter development of a uniquely American social order and "civil religion" and, by implication, a paradigm for the emerging civilization of modernity in the West.

In brief, this study attempts to place developments in New England within wider theoretical and comparative perspectives. Through relating the above perspectives with Weberian insights on the nature of ascetic Protestantism and the construction of posttraditional social centers and collectivities, this study treats seventeenth- and eighteenth-century New England as a "case-study of modernity." The specificities as well as shared characteristics of this new culture are, in the final chapter, placed within a wider historical and analytic framework.

The major theoretical assumptions underlying the mode of historical and sociological analysis used in this study were developed in response to the dual and related problems of (a) the relations of symbolic systems to constraining social structures, and (b) the dynamics of historical development in the West that saw, in the eighteenth century, civic and secular political structures emerge out of the religious and often apocalyptic visions of the seventeenth century.

These issues are addressed through a return to, and development of, the concept of charisma as originally formulated by Max Weber. The concept of charisma is developed as central to any understanding of the workings of the social order with special emphasis on its relation to the salvational doctrines of the great world-historical civilizations. Some of the core values of modernity as a civilization are further developed in terms of the secularization and transformation of charisma in the seventeenth and eighteenth centuries. The transformation of the genuinely charismatic dimension of sectarian-Protestantism is analyzed in terms of the three distinct processes of routinization, codification, and institutionalization. Though these distinctions are latent in Weber's own work, their implications for the emergence of modern civilization are not always made explicit. Thus, for example, Weber himself interpreted the developments of mid-century New England in terms of the loss of its sectarian character.[1] This study claims, rather, that a detailed study of the institutionalization of charisma within New England Puritanism reveals a fundamental restructuring of the relations between the Church and the world and so also between the Church and the sect (as sociological categories of analysis).

Charisma of course means the "gift of grace." In Weber's own work this definition was substantially broadened beyond the boundaries of Church history proper to define a mode of social organization and legitimation that was universal in its implications. This was the basis of his critique of Rudolf Sohm's relatively circumscribed usage of the term, in the context of the development of the Christian church.[2] Charisma, as originally defined by Max Weber, "applied to a certain quality of the individual personality by virtue of which he is set apart from ordinary men and treated as endowed with supernatural, superhuman, or at least specifically exceptional powers and qualities."[3] Knowing only "inner determination and inner restraint" the "call" of charisma does away with all hierarchy and differentiated spheres of authority as with all forms of economic (material) considerations.[4] Those united or subjected to its "call" are bound together by purely emotional forms of membership, by participating in its mission, by fulfilling their spiritual duty. Charismatic authority, which is "specifically outside the realm of every-day routine and the profane sphere," is thus the antithesis of all forms of traditional, rational (and bureaucratic) authority. Authority, like community, is defined, legitimized, and based solely on the continuing "proof" or "recognition" of its "call."

Elaborating on this definition, Edward Shils defined charisma as:

> the quality which is imputed to persons, actions, roles, institutions, symbols, and material objects because of their presumed connection with "ultimate," "fundamental," "vital," order-determining powers. This presumed connection with ultimately "serious" elements in the universe and in human life is seen as a quality or a state of being, manifested in the bearing or demeanor and in the actions of individual persons; it is also seen as inhering in certain roles and collectivities. It can be perceived as existing in intense and concentrated form in particular institutions, roles and individuals—or strata of individuals. It can also be perceived as existing in attenuated and dispersed form.[5]

This definition substantially broadens our understanding of charisma—organizationally, to include different types of actions, institutions, status incumbents, and collectivities, and symbolically to the notions of ultimate, fundamental, vital, and order-determining powers. The unique or "extraordinary" character imputed to charismatic personalities, institutions, or collectivities is by virtue of their contact with some transcendent power.[6] In Talcott Parsons's terms: "It is the quality which attaches to men and things by virtue of their relations with the 'supernatural,' that is, with the nonempirical aspects of reality in so far as they lend teleological 'meaning' to men's acts and events in the world."[7] Moreover, and as Talcott Parsons made clear, "men's ultimate value interests are in the nature of the case inseparably linked to their conceptions of the supernatural."[8] It was this contact with the transcendent realm, and so with the source of ultimate meaning and values, that for Weber, as for some of his followers such as Talcott Parsons and Edward Shils, constituted the source of charismatic authority. Indeed, Weber's notion of charismatic legitimation or domination was expanded by Shils, and by others such as S. N. Eisenstadt, to characterize that ultimate or "divine force" that is at the root of all authority.[9]

Consequently and in this reading, authority as well as the sources of community always maintain some charismatic dimension (however routinized it may become). This is rooted in their perceived connection to "some very central feature of man's existence and the cosmos in which he lives."[10] This central feature, and in fact power, resides in those laws or principles (indeed those "world images" noted previously) governing the universe and "creating, transforming, maintaining or destroying what is vital in man's life." Often conceived in divine terms or religious precepts (which is the sense in which we shall be using them) these can also be expressed in other terms, such as "scientific discovery, ethical promulgation, artistic creativity, political authority." All are, as Edward Shils has noted, just as much categories of the charismatic as is the prototypical case of religious prophecy.

Related to these perspectives—and as can be ascertained by reflecting on the course taken by these phenomena over history—is, what can be termed, the dual nature of charisma; that is to say, the particular propensity of charisma to be both at the root of any perduring pattern of normative order and as a force (creative or destructive) in the development of new patterns of meaning and social ordering.11 This dual nature of charisma has been treated in different ways by different social analysts. S. N. Eisenstadt, for example, has connected both the destructive and creative aspects of charisma to its inherent connection to the roots, or essence of the cosmic, social, and cultural orders.[12] This "ultimate" cast of the charismatic, according to Eisenstadt, explains its role not only in the construction of social institutions, but also in questioning the social order. For, as he notes:

> such a fervor may also contain a strong predisposition to sacrilege, to the denial of the validity of the sacred, and of what is accepted in any given society as sacred. The very attempt to reestablish direct contact with these roots of cosmic and of socio-political order may breed both opposition to more attenuated and formalized forms of this order, as well as fear and hence opposition to the sacred itself.[13]

In a somewhat different vein, the dual nature of charisma has been related to the distinction between "genuine," "pure," and institutionalized or "routinized" charisma. In this case, pure charisma is seen as a short-lived, "creative" force, erupting in times of "mass emotion" and with "unpredictable effect."[14] The creative element in this context is one of questioning existing normative order, institutional arrangements, and social structures.[15] To this may be contrasted that routinized charisma that "remains a very important element of the social structure, even though it is much transformed."[16] Addressing the dynamics of routinization in terms of its role in legitimizing authority, Weber has stressed how charisma loses its revolutionary (and hence both creative and destructive) character and, in fact, its essence:

> Instead of upsetting everything that is traditional or based on legal acquisition (in the modern sense), as it does in statu nascendi, charisma becomes a legitimation for "acquired rights." In this function, which is alien to its essence, charisma becomes a part of everyday life; for the needs which it satisfies in this way are universal.[17]

According to this view, pure charisma can be seen to be opposed to any existing social order—including those social institutions that "order" and "organize" social life through that very routinized charisma noted above.

It is in the above sense and as an "analytic instance" or "moment" of pure charisma that we shall approach the soteriological doctrines of early seventeenth-century New England Puritanism. These doctrines will therefore be seen as addressing the ultimate questions of meaning and establishing contact with that extraordinary (*ausseralltaglich*) dimension of existence.

In line with this approach, the original communities of Puritan "saints" who settled New England as part of a grand and transcendent "errand" will be treated as a charismatic community. Characterized by an immediately felt connection to the ultimate terms of salvation, these "communities of shared grace" were imbued with an *impersonalized* charisma that served as the basis of the social order.[18]

Similarly, the institutionalization of these doctrines into the fundamental terms of collective and individual identity over the course of the seventeenth century will be treated as a special case of the institutionalization of charisma in society. Such a process of institutionalization was, however, in its very nature unique. For that charismatic connection to the ultimate and vital elements of the cosmic and social orders was, within seventeenth-century New England Puritanism, posited in terms of the transcendence of history and mundane existence. When the answers to the problem of meaning are given in terms of ultimate and imminent salvation, their institutionalization becomes highly problematic. Indeed, and as we shall explore in the following chapters, the institutionalization of the original religious doctrines of New England Puritanism involved a fundamental restructuring of their soteriological assumptions and hence models of the social order. It was, we shall argue, this restructuring that proved so crucial for the ultimate emergence in the New World of modern forms of social life.

Chapter 1 reviews the historical forms through which charisma was articulated in Western Christendom, concentrating on their institutionalization in the early Church and their transformation in the Protestant Reformation of the sixteenth century. It describes the rejection of the Eucharist and of the hierarchy of apostolic succession, which were replaced by Calvinist and later Puritan "blueprints" for the reorganization of collective life through the ideas of the "holy community" of saints, bounded by the covenant. These changes are seen as essential to the construction of a this-worldly soteriology. Crucial to Puritan endeavors was the significance given to the construction of isomorphic totalities of belief, sacredness, and community. All are analyzed as critical in the reorientation of Christian salvational doctrines.

Chapter 2 takes up the prototypical model of Church and community of the Puritans who emigrated to the American Strand. Of particular importance was the idea that community and collective identity were encompassed within the Church, such that the latter established criteria of membership and boundaries of collectivity (via the covenant) that were also those of charismatic sacredness and purity. This model of the social order, built on covenanted communities of visible saints, is studied both in terms of similarities and variance from English Puritanism and, more analytically, as an instance of precisely those forms of charismatic communities generated by the break of ascetic-Protestantism with the soteriological and social doctrines of the Christian Church. Hence, definitions of both community and authority are seen to be inexorably tied to a new charismatic locus of existence defined by the gathered churches of regenerate saints (rather than by a sacerdotal order). Moreover, the very real attempt to construct the "Holy Commonwealth" within the workings of historical time is presented as both the defining element of the Congregational "errand into the wilderness" as well as the source of contradictions and inherent conflicts.

Chapters 3 and 4 deal in fact with the attempts to codify and institute sacred modes of social order, which generated alternative models of ordering society and so also alternative loci of collective identity and social authority. Thus, the Antinomian crisis (analyzed in chapter 3) was itself the product of the very attempt to implement those Puritan symbolic models (discussed in chapter 2) as the basis of the social order. The very terms of institutionalization tended to be diffuse and to open a variety of competing ways to interpret the moral and social orders. Attempts to establish a genuinely charismatic definition of social existence generated limits on the actualization of charismatic qualities in social life. Thus, for example, the institutionalization of Church authority conflicted with the symbolic model of the holy community of saints participating in the experience of grace. The continuing interplay of disjunction and contradiction, generated by the attempts to institutionalize charisma did not however produce routinization and stabilization, but rather a ferment of opposition and schism. In attempting to address this reality, analysis concentrates on the dialectical relationship between authority and community as these were affected by the dynamics of social growth and development.

Chapter 5 analyses the two major and transformative developments of mid-seventeenth-century New England Puritanism—the Half Way Covenant and the jeremiad sermon. Both were attempts to resynthesize the symbolic models and organizational mechanisms of collective identity in the face of the emergent crises discussed in the previous chapters. Through these developments, both external and internal boundaries of collectivity were loosened. On the one hand, criteria for membership were relaxed, on the other, the moral boundaries of the community, those distinguishing between "visible saints" and unregenerate members, was broken down. In a sense, the "world" was brought fully into the Church. Concomitantly, there emerged an ideal and mythical view of past generations (through the jeremiads) that provided the basis for the crystallization of a new collective identity.

Chapter 6 analyses the mechanisms through which charisma moved beyond the original "religious" premises of New England Puritanism, toward an embryonic civil tradition within which the Church (the sacred order) and the profane order were interwoven. Through such developments as Stoddard's form of Church organization, Cotton Mather's religious societies, the rise of "sacramentalism," the rise of a new piety, and religious revivalism, the Church was brought into the "world." More significantly, the interplay of sacred and profane was itself moved from the public sphere of religious and social action into the private soul of the individual. This "interiorization of boundaries" located the normative order and the responsibility for its upkeep within each individual. In turn, this led to the sacralization of the political sphere, to the idea of citizenship (perhaps peculiar to the United States) as infused with a sacred dimension through the "privatization of collective grace."

Chapter 7, the concluding chapter, argues how a genuinely charismatic, religious locus of collective identity and authority became integral to both the political and religious spheres and so to the future of revolutionary political action in the United States. The above noted perspectives, of the sacralization of this-worldly political action and the interiorization of grace, are presented as central components of modernity as a form of civilization. By placing developments in New England within a broader and comparative perspective both the shared components and unique nature of this development are highlighted.

It is my hope that this study can contribute to the development of new approaches to historically oriented sociological research, ones that will integrate (empirical) historical and (theoretical) sociological methods and perspectives. Ultimately, any truly informed sociological analysis of historical developments must take account of the importance of what Weber termed "ideal interests" and structures of significance in the formation of the more organizational and structural aspects of social life.[19] Along these lines, the current study attempts to use early American society as a laboratory to develop and elucidate some of the central problems of sociological theory and it uses this theory to illuminate broad patterns of this early American history in turn.

In sum, this study addresses not only such major issues of sociological inquiry as social change, the emergence of process from structure and structure from process, and the role of charisma in social ordering. More substantively, it seeks also to increase our understanding of the ideological and social processes underpinning early American history and of their contributions to the formation of modern forms of civil identity from the religious visions of the seventeenth century.

Notes
1. Max Weber, *Economy and Society* (Berkeley: University of California Press, 1978), 1208.
2. Ibid., 1112.

10 Innerworldly Individualism

3. Ibid., 241.
4. Max Weber, *On Charisma and Institution Building,* ed. S.N. Eisenstadt (Chicago: University of Chicago Press, 1968), 19, 68, 20, 50.
5. Edward Shils, *Center and Periphery: Essays in MacroSociology* (Chicago: University of Chicago Press, 1975), 127.
6. Weber, *On Charisma,* 19.
7. Talcott Parsons, *The Structure of Social Action* (New York: The Free Press, 1968), 668.
8. Ibid., 669.
9. The term, significantly, is Weber's own appearing in *Economy and Society,* 1147.
10. This and the following quotes in this passage are taken from Shils, *Center and Periphery,* 258–59.
11. Weber, *On Charisma,* xviii-xxxiv.
12. S. N. Eisenstadt, "Comparative Liminality, Liminality and the Dynamics of Civilizations," *Religion* 15 (1985): 321–22.
13. Weber, *On Charisma,* xli-xlv.
14. Weber, *Economy and Society,* 1146.
15. On the revolutionary nature of charisma, see Weber, *Economy and Society,* 1115–17.
16. Ibid., 1146.
17. Ibid., 1122–23.
18. On this concept, see Wolfgang Schluchter, *The Rise of Western Rationalism: Max Weber's Developmental History* (Berkeley: University of California Press, 1981), 124.
19. On this concept, see Max Weber, "The Social Psychology of the World Religions," in *From Max Weber: Essays in Sociology,* ed. H. H. Gerth and C. W. Mills (New York: Oxford University Press, 1946), 267–301.

1

Charisma, the Church, and the Reformation

If, as I hope to show, the category of charisma and its institutionalization will prove a useful tool in understanding the organizational and symbolic transformation of seventeenth-century New England Puritanism, and so also of the emergence of certain salient aspects of modern consciousness, some preliminary spadework is needed. For the definition of charisma as well as the dynamics of its routinization are different in different historical societies. Charisma is represented very differently in Western Christendom and in Theravada Buddhism, for instance. Moreover, its routinization within Christian civilization in general and New England Puritanism in particular took place along very particular lines. In the former case this was characterized by the differentiation of the Church from the world, and in the latter, as we shall see, by a unique form of their reintegration. More to the point, and as will be argued below, the very nature of its institutionalization within Christendom, underwent a major transformation with the Protestant Reformation.

Accordingly, the first task of this study is to place New England Puritanism within its historical and analytical context. This can be accomplished by studying the nature and modes of institutionalization of charisma within the Western Christian tradition.

Preliminary Distinctions

One of the most important, if preliminary, differentiations that must be made in analyzing Christian civilization is the "Axial" nature of this civilization.[1] That is to say, Christianity was one of the civilizations in which there emerged and became constitutionalized in the period between 500 B.C.E. AND 600 A.D.

> a conception of a basic tension between the transcendental and the mundane orders, a conception which differed greatly from that of a close parallelism between these two orders or their mutual embedment which was prevalent in so-called pagan religions, in those very societies from which these post-Axial Age civilizations emerged.[2]

The emergence of these Axial civilizations followed a period of institutional breakdown characterized by a similar breakdown of cosmological symbolism. This period, in Eric Voeglin's terms, of "cosmological disintegration" during different "times of troubles" resulted in a new appreciation of the relations between the individual and society to the cosmic order.[3] The change was accomplished through the fundamental restructuring of the terms of relations between mundane and transcendent orders. As has been noted by S. N. Eisenstadt and others, the emergence of this conception in the civilizations of ancient Israel, ancient Greece, China, and Islam, and in the religions of Christianity, Hinduism, and Buddhism constituted a major force in the restructuring of the terms of collective life and of the principles of political legitimation.[4] For with the conception of a "higher," transcendent order to which the political realm had to orient and legitimize itself, the "King-God" disappeared and the notion of the accountability of rulers and collectivities to a higher order arose.

In the context of the present study the differentiation between Axial and non-Axial civilizations is of utmost importance. For the Axial break (and the emergence of what has in other contexts been termed the *Great Civilizations* or *Historical Religions*) presumed a fundamental reordering of the nature of relations between society and "the powers governing the cosmos."[5] Breaking down their mutual interpenetration, the Axial age posited a new conception of the social order, autonomous of, but in tension with, the cosmic (henceforth conceived of as transcendent) sphere. Moreover, without the institutionalization of such a conception of the chasm between mundane and transcendental orders (between society and the cosmos) and the concomitant search to overcome this chasm, no salvational tradition is possible. Henceforth, in those Axial civilizations where this conception developed, the charismatic dimension of existence became identified with the soteriological bridge, with the process of salvation.

Central, and in fact, illustrative of this transformation is the time sense inherent in salvational religions, and most saliently, the notions of "final time," a cultural orientation that does not exist as such in pre-Axial social settings. As pointed out by G. Van der Leeuw, the primitive (non-Axial) man

> knows primordial time, which for him dominates all life, which is renewed over and over again in the present day occurrences that are the guarantee of this life. As long as he performs the rites correctly, he creates his world anew each day, in a manner of creatio continua. The creative word of myth renews the world for him.[6]

Compare this characterization with that break in temporal conceptions that marked the emergence of Axial civilizations:

> On the one side, time takes a cyclical course, on the other it has a beginning before which there was nothing and an end with which it stops. On the one side every sunrise is a victory over chaos, every festival a cosmic beginning, every sowing a new creation, every holy place a foundation of the cosmos, every historical event a rise or fall according to the regular course of the world and even the law that sustains society is nothing other than the rule of the sun's course. . . . On the other side, everything is exactly the same except that at a certain point in the cycle someone appears who proclaims a definitive event, the day of Yahweh, the last judgement, the ultimate salvation, or the final conflict as in Iran. The images used are all borrowed from the course of nature: day and night, summer and winter. But the ethos has changed; a hiatus has been made between, a tempus in the strict sense, which changes everything.[7]

This conception of final time, of an eschatology, a notion of both the beginning and end of historical time, was unique to certain Axial civilizations. Christianity was one of those civilizations whose soteriological orientations were concerned not with the restructuring of a once dominant cultural system but with annihilating the temporal and historical nature of both individual and collective existence. Its *locus classicus* was not in a return to a past state but in overcoming the insecurities and exigencies of *any* historical order.

In the Christian context, especially given our concern with developments following the Protestant Reformation, this perspective necessitates analysis of the connection between charisma and the major salvational doctrines of the Christian religion. Similarly and crucially, analysis must isolate those specific institutional arenas in which this connection was made. For it was primarily through a break with existing symbolic orders and organizational frameworks that new charismatic images were institutionalized and Puritan religiosity was defined. Moreover, any understanding of the specific role of Puritan religious orientations in constituting patterns of authority and collective identity in seventeenth-century New England (and anywhere else for that matter) must take into account the above connections and their sociological determinants.

It must further be noted that the intimate link between charisma and the construction of new models of authority and collective identity was not a peculiarly Protestant or Puritan phenomenon, but, as one parameter of the institutionalization of charisma, was constitutive of Christian civilization in general. What was unique to certain post-Reformation collectivities, however, was precisely the break effected with the dominant post-Augustinian notions of authority and community—a break that was itself related to the transformation of charisma and with it to the articulation of new models of social action.

Charisma and Its Transformation in the Early Church

As we have seen, the specific nature of charisma within Western Christendom stood in direct relation to the "Axial" nature of Christian civilization. That is to say, the locus of charisma and the sacred within society became linked to the particular soteriological message of Christianity. In the broadest of terms, this implied the restructuring and indeed the total negation and subsequent transformation of the mundane world in line with the image of the Kingdom of God. The coming of the Kingdom and the replacement of all the existing material and spiritual orders with the order of grace where "His will be done on earth as it is now being done only in Heaven" was of course the core of Christian soteriology. The coming of the Kingdom would thus replace the damaged and inherently faulty (since the Fall) world of nature (and of man) with the perfection of grace. And it was in preparing for this Kingdom—in line with Jesus's summons—that many of the early Christian communities, "in looking out for the Kingdom of God," became identified with the Kingdom itself.[8] In early Christianity, this resulted in the linkage of charisma (as "the gift of grace") with eschatological expectations of final salvation, the expectation of the

Parusia and the message of ultimate transcendence and end to historical time as prophesied in the *Book of Revelation*.

Indeed, until the fifth century, what may be termed *millennial orientations* (in the sense of expectation of "imminent, total, ultimate, this-worldly, collective salvation") were an integral component of Christian belief.[9] Among the different groups that constituted the early Christian communities, millenarian doctrines and orientations emerged with various degrees of saliency, with the Montanists of the second and third centuries being the most important and influential.

With the growing institutionalization of the Church and the need for the Christian faith to legitimize itself in the face of the alternate world visions of Hellenism and Judaism on the one hand and the Eastern mystery religions on the other, the apocalyptic visions of the early Christians underwent a fundamental reorientation.[10] Central to this process were the ideas of Augustine of Hippo, who transformed the City of God from an eschatological vision into a mystical territory incarnate in the Church and united by no temporal bonds other than common participation in the sacraments. Augustine's *City of God* appeared between 413 and 426 and that dualism between sacred and profane realms, which characterized his thinking, was to leave its mark on the Christian interpretations of the *Book of Revelation* (and the other eschatological texts of *Daniel* and *Enoch*) for over a millennium.

Thus, by the fifth century, the this-worldly doctrine of grace underwent a drastic change as the City of God was projected into a transcendent, unhistorical, and otherworldly realm.[11] So to and from 431 and the denunciation of millennialism by the Council of Epheson, millennialism as a sociocultural orientation achieved in Christian Europe a dual articulation: on the one hand, a nonradical, allegorical interpretation locating the millennium in the present community of believers organized into the Church; and, on the other, a radical, earthly, historically perceived, and future directed articulation of millennial doctrines. This more this-worldly interpretation of millennial doctrines continued to be articulated throughout pre-Reformation Europe as part of a radical tradition of protest.[12]

This marginalization of eschatological visions notwithstanding, it is nevertheless necessary to differentiate between the nature of charisma among the early Christian communities and the particular modes of its institutionalization within the organizational frameworks of society from the fourth century on. For, as we shall see in the following, the Reformation represented, to a great extent, a break with the patterns of institutionalized charisma that had characterized Western Christendom and an attempt, similar to that of the early Christians to construct a new moral order for the organization of social life.[13]

Symbolically, the original Christian vision posited new models of bridging the "transcendental chasm" through a greater interweaving of this- and otherworldly activities, a new stress on individual salvation and a linear and teleological time perspective that posited both a definite beginning and an end to historical time.[14] These dimensions of Christian salvation contained a strong eschatological element, which, as noted, was a strong "defining" element of the early Christian communities.

On the institutional level, the development of early Christianity saw the construction of a new "moral community" of believers differentiated from the societies in which they lived and united by bonds of exclusive communal fellowship.[15] These groups of early Christians, scattered across the Roman Empire, were united by social ties of a charismatic nature. Cutting across existing solidarities of kith and kin, the message of the early Church was one of a social solidarity rooted only in a shared experience of the sacred. In the words of St. Paul, "There is neither Jew nor Greek, there is neither bond nor free, there is neither male nor female: for ye are all one in Christ Jesus."[16] These new communities epitomized the "communitas" that stood at the root of the Christian charismatic organization.[17] Explicitly enjoined to see themselves as a community apart from the social world in which they existed, the early Christians shared with all charismatic groups a tie rooted in their immediate relation to that ultimate source of meaning and values beyond the immediacies of everyday life. This tie to the transcendental locus of meaning was expressed in the Christian context in the mystery of the Corpus Christi:

> For as the body is one, and hath many members, and all the members of that one body, being many, are one body: all also is Christ. For by one Spirit are we all baptized into one body, whether we be Jews or Gentiles, whether we be bond or free; and have been all made to drink into one Spirit.[18]

It was symbolized ultimately in the sacrament of the Eucharist wherein "each individual formed a part of the community of true communicants, sharing together the promise of eternal life."[19]

Early Christianity thus presented an alternative locus of social identity and of community that was rooted in the experience of grace. The bond established between communal members was one rooted not in primordial givens, but in an immediate connection to the fount of transcendental order. The new locus of communal solidarity and of the moral order was epitomized in St. Paul's rejection of the "ascriptive confines of Jewish ethical monotheism."[20] This rooting of the definitions of community in the experience of grace and a direct relation to the source of cosmic order and salvation (and not in legal prescriptions or primordial networks) allows us to speak of the early Christian ties of community and authority as essentially of a genuinely charismatic nature.

The purely charismatic state is, however, as Weber pointed out, only existent "in statu nascendi"—constituting, as it does, the negation of all ordered and institutionalized modes of social action.[21] In terms of Christian doctrine, this meant that the transformation of the early and "charismatic" communities of Christian believers into one Church, holy and apostolic, involved the institutionalization of the charismatic dimension of the early Christians.

Of major analytic importance to the process of institutionalization was the specific nature of charisma in Christian civilization. For, with charisma originally defined in terms of imminent, total, ultimate, and this-worldly salvation, the very act of its routinization and institutionalization in the world involved a fundamental contradiction. Expectations of final time and ultimate transcendence stood, after all, in continual tension to the mundane exigencies of daily life. The very negation of the world and worldly affairs inherent in the idea of grace stood in constant contrast to the realities of historical existence. Consequently, the institutionalization of charisma within Christian civilization was symbolically structured by the continual existence of this tension between the specific definitions of charisma (as grace) and the very process of its institutionalization (within what were, by definition, the mundane organizational structures of the Church).

With time and the growing needs of maintaining an institutional structure, the early visions of Christianity, as well as its soteriological premises, underwent a fundamental transformation. The dynamics of institution building, of establishing pervading and long lasting definitions of communal membership and equally hegemonic structures of authority, resulted in a shifting emphasis that tended toward a relative

18   Innerworldly Individualism

separation of this- and otherworldly modes of salvation and an increasing otherworldly interpretation of the Christian *Endzeit*. As a result, the original expectations of the final transcendence of history, which had characterized the early Christian communities, were seriously attenuated.[22]

Thus, what was essentially a process of routinization saw, in the early Church of the second and third centuries, the development of fixed points of dogma, established models of social action, and, with the office of the bishopric, a hierarchic structure of roles and offices. In short, what occurred was the growth and development of hierarchic structures of authority at the expense of the earlier, relatively undifferentiated, "charismatic band" of the faithful.[23]

The developing structures of authority were, however, as with the new models of community, rooted in prior relation of the apostles to the savior, as indeed was expressed in the principle of apostolic succession.[24]

> Age has succeeded age, bishop followed bishop, and the office of bishop and the principle of Church government has been handed down, so that the Church is established on the foundations of bishops, and every act of the Church is directed by those same presiding officers.[25]

With the growing institutionalization of Christian life there thus emerged new structures of authority—bishoprics and holders of priestly office who, by the end of the third century, effectively monopolized all channels of communion with the transcendent order.[26] It was only through the ministrations of those holding these positions that the new Christian could participate in the new community and share its particular salvational promise.

This latter development of specific institutional roles whose incumbents were dispensers of grace was a crucial component in the transformation of primitive Christianity into an institutionalized religion capable of "world building," organizational expansion, and, in the final analysis, civilization construction.

The Sacraments and the Changing Soteriological Arena of Christianity

Within Christian civilization, the meeting of unfulfilled intimations of grace with the realities of historical existence and the need to perpetuate collective existence within the world led to a particular dynamic of institutionalization. The process of institution building and collectivity construction that characterized the growth of the Church involved a fundamental transformation of its original message. For that which had united the original "charismatic" communities of early Christianity, the belief in Christ's Second Coming, and the fulfillment of the eschatological prophecies laid out in the Revelation of St. John was transformed. In this transformation, the originally "purely charismatic" locus of eschatological belief was routinized and embedded in specific institutional structures and roles, as well as in a ritual system: that of the sacraments.[27]

Of crucial importance to the process of institutionalization in medieval Christianity was its underlying dynamic. Inherent to it was the growing separation of this-worldly and otherworldly realms of social action, as opposed to their imminently perceived union inherent in eschatological expectations. In more concrete terms, this dualism was expressed in the growing separation between religious and political realms and the increasing negation of historical, this-worldly action as relevant to the process of salvation. Reaching its apogee in the thirteenth century with the crystallization of an embracing sacramental theology, the dualism and inherent tension between this-worldly and otherworldly orders within Christendom was articulated in the contradiction between the world and the Church, between nature and grace.[28]

The organizational implications of this development were manifest in the relative separation between ecclesiastical and civil spheres and the need to define discrete loci of authority and community in each. The ensuing tension between this-worldly and otherworldly realms was articulated in various ways in the course of the medieval era. It was expressed not only in the conflicts between ecclesiastic and civil powers over spiritual or temporal supremacy, but in the Church itself, as the abiding dualism between the Church as *corpus mysticum* and as *corpus regens,* as the governing organ of Christendom. Central to the resolution of this tension both within the Church and between the Church and the world was the growth of a sacramental theology. And while a coherent sacramental doctrine only emerged in the thought of Thomas Aquinas, its importance to the routinization of charisma was realized well before, in the writings of Augustine.

Through the representation of the original charismatic locus of Christianity in the sacraments, the cosmological vision of the early Church became an element in the growth of its organizational structure. Evident in the third-century debates around baptism and the Eucharist and in the later Christological doctrine of Cyril (d.444) and Theodore (d. 428) the charismatic dimension of Christian existence was, with time, incorporated into the sacraments and through them into the institutional structure of the Church.[29]

A further aspect of this institutionalization was its effect on the temporal orientations of Christianity. For, as noted, the early Christian communities lived in an intense expectation of the Second Coming and the End of Days, which, until the third and fourth centuries, retained their "this-worldly" character. This belief was articulated temporally in the notion of linear time with its teleological thrust and kairotic dimension. As has been noted by scholars, the Christian notion of time stood in marked distinction from Greco-Roman views of cyclical, ever returning time, which were themselves interwoven with Greek cosmology, conceptions of *arete* and of the soteriological premises of Hellenistic civilization (as exemplified in the actions of the hero in his struggle contra *fortuna*).[30] Similarly, the temporal conceptions of Christianity were bound up with the overarching conceptions of order—especially as compared to the nature of the relation of mundane to cosmic orders. For the linear temporality of Christianity, in positing an end to historical/mundane time, also posited the ultimate reunion of historical and sacred dimensions of time through its eschatological notions.

This temporal conception, bearing as it does on Christian beliefs on the workings of grace within the orders of history, was, however, through its very nature, a centrifugal, antinomian force, working against the concrete needs of institution building as perceived by many of the early Church fathers (in both the ante-Nicene and post-Nicene periods). Indeed, this "centrifugal" tendency was manifest in the reigns of Constantine and Theodosius, when an "apocalyptic separatism" led many groups of Christians beyond the boundaries of a Church tainted by its compromise with secular authority. Its potentially disruptive force was fought by none as strongly as by St. Augustine, who, in his writings, especially in the *City of God* and his *Confessions,* laid out a different temporal scheme, which, while maintaining the linear structure of sacred time, removed its "end" from any possible embedment in the mundane sphere of secular historical processes.[31] In its stead, he posited the "end of time" beyond time proper and beyond history, thus separating salvation from society and history from eschatology. In temporal terms, the separation of the *civitas terrena* and *civitas Dei* effected an ultimate disjunction of sacred and mundane times, and "histories," by declaring events in the *saeculum* irrelevant to the schema of salvation.[32]

The disembedment of sacred time from mundane historical referents dictated, however, the necessity of positing a new realm where people and especially Christians could orient their lives to the fount of the sacred. On the most general level, this was achieved through the ministrations of the Church. As pointed out by J. G. A. Pocock:

> The papal church rested upon the Augustinian divorce between eschatology and history; it denied redemptive significance to the structure and history of any secular society, while claiming itself to act and exercise authority as a bridge between civitas Dei and saeculum, a kind of institutionalization of the nunc-stans.[33]

More concretely, the realization of the sacred was achieved in the sacraments, which took, in Augustinian theology, a foremost position. For the rites of the sacrament provided that arena in which the communicant could establish contact with the sacred dimension of existence. The sacraments thus became that arena where sacred and profane meet, as opposed to the previously imminent perceived union at the end of historical time.

The derivatives of this change in the articulation of sacred time were felt in the meaning ascribed to the sacraments in general, but most specifically to that of the Eucharist, which, from the ninth century, embodied not only the Corpus Christi, but one of the most important loci of the charismatic dimension of Christian belief.

The importance of the Eucharist was already existent in the fifth century when, through communion, the individual believer not only participated in Christ, but, through such participation in the "medicine of immortality" realized, if only momentarily, the promise of eternal grace.[34] Moreover, while baptism maintained its role as the most important sacrament through the twelfth century, the Eucharist slowly emerged in the Middle Ages as one of the most important channels of grace. Thus, the controversy in the ninth century over the "real presence," reopened in the eleventh century by Berangar of Tours (d. 1088), culminated in the thirteenth-century doctrine of the primacy of the Eucharist.³⁵ The sacrament of the Eucharist, which originally celebrated community and shared grace among the early Christians, became at this time the primary vehicle for institutionalized grace and so also the primary mode of constituting and maintaining the authority of the Church, as well as a central mechanism in defining the boundaries of collective identity.³⁶ Similarly, while it was only in the thirteenth century and in the thought of Thomas Aquinas that the sacrament of the Eucharist emerged as the most important source of grace, its intimate link with the charismatic (and eschatological) dimensions of Christian thought were evident much earlier.³⁷

That the articulation of grace within the early Christian Eucharist was essentially eschatological in nature is a point that has been noted by numerous scholars.³⁸ Some scholars, notably Gilles Quispel, go even further and contend a continuous articulation of "proleptic eschatology" into the period of patristic Christianity and beyond. The Eucharist as "Messianic banquet of rejoicing, an anticipation of the lord's eschatological *beraka* with his disciples in the Kingdom of God" was thus a ritual that united in one act individual salvation with the ultimate principles of meaning and cosmic ordering rooted in the Christian telos.³⁹ These principles were themselves rooted in the eschatological promise of Christianity. For the Christian ordering of the social world and of history was, as noted, rooted in their particular concept of rectilinear kairotic time, "bound up with Creation and the continuous action of God . . . unfolding unilaterally in one direction, beginning at a single source and aiming towards a single goal."⁴⁰

However, as we have seen, this temporal dimension of Christian belief had been transformed with the institutionalization of the Church. No longer embedded in the processes of historical time—in terms of this-worldly activities and soteriologies—grace and the promise of ultimate transcendence had been removed to a realm beyond time and history to that of otherworldly and ritual activity. The Eucharist thus became that ritual arena where the this-worldly intimations of divine grace (in the orders of the world), which had characterized early Christian belief, were transformed and separated from the process of historical time and activity in the *saeculum*. In brief, the realization of grace in the Eucharist precluded or substituted for its realization within history.

In channeling the early eschatological dimension of Christian belief into the ritual of the Eucharist, the Eucharist itself attained its meaning as the (institutionalized) charismatic locus of collective identity and also of social authority. The communicant participating in the sacrament asserted in the rite four interrelated dimensions of existence: his community with other Christians; his acceptance of the priest's authority rooted in the principle of apostolic succession; and the ("iconic") realization of his own salvation, as well as of that of other believers, in the ultimate end of history.

In terms taken from the sociology of religion, it is possible to express this set of relationships as a communion with the sacred and so with the charismatic locus of existence. Important for us is the fact that this sacred experience contained a temporal dimension.[41] Entering into the realm of the sacred, the communicant entered as well the arena of sacred time.[42] Indeed, the term *proleptic eschatology* is an expression of the particular temporal dimension contained in the sacrament of the Eucharist. For the sacred time defined by the sacramental rite was that eschatological time marked off by Christ's *kairos*.

The institutional delineation of this sacred time, bounded by the organizational restraints of the Church and the linking of this sacred/charismatic locus with the ultimate eschatological promise of Christianity, was indeed one of the fundamental prerequisites for the institutional expansion of the Church.[43] It is important to note in this context the intimate link of charisma with the notion of ultimate salvation, which was, in a sense, mandated by the Axial nature of the Christian belief system and the particular solutions it posited to the problem of salvation.

The channeling of charisma within the institutional framework of the Church meant, moreover, that the loci of both collective membership and of authority would be similarly channeled. This much is clear from the very Weberian definition of charisma and its routinization. What is more central to our own problem, however, is that this channeling united the structures of authority and of collective identity with the particular resolution of the soteriological problem in Christianity. Such a union, through the connection maintained between the rite of the Eucharist and existing structures of authority and definitions of community, bound Christian visions of ultimate salvation to the particular institutional structure of the Church that emerged in the fourth and fifth centuries. By defining sacred time in eschatological terms and uniting it on the level of social organization with the particular patterning of relations of authority and collective identity defined by the one holy and Catholic church, any alternative symbolic or institutional articulation of the sacred was essentially precluded.[44] From this perspective it is not at all surprising that the Eucharist achieved its primacy as a source of grace in the same period that the Church (through the papal bull *Unam Sanctum* of 1303) identified itself with the *corpus mysticum*. The otherworldliness of Christian salvation was at this time intimately linked to a definition of Christian community and authority centered in the Church.[45]

Change and Transformation in the Reformation

The soteriological beliefs of medieval Christianity were, as is well known, transformed in the Protestant Reformation of the sixteenth century and especially in the development of Calvinist theology.[46] Calvinism essentially implied the establishment of a new type of moral bond between communal members, and therefore a redefinition of the terms of collective membership and the legitimation of authority. More than Luther's "priesthood of believers," which, while positing a break with the Church, did not posit a similar break with the overriding social definitions of community, followers of Calvinist doctrine in England, Scotland, the Netherlands, France, and Geneva tended to be bounded by new ties of fellowship as well as by notions of a new type of moral authority based on inner conscience.[47]

In terms of our own interests the break effected within the Reformation with the dominant assumptions of the Church on the nature of collective identity and social authority was essentially a break with the institutionalized loci of charisma in society. This achieved its most salient expression in the thought of John Calvin on the primacy of grace and the subordination of natural law to divine sovereignty.[48] From this perspective the way was opened for a new mode of institutionalizing charisma, through uniting the hitherto disparate realms of nature and grace. In Ernst Troeltsch's words:

> At this point [in Calvinism] it was Protestantism alone which drew Nature and Grace together, since in its view the redeeming Will of Grace both gave each man his secular task in the World and made it the normal sphere, necessary for everyone, for the exercise of the spirit inspired by Divine Grace.[49]

The search for a new unity between the world and the Church, based on the primacy of grace and aimed at the creation of a "Holy Community," represented a major break with the pervading models of institutionalized charisma within Christendom, which—as we have seen—was based on the separation between this-worldly and otherworldly activity. By bringing the mundane sphere into the realm of grace, Calvinism opened the way for a new unity of this-worldly and otherworldly orientations and activities. This transformation, which, in a sense, nullified the dominant modes of institutionalized charisma, stood at the root of that "innerworldly" or "intramundane asceticism which logically and comprehensively recognizes all secular means, but which reduces them to means only, without any value in themselves, in order that by the use of all means available the Holy Community may be created."[50] Activity in the world thus became once again a means to salvation, a legitimate soteriological arena, and the core of those transformations engendered by Calvinism in the symbolic universe of Western Christendom. As such, it was integral to the construction of new symbolic definitions of collective identity and new models of legitimizing authority that developed in sixteenth- and seventeenth-century Europe.

The redefinition of these two fundamental parameters of institutionalized social interaction were rooted in the primacy of the "Word" and the renewed stress on the indwelling of grace as opposed to the dictates of natural law as the basis of individual and collective existence. Negating the efficacy of externally applied grace, Calvinism did away as well with the mediating function of priestly authority. In terms of sacramental theology, this was expressed in the "de-sacralization" of the Eucharist and its annulment as a means of grace.[51] Doing away similarly with the soteriological efficacy of externally enforced norms, Calvinism posited voluntary obedience to God's law as the only true basis of Christian life.[52] This doctrine served as the basis of a new conception of cosmic order with important implications for the reorganization of the two interwoven spheres of identity and authority. For the basis of the new ideal order, the new *ecumene*, was henceforth to be the "Holy Community" of "saints," voluntarily participating in Christ.[53] Henceforth, the boundaries of the Christian community were not those of common participation in the sacrament of the Eucharist, but a common and voluntary subjugation of each individual will to the will of God. By willful participation in the Body of Christ, a new community was defined, one which, like that of the early Church, existed in the body of the old but yet was distinct from it. In Calvin's words:" It is the godly man's duty to abstain from all familiarity with the wicked, and not to enmesh himself with them in any voluntary relationship."[54] Such a code of conduct led to the effective separation within each parish of two bodies of communicants—"on one side there were the true, genuine, faithful and active Christians, and on the other those who were merely nominal and worldly." There thus was effected, in Troeltsch's words, "the separation of the pure body of communicants from the impure."[55]

The voluntary nature of the true Christian community was expressed in the covenantal or consensual nature of the ties assumed by its participants. This new community, based on a consensual notion of membership was to be governed by elected officials whose authority was rooted in "the general voice" of the community.[56] As the role of the ecclesiastical official was one of *administratio spiritus* and of building the community, his election or "calling" by the "elect" was essential, "not to diminish any part of the common right and freedom of the Church."[57] In this conception the role of the ministry underwent a fundamental change: from a hierarchic position mediating between communicant and the Deity, to assuming a purely functional and administrative role. Thus, for example, Archbishop Thomas Cranmer, in arguing against the Catholic conception of a priest's sacramental duties, stated that

> Christ made no such difference between the priest and the layman, that the priest should make oblation and sacrifice the Christ for the layman, and eat the Lord's supper from him all alone, and distribute and apply it as him liketh. Christ made no such difference; but the difference that is between the priest and the layman in this matter is only in the ministration: that the priest, as a common minister of the Church, doth minister and distribute the Lord's supper unto other, and other receive it at his hands.[58]

Through such doctrines, Calvinist thought prepared the way for a breakdown of the existing solidarities of Christian society and posited a new set of ties between people—in Donald Kelley's telling phrase, "a kind of sublimation of blood into belief."[59] In so doing it redefined the nature of society and, as we shall see, the locus of the sacred as well. As part of the same dynamic, it articulated a new notion of the relationships of domination within society. For while accepting in practice the need for positive law and structures of domination (until the establishment of the Kingdom of God), it negated their locus in any ultimate principles of order (as articulated in Thomist philosophy).[60] In its stead, it posited in the sphere of Church polity a conception of the ministry based on consent, collective agreement, and the fundamental equality of believers and ministers before God.

Given these orientations, it was perhaps not surprising that new loci of social solidarity and collective identity, as well as new models of legitimizing ministerial authority developed primarily among those groups of Puritan "saints" who emerged within the English Protestant movement. Moreover, by restructuring the basis of both collective identity and authority, the fundamental premises of Calvinist doctrine as reinterpreted by English Puritans paved the way for a radical change in the articulation of charisma. By breaking down the existing unity between the Eucharist and the sacred or charismatic locus of existence, the former came to be replaced by the idea of the covenant, which, as we shall see, served as the basis for the construction of new social and political centers and for the establishment of new social and collective entities.

The Puritan Context

The new conceptions of the social and cosmic order implicit in Calvin's "active ideal of holiness," tied, as they were, to the "ideal of the Holy Community," developed differently in different historical communities.[61] Our concern is with their development among those groups of English Puritans that emigrated to New England in the third decade of the seventeenth century.

Among all the different attempts to implement the Calvinist concept of the "Holy Community," the New England Congregationalist notion of a "Holy Commonwealth" was ultimately the most successful. It provides, therefore, the best example of the problems and solutions to the routinization of charisma according to the dictates of Calvinist religious sentiment.

The New England Congregationalists were, however, but one wing of that broad and labile movement of social and religious reform called Puritan that developed in England from the 1560s to the 1640s. In many ways, they took the implications of reform well beyond the point advocated by other elements of the English reform movement. Their radicalism was primarily evident in the development of new loci of communal identification and membership, first on the local level of villages and parishes and later in the formation of the larger collective entity of New England.[62] The development of what was essentially a new social and political center across the ocean was, therefore, rooted in the prior establishment of new models of collective identity and solidarity, as well as new models of authority and hierarchy within the Reformed churches of England.

The development of novel forms of social organization, following the return of the Marian Exiles, took a particularly intense expression in the context of Elizabethan England. Thus, there developed new forms of religious expression and communal bonds, both characterized by a break with existing models of authority, community, and notions of the sacred. In all spheres, the break with existing models was manifest in both institutional and symbolic spheres of social action.[63]

More than in any other social act, the drawing up of "covenants" between and among Puritans in Tudor England provided the basis for the reworking of the terms of social life in line with a new model of social organization.[64] In the covenanted communities and the "gathered churches" of the later sixteenth and early seventeenth centuries, diverse groups of English Puritans laid down, as it were, the blueprint for a fundamental reorganization of the principles of collective life.[65] This reorganization implied on the doctrinal level, a new form of interweaving of what has been termed this-worldly and otherworldly orientations and what was more "emically" designated as the law of nature and the law of grace. "A double law," as John Winthrop preached aboard the *Arbella*, "by which we are regulated in our conversacion one towards another . . . the lawe of nature and the lawe of grace, or the moralle lawe or the lawe of the gospell."[66] In line with their emphasis on uniting these two realms in a new moral order, the Puritan saints sought to realize and enact the law of grace in the sphere of mundane this-worldly activities. The principal social mechanism for this realization was within the covenant, for it was primarily in the covenant that the Puritans attempted to construct a new "metaphysical universe" where the hitherto contradictory spheres of nature and grace would be reconciled and produce a new man, one "in Christ," as well as a new and reformed social order. This social order would, moreover, lead to the fulfillment of age-old Christian eschatological hopes and visions.

The sociological concomitants of this new conception of social order have been attested to by historians from William Haller and Patrick Collinson to William Hunt and J. G. A. Pocock and we need only summarize them here.[67] On one level, they were manifest in a new mode of religious expression characterized by lay preaching, "prophesysings," as well as what later would be termed an "enthusiastic" religiosity of popular piety and noninstitutionalized manifestations of grace.[68] On the level of social organization, the covenanting of communicants implied primarily a break with existing solidarities of both Church and neighborhood.[69] Covenanting together, the Puritans also covenanted themselves off from the major existing institutional loci of solidarity—the Church, village, or parish—and so also from those social identities that prevailed in English society.[70] The withdrawal from existing loyalties both national and ecclesiastical to the Church of England and the growth of a new set of commitments, loyalties, and identities to the individuals covenanted together in pursuit of a new spiritual and moral life was a fundamental element in the construction of new loci of collective meaning and identity.[71]

Along with the positing of a new type of bond between community members, the covenant implied also a new concept of authority and of relations of hierarchy and domination within the covenanted communities of Puritan saints. In fact, the covenant, especially as developed by those groups of Puritans who at a later date would be termed Congregationalists, represented a unique realization of those models of Church organization propounded by the sixteenth-century reformers, such as Thomas Cartwright and William Perkins. Though the later New England Congregationalists did not justify their practice in terms of Cartwright's doctrine, their own organizational models were rooted in the more general demands for reform advocated in the sixteenth century. In the crucial sphere of ministerial authority, these reforms called for a redefinition of the terms of the relationship between the minister and his congregation. These were conceived as being intimately linked and ultimately inseparable. For, in line with the consensual conception of authority, the ministers were to be freely elected by the congregation so that, in the words of, Thomas Cartwright, one of the most articulate exponents of sixteenth-century English reformed thought:

> The consent of the churche in the election of the ministrie being profitable unto the godlie and those which are trewe sheepe that their love maie abounde towards their minister and in respect of Hypocrites and goates that they maie be more inexcusable before God and lesse hurtefull to men.[72]

Indeed, Cartwright in his opposition to the customs of the Church of England, to pluralism and non-residency, to the hierarchic and authoritarian form of Church organization, to the offices of archdeacon and archbishop, voiced the objection to English church practice that was at the heart of the Puritan reform movement. Although Cartwright ultimately failed in his attempt to reform English church practice, in their rejection of the hierarchic structure of the Church, the Puritans in general advanced a totally new conception of the ministry, one in which the role of the minister could be conceived only in the context of his direct relations with one congregation.[73] By defining in this novel manner the relations of the ministry to the congregants, the Puritans essentially posited new principles of the legitimation of authority. Instead of rooting authority in a "traditional" mode of legitimation whose ultimate referent was in the charismatic moment of the Passion (institutionalized through the principle of apostolic succession), the authority of the minister was henceforth grounded, on the one hand, in the "rational" practices of "plain preaching" and, on the other, in a direct communion with the congregants.[74]

On the symbolic plane, this new notion of authority—as rooted in the congregation—was manifested in the struggle against vestments and the surplice, both of which were seen as symbolic of the power of the priestly *office,* a power rooted in institutionalized grace as legitimized through the continuation of the apostolic tradition.[75] The struggle waged by the Puritans against these symbolic ornaments was precisely against the institutionalized channels of grace and charisma. Moreover, while the personal qualities of the minister were important to the calling of the ministry, they were ultimately tangential to his authority. This authority was rooted in the calling of the minister by the community (as opposed to a presbytery) and on the nature of the ties between minister and communicants.[76]

In the sphere of community and communal identity, as in that of authority, the Puritan movement was most essentially an attempt to build a new set of communal bonds within English society.[77] This fact amply explains their constant reference to the early Church as a legitimizing body of practices at odds with existing solidarities. Both groups defined themselves solely by the establishment of new institutional nexuses. In the case of the early Church this was accomplished in the rites of the Eucharist and in the case of the Puritan communities, in the ritual of the covenant. Indeed, the idea of the covenant, as it developed among certain groups of self-governing Puritan churches, effectively replaced the sacraments, especially that of the Eucharist, as the primary mode of establishing and asserting the development of these new ties within the emerging communities of Puritan "saints." It was then both the institutional locus and symbolic expression of a new moral community, bounded by different institutional and symbolic parameters from that of the society within which they coexisted.

These developments represented, in fact, a new definition of the social order and of the parameters of social interaction. In defining anew the nature of the bonds uniting community members (as opposed to solely the extent or meaning of membership), those communities of Puritan saints who covenanted among themselves to form their own churches established as well a redefinition of the locus of the sacred. No longer bounded by sacramental ritual, the sacred, too, moved both its institutional and symbolic locus from the rituals of the Church to other social and political spheres.

Nowhere was this clearer than in the reinterpretation given to the Eucharist, no longer an entity in its own right, but a "seal of the covenant," which itself represented the new sacred dimension of existence. It is in this context that we must view the specific changes instituted in Puritan churches in the manner of administrating the Host. For the destruction of altar rails and the change from altar to table, level with the congregants, represented in symbolic terms the destruction of that sacred space within which the sacred was confined.[78]

This deconstruction of sacred space was one moment in a dynamic that saw the emergence of a new notion of sacred time. For, no longer bounded by the otherworldly interpretation of soteriological activity formulated by the pre-Reformation Church and free of its physical embedment in the ritual formulation of the Church, the temporal articulation of the sacred dimension was, as its spatial parameters, transformed.

It is in the general transformation in the nature of the sacred that we must look for the symbolic roots of the early Puritan migration to the New World. Perhaps most evident in their particular conception of time and providential history, those Puritans who emigrated to the American Strand lived in an expectation of the eschaton, in a sacred time, in which they participated in the making of sacred history.[79] This participation was effected through the covenants that each individual contracted with God, as well as those among the godly, to further the work of reformation and so to hasten the coming of the Kingdom of God on earth.

Interestingly enough, the connection between the Puritan doctrine of the covenant and their very move to New England has only recently been explored, notably in the work of Avihu Zakai.[80] And yet an explication of this phenomenon, from either of the two major paradigms dealing with the sociology of religion, that is, from either a Durkheimian or Weberian perspective respectively, is almost implored. For the particular mode of reconciliation of nature and grace in covenant theology assumed a reconstruction of the sacred. No longer embedded in the sacramental rituals of the Church or transmitted through participation in the sacrifice of the Eucharist, the sacred was expressed in Puritan practice in the new social ties of the covenant. This social covenant, which, in the words of Richard Rogers, "did knit them in that love, the bond whereof could not be broken either on their part which now sleepe in the Lord, whiles they heere lived, nor in them which yet remaine, by any adversarie power unto this day," was, in fact, the organizational form taken by a new "moral community."[81]

From a Durkheimian perspective, the symbolic and institutional relocation of the sacred was totally congruent with the changing boundaries of collectivities, with the new ties engendered among and between Puritan communicants.[82] As new forms of solidarity emerged and were constituted, new definitions of the sacred—as expressions of this solidarity—were proffered. The desacralization of the sacraments, and indeed, of ritual in general is but the symbolic concomitant of the establishment of new ties of affinities between social actors leading to the establishment of new collective entities (as in New England), or to the redefinition of existing ones (as was the case among Puritans in England).

From the Weberian perspective, a very different, but certainly not at all contradictory, dynamic can be seen to be at work.[83] For, as noted throughout, the particular dynamic that characterized the emergence of

Puritan social groups can be usefully conceived of as a return to the original or genuinely charismatic band type of social organization. Such an organization would be, like the early Church, based on a direct, unmediated contact between the leader and the led, unrestricted by previous prescriptions, norms or laws; an organization, moreover, devoted to the teaching of moral laws and commands, of revealed and therefore indisputable truths acceptable on the basis of faith alone.[84] Thus, on the one hand, more immediate bonds were established both between members of the groups and between them and the different loci of authority. On the other hand, there emerged a new stress on inward piety and the indwelling of grace, as opposed to its more institutionalized realization and in a more direct relation to the ultimate sources of cultural meaning and order.

Moreover, as stressed by Weber this return to the original charismatic locus of social action and organization, though possible only "in statu nascendi," provides the basis both for reevaluation of existing institutional arrangements and, under the proper structural conditions for the establishment of new models of social action, definition of collective entities and models of social order. Such a process involves a reroutinization and institutionalization of charisma if it is to be successful. Indeed, as has been most critically determined in the writings of Max Weber as well as in more recent sociological and anthropological work, it is impossible to divorce the process of institution building proper, whether in its "initial" or more "routine" moments, from the "charismatic" dimension of existence.[85]

The crux of this connection, through the relation of charisma to the search for order and ultimate meaning, has been most cogently stated by Edward Shils:

The charismatic quality of an individual as perceived by others, or himself lies in what is thought to be his connection with (including possession by or embodiment of) some very central features of man's existence and the cosmos in which he lives. The centrality, coupled with intensity makes it extraordinary.... The centrality is constituted by its formative power in initiating, creating, governing, transforming, maintaining or destroying what is vital in man's life. That central power has often, in the course of man's existence, been conceived of as God, the ruling power or creator of the universe, or some divine or other transcendent power controlling or markedly influencing human life and the cosmos within which it exists.[86]

While Shils's statements address themselves in the main to the charismatic leader it should be remembered that Weber's own formulation, though dealing with charisma as a form of authority and legitimation, dealt less with the charismatic leader and more with the charismatic group or band. In so doing, Weber lay open the way for his prevailing concern with the connection of charisma to more institutional frameworks, as exemplified in the concepts of charisma of office (*Amptcharisma*), kinship (*Geltilcharisma*) and heredity (*Erbcharisma*), all of which are categories used to encompass the connection between charisma as a certain extraordinary quality existing beyond the formal structures of social action and their more institutional frameworks.[87] As such, and in terms of the relevance within the social realm proper, the charismatic dimension is, as noted by Eisenstadt, focused "in the construction of the boundaries of personal and collective identity, in the construction of social centers, the centers of society and of its major symbols of prestige."[88]

The connection between the charismatic dimension of existence and the different concrete processes of institution building is of major import for our own study, especially in light of the particular "separating" characteristic of the Puritan enterprise in New England. For, in the break posited with existing institutional structures and the concomitant construction of new ones that characterized the first generation of settlement, both aspects of social life were interwoven in a rather unique pattern. Having broken not only with existing institutional patterns, but with the ultimate matrixes of meaning-giving order as well, Puritan culture was led to rearticulate the charismatic dimension in Christianity in the novel terms of their own experience. This was expressed in what hitherto has been termed a relocation of the sacred, but what was as well a reformulation of the ultimate soteriological principles of individual and collective existence. For, through redefining the principles of salvation, which, *inter alia,* provided ultimate meaning, Puritan culture articulated a new notion of charisma, much closer to its original or pure form, unattenuated by institutional structures, hierarchies, and offices.[89]

These two theoretical perspectives taken together, that is, the redefinition of the sacred as part of the reestablishment of new communal ties on the one hand and the reassertion of direct charisma as a focus for both the reevaluation of existing social institutions, hierarchies, and models of social order and the establishment of new ones on the other, present the necessary context for the analysis of events in the first three generations of New England settlement. For it was in those years that the basis of collective and individual identities crystallized in large part through the institutionalization of the original charismatic dimension.

Notes

1. Karl Jaspers, *The Origin and Goal of History* (London: Routledge and Kegal Paul, 1952); Bernard Swartz, ed., "Wisdom Revelation and Doubt: Perspectives on the First Millennium B.C.," *Daedelus* (Spring 1975); S. N. Eisenstadt, "The Axial Age—the Emergence of Transcendental Visions and the Rise of Clerics," *European Journal of Sociology* 23 (1982): 294–314.
2. Eisenstadt, "Axial Age," 294, 296.
3. On the symbolization of cosmic order and on times of troubles, see Eric Voeglin, *Order and History,* vol. 1 (Baton Rouge: Louisiana State University Press, 1954), 1–13, 52–110.
4. Eisenstadt, "Axial Age," 300, 301.
5. For this terminology and additional perspectives on religious evolution, see Robert Bellah, "Religious Evolution," *American Sociological Review* 29 (1964): 358–74.
6. G. van der Leeuw, "Primordial Time and Final Time," in *Man and Time: Papers from the Eranos Yearbook* (Princeton: Princeton University Press, 1973), 337.
7. Ibid., 339.
8. Ernst Troeltsch, *The Social Teachings of the Christian Churches,* vol. 1 (New York: Harper and Row, 1960), 52.
9. Yonnia Talmon, "Millenarian Movements," *European Journal of Sociology* 7 (1960): 125–48; Rudolph Bultmann, *Primitive Christianity* (Philadelphia: Fortress Press, 1956), 180–208; Oscar Cullman, *Christ and Time: The Primitive Christian Conception of Time and History* (London: SCM Press, 1953). For the roots of Christian eschatological visions in Judaism, see Yoseph Klausner, *The Messianic Idea in Israel* (Tel Aviv: Massada Press, 1950) in Hebrew; Gershom Scholem, *The Messianic Idea in Judaism* (New York: Schocken Books, 1971). For additional perspectives on the relation of early Christianity to Judaism, see David Flusser, *Jewish Sources in Early Christianity, Studies and Essays* (Tel Aviv: Siphriat Hapoalim, 1982) in Hebrew.
10. For perspectives on the competition between different transcendental visions, see George Bowersock, "Architects of Competing Transcendental Visions in Late Antiquity," in *The Origin and Diversity of Axial Age Civilizations,* ed. S. N. Eisenstadt (Albany: SUNY Press, 1986), 280–87; Charles Cochrane, *Christianity and Classical Culture* (New York: Oxford University Press, 1957), as well as the more classical formulations of Max Weber, *Ancient Judaism* (New York: The Free

Press, 1952). Additional perspectives on the reorientation of the Church are provided by Peter Brown, "Approaches to the Religious Crises of the Third Century A.D.," *English Historical Review* 83 (1968): 542–58; idem, *Augustine of Hippo* (Berkeley: University of California Press, 1969); Hans Lietzmann, *Mass and the Lord's Supper: A Study in the History of Liturgy*, vol. 1 (Leiden: E. J. Brill, 1949); H. J. D. Drijivers, "Early Christian Asceticism and Monasticism" (Paper presented to the Conference on Max Weber and the Analysis of Late Antiquity, Bad Homburg, 1982). On Gnosticism, see Hans Jonas, *The Gnostic Religion* (Boston: Beacon Press, 1958); Elaine Pagels, *The Gnostic Gospels* (New York: Vintage Press, 1981); R. Wilson, *The Gnostic Problem: A Study of the Relation between Hellenistic Judaism and the Gnostic Heresy* (New York: AMS Press, 1958); as well as A. Logan and A. J. Wedderburn, eds., *The New Testament and Gnosis: Essays in Honor of Robert Mc. L. Wilson* (Edinburgh: T. & T. Clark), 1983.

11. On the temporal dimension in the thought of St. Augustine, see Robert Markus, *Saeculum: History and Society in the Theology of Saint Augustine* (Cambridge: Cambridge University Press, 1970).

12. On medieval protest, see Norman Cohen, *The Pursuit of the Millennium* (New York: Oxford University Press, 1977); Howard Kaminsky, "Hussite Radicalism and the Origins of Tabor," *Medievalia et Huamistina* 10 (1956): 102–30; idem, "Chilianism and the Husseite Revolution," *Church History* 26 (1957): 43–71; idem, *The History of the Hussite Revolution* (Berkeley: University of California Press, 1967); M. Lambert, *Medieval Heresy: Popular Movements from Bogomil to Hus* (London: E. Arnold, 1977); Gordon Leff, "In Search of the Millennium," *Past and Present* 13 (1958): 89–95; idem, "The Pursuit of Holiness in Late Medieval and Renaissance Religion" (Papers from the University of Michigan Conference, 1974); Marjorie Reeves, *The Influence of Prophecy in the Late Middle Ages: A Study of Joachinism* (Oxford: The Clarendon Press, 1969); Frederick Heywood, *John Zizka and the Hussite Revolution* (Princeton: Princeton University Press, 1956). For the religious sources of these movements, see Ann Williams, ed., *Prophecy and Millenarianism, Essays in Honor of Marjorie Reeves* (Harlow, Essex: Longmans, 1980).

13. On the importance of the new moral order implied in the Christian vision, see Peter Brown, *The Making of Late Antiquity* (Cambridge: Harvard University Press, 1978).

14. On the Christian conception of time and history, see Robert Cushman, "Greek and Christian Views of Time," *Journal of Religion* 33 (1953): 254–65; Lynn White, "Christian Myth and Christian History," *Journal of the History of Ideas* 3 (1942): 145–58; Anton Chroust, "The Metaphysics of Time and History in Early Christian Thought," *New Scholasticum* 19 (1945): 322–52; Oscar Cullmann, *Early Christian Worship* (London: SCM Press, 1953). A comparative, if somewhat unmethodical perspective is provided by S. G. F. Brandon, *History, Time and Deity: A Historical and Comparative Study of the Conception of Time in Religious Thought and Practice* (Manchester, England: University of Manchester Press, 1965).

15. See Sheldon Wohlin, *Politics and Vision* (Boston: Little, Brown and Co., 1960), 95–140; Cochrane, *Christianity and Classical Culture*; Brown, *The Making of Late Antiquity,* 56–77.

16. Gal. 4:28.
17. On "communitas," see Victor Turner, *Dramas Fields and Metaphors* (Ithaca, NY: Cornell University Press, 1969), 131–65. On the community of grace as a form of social organization, see Troeltsch, *The Social Teachings*, 39–89. On Weber's claim to the universality of the charismatic experience as opposed to its specificity in Christian culture, see Weber, *Economy and Society,* 1112.
18. 1 Cor. 12:12, 13.
19. Wohlin, *Politics and Vision,* 101.
20. Schluchter, *The Rise of Western Rationalism,* 152.
21. For this characterization of genuine charisma, see Weber, "Economy and Society," 246, 1121 and also Liah Greenfeld, "Reflections on Two Charismas," *British Journal of Sociology* 36 (1985): 117–32.
22. This can be assessed in, among other things, the transformation of the millennial visions of St. Justin Martyr (d.c.165), Ireaneus (d.c.200), and Tertullian (d.c.225) proclaiming the imminent resurrection of the dead and the impending Second Coming of Christ (within historical/mundane time), to the type of doctrine proposed by Eusebius (d.c.339), Dionysus the Great (d.c.264), Origen (d.c.254), and later in the post-Nicean period, by Augustine—all proponents of an allegorical millennialism, divorced from historical processes and events in the mundane sphere. The doctrine of a "de-eschatological history," by positing the millennium in an "other-worldly" present, effectively removed the Christian telos from history proper and circumscribed it in the sphere of Church history. Projection of the millennium beyond the secular sphere of human history was thus concomitant with the emergent patterns of orthodoxy, which made access to the deity dependent on the mediation of the consecrated priest whose legitimacy was established through the principle of apostolic succession. On the transformation of early Christian millennialism, see Jaroslav Pelikan, *The Christian Tradition: A History of the Development of Doctrine,* vol. 1 (Chicago: University of Chicago Press, 1971), 123–31. Further dimensions of the changing Christian view of history are treated in C. F. Patrides, *The Phoenix and the Ladder: The Rise and Decline of the Christian View of Time* (Berkeley: University of California Press, 1964); Karl Lowith, *Meaning and History* (Chicago: University of Chicago Press, 1949); Arnold Momigliano, "The Pagan and Christian Historiography in the Fourth Century A.D.," in *The Conflict between Paganism and Christianity in the Fourth Century* (Oxford: The Clarendon Press, 1963), 107–26; R. L. P. Milburn, *Early Christian Interpretations of History* (London: A. & C. Black, 1954). On St. Justin Martyr's eschatology, see Erwin Goodenough, *The Theology of Justin Martyr* (Amsterdam: Philo Press, 1968), 279–91. On Origen, see Gerard Caspary, *Politics and Exegesis: Origen and the Two Swords* (Berkeley: University of California Press, 1979). Eusebius, "the father of Ecclesiastical history," documented his own attitudes and those of Dionysus in his *Ecclesiastical History,* Book X.25 (see Eusebius, *The History of the Church,* translated by G. A. Williams [Harmondsworth: Penguin, 1965]).
23. This process, which witnessed the development of "authority" at the expense of "community" was already well under way by the second century, as illustrated in the writings of St. Cyprian:

38   Innerworldly Individualism

> The episcopate is one; the individual members have each a part, and the parts make up the whole. The Church is a unity ... the Church is made up of the people united to the priest as the flock that cleaves to the shepherd. Hence you should know that the bishop is in the Church and the Church in the bishop, and that if any one be not with the bishop he is not in the Church ... the Church is one and may not be rent or sundered, but should assuredly be bound together and united by the glue of the priests who are in harmony one with another. (*De Catholicae ecclesiae unitate*, 5; Epistle, lxvi, 7, quoted in Wohlin, *Politics and Vision*, 108)

24. C. H. Turner, "Apostolic Succession," in *Essays on the Early History of the Church and Ministry*, ed. H. Swete (London: MacMillan, 1921), 93–114.
25. St. Cyprian, Epistle, xxxiii, 1, quoted in Wohlin, *Politics and Vision*, 108.
26. Brown, *The Making of Late Antiquity*, 98; see also his "The Rise and Function of the Holy Man," *Journal of Roman Studies* 61 (1971): 80–101; Philip Rousseau, *Ascetics, Authority and the Church in the Age of Jerome and Cassio* (Oxford: Oxford University Press, 1978).
27. For one of the few attempts to deal with this transformation of the original charismatic element in Christianity in an anthropological manner, see Edmund Leach, "Melchisedech and the Emperor: Icons of Subversion and Orthodoxy," in *Structuralist Interpretations of Biblical Myth*, ed. E. Keach and D. A. Aycock (Cambridge: Cambridge University Press, 1983), 67–88.
28. This conflict, inherent to medieval Christendom, achieved one of its most salient expressions during the Investiture Contest when Pope Gregory VII attempted to unite both realms under Church authority. On this period, see Gerhard Tellenbach, *Church, State and Christian Society at the Time of the Investiture Contest* (Oxford: Basil Blackwell, 1959).
29. Pelikan, *The Christian Tradition*, vol. 1, 166–71, 236–38.
30. On ancient conceptions of time, see A. Momigliano, "Time in Ancient Historiography," *History and Theory Beiheft* 6 (1966): 1–23; John Callahan, *Four Views of Time in Ancient Philosophy* (Cambridge: Harvard University Press, 1948); Anton Chroust, "The Meaning of Time in the Ancient World," *New Scholasticum* 21 (1947): 1–70. On the relation between Greek and Christian views, see Robert Nisbet, *Social Change and History* (New York: Oxford University Press, 1969), 15–103; J. G. A. Pocock, *The Machiavellian Moment* (Princeton: Princeton University Press, 1975), 31–48; Ernst Hoffmann, "Platonism in Augustine's Philosophy of History," in *Philosophy and History, the Ernst Cassirer Festschrift*, ed. R. Klibansky and H. Paton (New York: Harper and Row, 1963), 173–90. Further and related discussion of the meeting between both civilizational concepts can be found in Werner Jaeger, *Early Christianity and Greek Paideia* (Cambridge: Harvard University Press, 1961).
31. Augustine, *The Confessions of Saint Augustine*, Books XI and XII, translated by Edmund Pussy (New York: Modern Library, 1949); idem, *The City of God*, Books XII–XVI, translated by Henry Bettenson (Harmondsworth: Penguin, 1972). See also Theodore Mommsen, "St. Augustine and the Christian Idea of Progress: The Background to the City of God," in *Medieval and Renaissance Studies*, ed. Theodore Mommsen (Ithaca, NY: Cornell University Press, 1959), 265–89; Herman

Hausees, "St. Augustine's Conception of Time," in *Aspects of Time,* ed. C. A. Patrides (Manchester: University of Manchester Press, 1976), 30–37. On more general aspects of St. Augustine's writings see the collection edited by Roy Battenhouse, *A Companion to the Study of St. Augustine* (New York: Oxford University Press, 1955).

32. Markus, *Saeculum*. For an important note on the relation of the *aevum* to the *saeculum* in the thought of St. Augustine, see Pocock, *The Machiavellian Moment,* 42.
33. Ibid., 45.
34. Wohlin, *Politics and Vision,* 101; Pelikan, *Christian Tradition,* vol. 1, 169.
35. For a social contextualization of this development, see Steven Ozment, *The Age of Reform 1250–1550: An Intellectual and Religious History of Late Medieval and Reformation Europe* (New Haven: Yale University Press, 1980), 90–98.
36. For historical perspectives on this development, see John Bossy, "The Mass as a Social Ritual," *Past and Present* 100 (1983): 29–61; for its more theological aspects, see Gary Macy, *The Theologies of the Eucharist in the Early Scholastic Period* (Oxford: Clarendon Press, 1984); also E. R. Mascall, *Corpus Christi: The Church and the Eucharist* (London: Longman, 1953).
37. Geoffrey Wainwright, *Eucharist and Eschatology* (New York: Oxford University Press, 1981).
38. See especially Bultmann, *Primitive Christianity*; Cullmann, *Early Christian Worship,* 14–20; Gilles Quispel, "Time and History in Patristic Christianity," in *Man and Time: Papers from the Eranos Yearbook* (Princeton: Princeton University Press, 1973), 85–107. A more general discussion of Christian eschatology including of modern thinkers is to be found in R. H. Charles, *Eschatology: The Doctrine of a Future Life* (New York: Schoken Books, 1963). For more anthropological discussions of the Eucharist, see S. W. Sykes, "Sacrifice in the New Testament and Christian Theology," in *Sacrifice,* ed. M. F. C. Bourdillon and M. Fortes (New York: Academic Press, 1980), 61–83; G. Feeley-Harnik, *The Lord's Table: Eucharist and Passover in Early Christianity* (Philadelphia: University of Pennsylvania Press, 1981); and the older but still interesting work by Alice Gardiner, *History of Sacrament in Relation to Thought and Progress* (London: Williams and Norgate, 1921).
39. Quispel, "Time and History," 89.
40. Henri-Charles Puech, "Gnosis and Time," in *Man and Time,* 38–84.
41. On the temporal dimension of the sacred, see Edmund Leach, "Two Essays Concerning the Symbolic Representation of Time," in *Rethinking Anthropology,* ed. E. Leach (London: Athlone Press, 1961), 124–36.
42. See for example C. G. Jung:
    The Mass is an extramundane and extemporal act in which Christ is sacrificed and then resurrected in the transformed substances, and this rite of his sacrificial death is not a repetition of the historical event but the original, unique and external act. The experience of the Mass is therefore a participation in the transcendence of life, which overcomes all bounds of space and time. It is a moment of eternity in time. (1969, 118)
43. On the connection of charisma to institution building, Weber, *On Charisma*; Edward Shils, "Charisma Order and Status," in *Center and Periphery,* ed. E. Shils

(Chicago, University of Chicago Press, 1975): 256–75. See also the perspectives opened by Peter Berger, "Charisma and Religious Innovation: The Social Location of Israelite Prophecy," *American Sociological Review* 28 (1963): 940–50.

44. The growing preoccupation in the fifteenth century with a collective identity based on lineage as opposed to collective participation in the community of the Eucharist bears witness to the continuing tension engendered within Christian civilization by its novel definition of the boundaries of community. See John Bossy, *Christianity in the West 1400–1700* (Oxford: Oxford University Press, 1985), 86.

45. Wohlin, *Politics and Vision*, 134. Given this linkage, it is no wonder that the different protest movements of the Middle Ages, which articulated millennial orientations, broke at the same time with the sacramental doctrines of the Catholic church and with its institutional structures. For by propounding a this-worldly millennialism, one seen to take place within mundane history, they effectively broke down the institutional constraints that had, within the Catholic church, tied apocalyptic images to otherworldly interpretations and pursuits. Breaking down the boundaries of the "sacred," they strove to realize the promise of Christianity to make all of history *Heilesgeschichte*. Their break with the sacramental dogma of the Church as well as their this-worldly millennialism were thus in essence two elements of one dynamic. Its sociological implications were felt in their concomitant redefinition of the boundaries of collective membership, trust, and affiliation. Thus, in many medieval millennial movements, such as the Waldensians and later the Taborites, there developed, concurrently with a break with the sacramental doctrine of the Church, the positing of new boundaries of collective membership and of the salvational collective. Similarly, they posited new principles and structures of authority, which were, moreover, rooted in a less hierarchic manner to the fundamental terms of collective solidarity. We may in fact say that in the break posited by these protest movements with existing institutional structures, as well as with their ritual concomitants (the sacraments), within which the sacred was bounded, they opened up the possibility of moving the sacred back into history, a process that was throughout parallel and integral to their reassertion of a genuine charismatic bond among collective members. For studies of these movements, see Kaminsky, *The History of the Husseite Revolution;* Lambert, *Medieval Heresy;* Michael Mullett, *Radical Religious Movements in Early Modern Europe* (London: George Allen and Unwin, 1980).

46. For a general and historical review of these transformations, see H. Trevor-Roper, *Religion, the Reformation and Social Change* (London: Macmillan Press, 1967), 1–45. For only some sociological perspectives on the Weberian thesis, see Reinhart Bendix, "The Protestant Ethic Revisited," *Comparative Studies in Society and History* 9 (1966/67): 266–73; idem, "Max Weber's Interpretation of Conduct and History," *American Journal of Sociology* 51 (1945/46): 511–26; A. Bieler, "Calvinism and Capitalism," *Reformed Presbyterian World* 19 (1959): 145–59; S. N. Eisenstadt, ed. *The Protestant Ethic and Modernization: A Comparative Perspective* (New York: Basic Books, 1968), 3–45; Amintore Fanfani, *Catholicism, Protestantism and Capitalism* (London: Sheed and Ward, 1939); Gianfranco Poggi, *Calvinism and the Capitalist Spirit: Max Weber's Protestant Ethic* (London:

Macmillan Press, 1983); Guy Swanson, *Religion and Regime: A Sociological Account of the Reformation* (Ann Arbor: University of Michigan Press, 1967).
47. On these aspects of Calvinism, see Harvo Hopfl, *The Christian Polity of John Calvin* (Cambridge: Cambridge University Press, 1982); Sheldon Wohlin, "Calvin and Reformation: The Political Education of Protestantism," *American Political Science Review* 51 (1957): 425–54; Troeltsch, *The Social Teachings,* vol. 2, 576–690; David Little, "Max Weber Revisited: The Protestant Ethic and the Puritan Experience of Order," *Harvard Theological Review* 59 (1966): 415–28; idem, *Religion, Order and Law: A Study in Pre-Revolutionary England* (Chicago: University of Chicago Press, 1984); Michael Waltzer, *The Revolution of the Saints* (Cambridge: Harvard University Press, 1965). For an opposing view to those of David Little and Michael Waltzer, see John McNeill, "Natural Law and the Teachings of the Reformers," *Journal of Religion* 26 (1946): 168–82; John McNeill, *The History and Characters of Calvinism* (New York: Oxford University Press, 1954). On the place of Calvinism in the history of Western European political thought, see Quinten Skinner, *The Foundations of Modern Political Thought* (Cambridge: Cambridge University Press, 1979), 189–348. On some of its social implications, see Steven Ozment, *The Reformation in the Cities* (New Haven: Yale University Press, 1975); Norman Birinbaum, "The Zwinglian Reformation in Zurich," *Archive Sociologie Religion* 4 (1959): 15–30; J. E. Ellemers, "The Revolt of the Netherlands: The Part Played by Religion in the Process of Nation-Building," *Social Compass* 14 (1967): 93–103.
48. For a somewhat different perspective on charisma in the context of Calvin in Geneva, see William Swatos, Jr. "Charismatic Calvinism: Forging A Mission Link," in *Charisma, History and Social Structure,* ed. R. Glassman and W. Swatos, Jr. (New York: Greenwood Press, 1986), 73–82.
49. Troeltsch, *The Social Teachings,* vol. 2, 609.
50. Ibid., 607.
51. For discussion of the different views on the "real presence" in the Eucharist among the English reformers, see Francis Clark, *Eucharist Sacrifice and the Reformation* (London: Darton, Longmans and Todd, 1960), 127–76.
52. Little, *Religion, Order and Law,* 41.
53. Troeltsch, *The Social Teachings,* vol. 2, 590–92.
54. John Calvin, *Institutes of the Christian Religion,* Book IV, ed. John McNeill (Philadelphia: Fortress Press, 1956), 1, 15.
55. Troeltsch, *The Social Teachings,* 596–97. In Calvin's thought the freedom within which the true body of believers lived must be differentiated from the state of existing political society and from the unregenerate, among whom the command of God had to be enforced by coercion until the coming of the Kingdom of God. At its coming, according to Calvin, the separation between those "in Christ" participating in the world of freedom and those still subject to coercion would be dissolved.
56. Little, *Religion, Order and Law,* 71.
57. Calvin, *Institutes,* Book IV, 3, 15.
58. Quoted in Clark, *Eucharist Sacrifice,* 131.
59. Donald Kelley, *The Beginnings of Ideology* (London: Cambridge University Press,

1981), 80.
60. It must be noted that when approaching the realm of political society Calvin realized the inability of distinguishing the visible Church from the invisible Church of the elect and so accepted the necessity of ministerial prerogative and power. These formed the basis of the particular notion of Calvinist "theocracy," where the powers of Church and State were to work together toward the establishment of God's Kingdom on earth. And, in fact, the different forms of national covenants, whether the Genevan Confession of Faith (1536), the Scottish National Covenant (1638), the English Solemn League and Covenant (1643), or those of the New England town churches, effectively attempted just such a total reformulation of collective life.
61. Troeltsch, *The Social Teachings,* vol. 2, 595. For a recent study of Puritan religious practice in a comparative perspective, see Mary Fulbrook, *Piety and Politics, Religion and Absolutism in England, Wurttenberg and Prussia* (Cambridge: Cambridge University Press, 1983).
62. A good discussion of this process on a local level can be found in William Hunt, *The Puritan Moment: The Coming of Revolution in an English County* (Cambridge: Harvard University Press, 1985), 90–91, 131–36.
63. Much has been written on the institutional implications of Puritan religiosity. For some of the more relevant analyses, see Michael Waltzer, "Puritanism as a Revolutionary Ideology," *History and Theory* 3 (1963): 59–90; George Mosse, "Puritanism and Reasons of State in Old and New England," *William and Mary Quarterly* 9 (1952): 67–80; idem, "Puritan Political Thought and the Case of Conscience," *Church History* 23 (1954): 109–25; idem, *The Holy Pretense: Christianity and Reasons of State from William Perkins to John Winthrop* (Oxford: Basil Blackwell, 1957); C. and K. George, "Puritanism as History and Historiography," *Past and Present* 41 (1968): 77–104; C. H. George, "Protestantism and Capitalism in Pre-Revolutionary England," *Church History* 27 (1958): 351–146; W. Lamont, "Puritanism, History and Historiography," *Past and Present* 44 (1969): 133–46; Jerald Brauer, "The Nature of English Puritanism: Three Interpretations," *Church History* 23 (1954): 99–108; Gordon Marshall, *Presbyteries and Profits: Calvinism and the Development of Capitalism in Scotland 1560–1707* (Oxford: Clarendon Press, 1980).
64. On the centrality of the covenant in the lives of the Puritans, see Patrick Collinson, "Towards a Broader Understanding of the Dissenting Tradition," in *The Dissenting Tradition,* ed. C. Cole and M. Moody (Athens: Ohio University Press, 1975), 3–38. On the relation of covenant theology to Calvinist doctrine, see Everett Emerson, "Calvin and Covenant Theology," *Church History* 25 (1956): 136–44; Perry Miller, *Errand into the Wilderness* (New York: Harper and Row, 1964), 48–98; J. Moller, "The Beginnings of Puritan Covenant Theology," *The Journal of Ecclesiastical History* 14 (1963): 46–67. Further theological issues are explored in Klaus Baltzer, *The Covenant Formulary* (Philadelphia: Fortress Press, 1971); C. Burrage, *The Church Covenant Idea: Its Origins and Development* (Philadelphia: American Baptist Publication Society, 1904). Different political aspects of the covenant are developed by S. A. Burell, "The Covenant Idea as a Revolutionary Symbolic: Scotland 1596–1635," *Church History* 27 (1958): 13–58; David Zaret, *The Heav-*

enly Contract: Ideology and Organization in Pre-Revolutionary Puritanism (Chicago: University of Chicago Press, 1984).

65. The extent to which the covenants regulated the lives of those who entered into them, especially in maintaining the symbolic and physical boundaries of the new community is evinced in the 1642 Independent Covenant presented by John Bastwick and reproduced by Michael Tolmie, *The Triumph of the Saints: The Separate Churches of London 1616–1649* (Cambridge: Cambridge University Press, 1977), 196. See also Michael Watts, *The Dissenters* (Oxford: Oxford University Press, 1978), 30, 31, 41, 42, 55, 56.

66. John Winthrop, (1630) in *The Puritans: A Sourcebook of Their Writings,* ed. P. Miller and T. Johnson (New York: Harper and Row, 1963), 196.

67. William Haller, *The Rise of Puritanism* (Philadelphia: University of Pennsylvania Press, 1972). In addition to the above noted references, see Michael Knappen, *Tudor Puritanism: A Chapter in the History of Idealism* (Chicago: University of Chicago Press, 1939).

68. For these aspects of Puritanism see: Geoffrey Nuttal, *The Holy Spirit in Puritan Faith and Experience* (Oxford: Basil Blackwell, 1946); Norman Pettit, *The Heart Prepared: Grace and Conversion in Puritan Spiritual Life* (New Haven: Yale University Press, 1966). For a less theological and more historical view see: Hunt, "The Puritan Moment," 94. For the importance of this form of religious expression among the separatists see: Watts, "The Dissenters," 26. For a general history of Christian enthusiasm see: Ronald Knox, *Enthusiasm: A Chapter in the History of Ideas* (Oxford: Oxford University Press, 1950). For a discussion of its changing temper in the seventeenth century see: Michael Heyd, "The Reaction to Enthusiasm in the Seventeenth Century" *Journal of Modern History* 53 (1981): 258–280. From a sociological standpoint these expressions of a noninstitutional grace were manifestations of a genuinely charismatic dimension whose importance in the process of social restructuring will be taken up in the following chapters.

69. Just how drastic this "dichotomizing" of society was is a matter of some historical debate, though there is a relative consensus among historians that by the early decades of the seventeenth century it was radically more evident than in the Elizabethan period. By this, later, period the desire to make the community of the godly "real and visible" led to palpable tensions between the community of the gathered Church and the rest of the "Christian nation". Recent discussion of this problem can be found in Patrick Collinson, *The Puritan Character: Polemics and Polarities in Early Seventeenth-Century English Culture* (Los Angeles: William Andrews Clark Memorial Library, 1989).

70. A slightly different view is offered by Patrick Collinson in his *The Elizabethan Puritan Movement* (Berkeley: University of California Press, 1967); see especially the idea of *ecclesiola in ecclesia* on p. 375.

71. Avihu Zakai, "The Gospel of Reformation, the Origins of the Great Puritan Migration," *Journal of Ecclesiastical History* 37 (1986): 14. Impressive discussions of this process whereby new loci of community were formed within the overall Puritan movement and its separatist tradition can be found in Collinson, "A Broader Understanding," 3–38; Watts, *The Dissenters,* 14–26; Tolmie, *Triumph of the Saints,* 1977; Haller, *The Rise of Puritanism,* 1972. The tension formed within society by

44   Innerworldly Individualism

the growth of Puritanism is amply attested to in such satires as "Zeal-of-the-land-Busy" in Ben Jonson's *Bartholomew Faire* or in the 1633 *Declaration of Sports*, which explicitly ordered the Puritans "to conform themselves or to leave the country" if they would not abide "our good people's law for recreation," for which the king's pleasure decreed "that after the end of divine service our good people be not disturbed, letted or discouraged from any lawful recreation, such as dancing, either men or women; archery for men, leaping, vaulting, or any other such harmless recreation, nor from having of May-games, Whitsunales, and Morris-dances; and the setting up of May-poles and other sports therewith used" (S. R. Gardiner, ed., *The Constitutional Documents of the Puritan Revolution 1625–1600* [Oxford: Clarendon Press, 1906], 101). A good understanding of the social importance of the local games, rites, and feasts (with which the Puritans broke) can be found in V. A. Kolve, *A Play Called Corpus Christi* (Stanford: Stanford University Press, 1966); James Mervyn, "Ritual Drama and Social Body in the Late Medieval English Town," *Past and Present* 98 (1983): 3–29; Peter Laslett, *The World We Have Lost* (London: Methuen and Co., 1965). Other aspects of the Puritan break with established authority can be found in J. F. New, *Anglican and Puritan: The Basis of Their Opposition 1558–1648* (Stanford: Stanford University Press, 1964). Comparative perspectives on ritual among Protestants and Catholics on the continent can be gained from Natalie Davis, "The Sacred and the Body Social in Sixteenth Century Lyon," *Past and Present* 90 (1981): 40–70. Further perspectives on the Puritan aversion to the *Declaration of Sports* can be found in W. DeLoss, *The Fast and Thanksgiving Days of New England* (Boston: Houghton Mifflin Co., 1895), 1–27.

72. Quoted in Little, *Religion, Order and Law,* 92–93.
73. It is important to note that while the developing historical trajectory of the Puritan movement led to different stands taken on these issues by Presbyterians, on the one hand, and Congregationalists or Independents on the other, the rejection of residency was shared in the 1570s by both Cartwright's Presbyterian movement as well as the different Separatist sects. See Watts, *The Dissenters,* 25.
74. The style of plain preaching is discussed by Haller, *The Rise of Puritanism,* 19, 23, 129–72 and by Lazer Ziff, "The Literary Consequences of Puritanism," in *The American Puritan Imagination: Essays in Reevaluation,* ed. S. Bercovitz (New York: Cambridge University Press, 1974), 34–44.
75. Watts, *The Dissenters,* 18; Hunt, *The Puritan Moment,* 115.
76. On the calling of ministers see: Haller, *The Rise of Puritanism,* 53; Watts, *The Dissenters,* 25.
77. This fact is also stressed in Theodore Bozeman, *To Live Ancient Lives* (Chapel Hill: University of North Carolina Press, 1988).
78. On the importance of sacred space in the ritual of the Eucharist and elsewhere, see Edmund Leach, *Culture and Communication: The Logic by which Symbols are Constructed* (Cambridge: Cambridge University Press, 1976), 81–93. On the conflict between the Puritans and Archbishop Laud on the nature of the sacramental rite, see Watts, *The Dissenters,* 65. See A. Morton, *The World of the Ranters* (London: Lawrence and Wishart, 1970), 11 on the destructuring of sacred space. On the provisory and profane nature of the communion table among Puritans in

New England, see Elizabeth Winslow, *Meetinghouse Hill 1630–1783* (New York: Norton, 1972), 52, 56. Explicit injunctions on the profane nature of the communion table can be found in Nicholas Ridley's *Reasons Why the Lord's Board Should Rather be After the Form of a Table than of an Altar,* where he states: "The form of a Table shall more move the simple from the superstitious opinions of the popish Mass, unto the right use of the Lord's Supper. For the use of an altar is to make sacrifice upon it: the use of a table is to serve men to eat upon." Quoted in Clark, *Eucharist,* 132.

79. Avihu Zakai, *Exile and Kingdom: History and Apocalypse in the Puritan Migration to America* (Cambridge: Cambridge University Press, 1992).
80. Ibid.
81. Richard Rogers, *Seven Treatises . . . Called the Practice of Christianitie,* 2d ed. (London, 1605), 497–98.
82. For the relation of the sacred to the collective, see Emile Durkheim, *The Elementary Forms of Religious Life* (London: George Allen and Unwin, 1968), 23–47. Explications of Durkheim's theory may be found in Anthony Giddens, *Capitalism and Modern Social Theory* (Cambridge: Cambridge University Press, 1971), 105–18. The importance of moral authority and moral community as aspects of this connection in Durkheim's thought can be found in Talcott Parsons, "Durkheim on Religion Revisited: Another Look at the Elementary Forms of Religious Life," in *Action Theory and the Human Condition,* ed. T. Parsons (New York: The Free Press, 1978), 213–32. See also Parsons, *Social Action,* 378–90.
83. On the parallel nature of Durkheim's sacred and Weberian charisma, see Parsons, *Social Action,* 658–72. See also A. Piepe, "Charisma and the Sacred: A Re-evaluation," *Pacific Sociological Review* 14 (1971): 147–61, and for an opposing view to that of Parsons, see W. Pope, "On the Divergence of Weber and Durkheim: A Critique of Parson's Convergence Theory," *American Sociological Review* 40 (1975): 417–27.
84. On these aspects of charisma, see Greenfeld, "Two Charismas," 117–32; Shils, ed., *Center and Periphery,* 127–34. On charismatic leadership, see also M. Spencer, "What is Charisma," *British Journal of Sociology* 24 (1973): 341–54; idem, "Weber on Legitimate Norms and Authority," *British Journal of Sociology* 21 (1970): 123–34.
85. In this context it is possible to see a close affinity between charisma as it is used by Max Weber and Durkheim's sacred or Turner's institutionalized communitas. All point to a similar phenomenon, one existing in the interstice of institutionalized social interaction, but are nonetheless fundamental to its workings.
86. Shils, ed. *Center and Periphery,* 259.
87. See Schluchter, *Western Rationalism,* 36–37; Weber, *On Charisma,* xxi.
88. Eisenstadt, "Comparative Liminality," 319.
89. On the importance of soteriological meaning to the construction of different realms of social action, see Weber, "The Social Psychology," 267–301.

2

The Origins of Settlement

The rearticulation of charisma as a mode of historical action took place among those Puritans who emigrated to the American Strand. Founding their "errand into the Wilderness" on the basis of the covenant—as locus of social authority and communal identity—they saw in their settlement an instrument of cosmic redemption. Central to the rearticulation of charisma among these Puritans was their vision of a "Holy Commonwealth," of a theocracy where the hitherto disparate realms of political-historical and religious action would be reintegrated. Mundane and transcendent realms would thus be reunited in a collective devoted to the this-worldly realization of otherworldly ends.

The following chapters will analyze these communities through concentrating on the following perspectives: (a) defining the original and charismatic nature of settlement; (b) analyzing the problems incumbent on the organization of social life in accordance with such a model of social existence; and (c) analyzing the process of its institutionalization into perduring patterns of normative action over the first hundred years of New England history.

Accordingly, in this chapter, the original impetus of the Puritan settlement in the New World as well as its early years are analyzed in terms of the immediately perceived linkage of social life to the ultimate matrixes of meaning and cosmic order.

In many ways, the communities founded in the New World were similar to those of the early Christians in the unattenuated nature of their connection to the charismatic dimension of existence. In this light, it is possible to characterize them as communities participating in a "genuinely" or "purely" charismatic experience, relatively unmediated by institutions or figures of authority. Organizationally this experience was manifest in the particular models of authority and community posited by the Congregational Puritans. In the early years of settlement, authority was seen as rooted in particular communities (Congregational churches) of saints, undifferentiated from them and sharing equally with them in the experience of grace. Community was defined in terms of sainthood and membership in the Church of covenanted saints. The early years of settlement witnessed many conversions and the expectation that all community members would experience regeneration and join the covenanted community of saints, which was the basis of their Holy Commonwealth.

Analytic Perspectives

In the third decade of the seventeenth century, thousands of English men and women, clergy and laity alike, migrated from England—primarily from East Anglia—to the New World.[1] Many of these emigrants were among those persecuted by the rule in England of Archbishop William Laud, who imposed strict religious conformity and insisted that "his clergy conform to the Prayer Book, wear the surplice, raise their communion tables up like altars at the east end of the chancel, rail them off from the laity, and compel their people to kneel at the rails to receive the sacrament."[2] These practices, at odds with their beliefs, drove many dissenting Puritans out of the country, first to the Netherlands and finally to New England. In the New World, they endeavored to construct a new social order, based on their conception of correct Church practice and on their understanding of the proper relations between civil and ecclesiastical orders, in other words, between the Church and the State.[3]

The basis of this new social order was the covenanted Church of "visible saints." Membership in these congregations defined, in the early years of settlement, not only the basis of political participation in the polity, but, more embracingly, the ideal model of collective identity and social solidarity.[4] Rooted in the covenants contracted between communal members for the mutual pursuit of a godly life, the Congregational churches of visible saints were an organizational arrangement of great import. For, rather than a retreat or rejection of the world, they were formed as the basis for a remaking of the world, for the reconstruction of civil, no less than religious life. In this sense, the attempt of seventeenth-century Congregationalists to build a "Christian Commonwealth," where even civil magistrates were "to serve Christ's ends for the good and welfare of his Churches," represents a major attempt to reunite this-worldly and otherworldly spheres of action.[5] That relative dissociation of this-worldly from otherworldly realms that had characterized the institutionalization of the original charismatic message of Christianity was here reformulated. Thus, even though the New England Congregationalists were not Calvinist in terms of their adherence to specific religious precepts (the covenant as such was hardly a critical component of Calvin's theology); analytically they represented a unique attempt to realize the Holy Community of free individuals sharing in divine grace, which stood at the heart of Calvinist belief.

This attempt to realize grace within mundane, historical, worldly actions and institutions and not in otherworldly rites, involved a reconstitution of the charismatic locus of organized social life—the organizational and institutional embodiment of which was in the covenanted churches of visible saints themselves. Moreover, by stressing the linkage of this-worldly historical action with otherworldly grace, the New England Congregational Puritans once again opened up the possibility of uniting mundane and providential history, of making of history, *Heilsgeschichte*. No longer defined solely in otherworldly terms, the possibility of realizing grace and of fulfilling the age-old prophecies of human redemption played an important role in ordering social existence in the early years of the Bay Colony.

Of central importance to the ordering of social life according to this conception was the very formulation, articulation, and enactment of the principles shared by communal members on the proper workings of the social order and of the locus of these in ultimate principles of individual meaning and cosmic ordering.

The construction of a meaningful framework of social ordering within which new models of authority and community were constituted in seventeenth-century New England was carried out in a particular set of circumstances. In the broadest of strokes, these were delineated by the new moral order inherent in the attempt to construct a "Godly Community," which involved the restructuring of: (a) communal ties; (b) the nature of authority; and (c) the sacred dimension of existence. Taken together these three elements formed the basis of a "return" to a more genuinely charismatic conception of the social order.

Admittedly, the Puritan attempt to reconstruct the moral and institutional bases of the social order was neither unique nor unprecedented. The attempt to construct a Holy Commonwealth of individuals, sharing in divine grace, that is, to establish some form of virtuosi religious ethic had many precedents within Christendom. Indeed, as analyzed by Ernst Troeltsch, this development was almost mandated by the contradictory injunctions of Christian civilization toward an absolute universalism (based on the community of love) and an absolute individualism (of the individual standing in relation to God).[6] What was unique to the Puritan "errand into the wilderness" was that, as opposed to other heretical and separatist sects (within pre-Reformation Christianity as well as, it should be noted, within the broad movement of the Reformation), New England Puritanism did succeed in institutionalizing its vision of the social order and in forming a crucial component of what came to be a lasting social and political tradition.

Thus, and to take a case in point, we may think of those types of millennial movements studied by Norman Cohen, Yonnina Talmon, Harold Kaminsky, and others.[7] These too attempted to return to a genuinely charismatic conception of the social order, to a relatively unmediated relation between authority and community, to a virtuosi religious ethic, which moreover sought, as did New England Puritanism, to make of history, sacred history. The Anabaptists in Munster for instance united an eschatological view of history with a general reorganization of the major institutional realms of social life: the restructuring of social hierarchies, division of labor, relations between the sexes, and distribution of resources.[8] However, all these movements failed or were repressed by external force. Within the English Reformation too, the history of the dissenting tradition and of radical ascetically orientated Puritanism was—as a major force in social life—cut short by mid-century.

The uniqueness of New England Puritanism both analytically and historically is thus not solely in its original conceptions of the nature of authority and community, and its vision of history. Some of these conceptions, such as those on the contractual relations between ministers and congregants and on the centrality of the covenant in providing new forms of individual and collective existence were—as noted in the previous chapter—shared by Puritans on both sides of the Atlantic. What was unique in the Puritan experiment in the wilderness was rather that these forms of organizing social life and providing meaning to individual and collective existence did, over the course of three generations, become institutionalized to form one of the foundations of what Seymor Martin Lipset has called the "first New Nation."[9] Over these three generations Peter Bulkeley's "Cittie set upon a hill, in open view of all the earth" did remain standing and if the "days of grace" passed, they nevertheless provided lasting foundations and are worthy of our attention.[10] The very process of change was thus, itself, part of the historical development we must attempt to understand.

For it was only in the reinterpretation and reformulation of the original terms of collective existence that what may be termed *the emergent properties of action* took form over the first hundred years of settlement.[11] What began in 1630 as an attempt to construct the organizational mechanisms necessary for the reproduction of a social order based on the covenanted churches of visible saints, ended by the early eighteenth century in the virtual transformation of that order. The very attempt to ensure continuity and duration of a social order dedicated to the realization of the principle of religious purity ended in the abrogation of the original principles upon which continuity was to be based.

Central to this process of cultural transformation was the emergence of a basic tension between the major structures of authority and community in the first thirty years of settlement (1630–1660) and its resolution over the course of the next two generations of social life. It was ultimately only through a complex dynamic of negotiation between different groups, as they were subject to changing circumstances (and as perceived through the prism of their symbolic universe), that a workable framework of social action was established. In its establishment, more changed than just the shared assumptions on the ultimate meaning and purpose of collective life. The very institutional arrangements through which authority was exerted and collective identity asserted, also changed.

Many factors played a part in structuring the dynamics of institution building in seventeenth-century New England: the protest of different sectarian groups advancing a doctrine of spiritualized grace; relations with the mother-country; conflict between ministers and congregations; conflicts within the colonizing families; the Indian Wars; the Civil War and Restoration in England; and the process of structural change itself, characterized by economic expansion, demographic growth, and the increasing strength of mercantile elites in the early decades of settlement.[12] All of these different factors contributed to the specific ways through which the original salvific doctrines of the settlers were institutionalized over the seventeenth century in New England. Often, they were themselves influenced and structured in turn by the particular soteriological visions of the early Puritans and their attempt to institute them as the basis for the social order.

It is thus possible to divide the time span between the 1630s and 1730s into three distinct periods. The first decade of settlement saw the original attempt to build a social order on the basis of a community defined in terms of a shared experience of grace. The second period, from the end of the 1630s until the early 1660s, experienced the failure of the original definitions of community and authority. The original attempt at building long-lasting and pervasive definitions of order and the frameworks thereof ended in this period in the much discussed mid-seventeenth-century crisis of authority and in the Synod of 1662. The third period, from the 1660s until the early decades of the eighteenth century, witnessed an attempt to construct new patterns of social ordering through a broadening of the terms of collective membership beyond its original "theocratic" ideal and through the positing of new bases of legitimation of authority. Through these changes, what we have termed the charismatic basis of social life was essentially routinized in society, and the major institutional models of social action were crystallized. It is these three periods, or "moments," that will be analyzed through the transformation of the primary meaning-giving frameworks of society as this change was registered in those social institutions in which notions of authority and identity were enacted. The first period will be analyzed through the original premises of settlement, the second through the emerging tension between authority and community as manifest in the dynamics of religious protest and legal codification, and the final period through the changing locus of communal identity.

Origins, Separation, Identity

In the second and third decades of the seventeenth century, some 20,000 people crossed the Atlantic in an attempt to construct a new social and moral order based on pure Church practice. The very attempt, however, to construct "a new culture in a new world" led to a redefinition of their ties to the Church, country, and communities they left behind.[13] One of the major themes around which these questions revolved was the separatist nature of the settlement in New England. Thus, although John Cotton, one of the major religious leaders of the emigration, attempted in 1648 to repudiate any connection between the New England Congregational Way and the (earlier) separatist tendencies within Puritanism, there is little doubt that the churches established in New England in the 1630s were separatist in nature.[14] For the "gathered churches" that the Puritan saints established in the New England wilderness were dedicated to dual and interwoven purposes: on the one hand, to the establishment of a Congregational church policy (outlawed in England before the 1640s) and, on the other, to hastening the coming of the Kingdom of God through the building of a "Godly civil government."[15]

Since Perry Miller's designation of the New England Way as "non-separatist Congregationalists," historians have been debating the precise nature of the move to the American Strand.[16] Different opinions exist as to whether or not it constituted a clear break with the English church or whether (as opined by the leaders of the emigration) its roots were in the old non-Conformist tradition of William Ames, William Bradshaw, and Robert Parker.[17] Such a tradition, while viewing the churches of England to be corrupt, considered them nonetheless true churches and sought to reform rather than separate from them.[18] In many ways, the confusion of contemporary historians as to the precise nature of Congregational church polity (especially with respect to the English church system) reflects the contradictory nature of the historical sources themselves, such as for instance John Cotton's correspondence with the separating church of Salem, which belies an affinity with their polity not expressed in writings meant for an English audience.[19] Moreover, as noted by David Hall, a partial explanation of this confusion is to be found in the dynamic of settlement itself, which imposed its own logic on the practice of the Puritan settler, and, in so doing, led them to a more radical interpretation of Church polity than they had advanced while still in England.[20] Indeed, whether or not the Puritan emigrants to the New World were "separatists" in the technical sense (a much debated point, both then and now), they did, through their quest for a "pure" social order based on the practice of restricting Church membership to the visible saints, separate themselves from the major traditions of English church policy. In so doing, they distanced themselves as well from the major loci of communal solidarity, social identities and foci of social ordering, and meaning represented in and by the English church.

In fact, and as recent historiography has made clear, the act of emigration itself was undertaken precisely to allow this radical transformation in foundation of Church membership.[21] Only through the act of emigration could a pure Church order be established—one that would maintain the purity of the visible saints (religious virtuosi) inviolate and apart from the unregenerate. Whatever its theological justification, this policy represented a radical rejection of existing Church practice (not possible in England until the 1640s and 1650s) and thus de facto separation from the Church of England (though, to be sure, Puritan theologians presented the emigration itself as an alternative to rigid separation and the "unchurching" of the English church).[22]

Now many of these ideas, together with the refusal to wear the surplice, using the sign of the cross in baptism, the opposition to godparents, kneeling during the sacrament, standing at the reading of the Gospel, and bowing in the name of Jesus, were, in the early decades of the seventeenth century, common to Puritans in both Old and New England. However, the very move to the New World, and with it the possibility of constituting a new civil and ecclesiastical polity based on "Godly Ordinances," exacerbated the distance (symbolic and not solely physical) of the Puritan immigrants from existing and longstanding loyalties.

Thus, on the one hand Puritans in New England shared with their English compatriots a profound sense of "otherness" occasioned by the original break posited by Puritanism with the local, regional, and primordial structures of identity existent in sixteenth-century England. Covenanting themselves and thus setting themselves off from their local villages, their social rites and rituals, ceremonies of collective solidarity, and "the hagiography of festivals, the sports and dancing, the magic and taboos," the early Puritans—in both societies—evinced, in Keith Thomas's words an "implacable hostility to more primitive society."[23] On the other hand, in New England the differences between visible saints and the unregenerate took an institutional form unmatched by other Puritan communities of their time. For the Bay Puritans defined the civil community in sacred terms of the visible saints—the regenerate. These "elect" were, in civil obligations, duties, and liberties, set apart from the "ungodly" who had not "owned the covenant" and who were barred from both political membership in the community (they were denied the franchise) and from symbolic participation in communal rites (specifically in the partaking of the Lord's Supper) in the first decades of settlement.[24]

It is important to note that the restriction of Church membership to the visible saints, while a practice originally imported from the separating churches of England and Holland, attained during the first years of settlement an importance it had not had in the other Puritan "diasporas." For the minority nature of the separating Puritan churches in these countries, their distance from political power and so from any possibility of imposing their model on society at large, precluded its acceptance or institutionalization within the polity. In New England, however, where the Puritan elites that articulated this doctrine were the major carriers of social models and molders of collective desiderata, a serious attempt was made in the first decade of settlement to impose on society as a whole this model of collective membership as the legitimate and defining one.[25]

This doctrine was an early and defining characteristic of New England Puritanism, growing out of the settlement itself. For, while the "covenanting" of a community of saints was, as noted above, a practice begun in late sixteenth-century England, the transformation of the ties so engendered into the major criteria for collective membership was, in the 1630s, a predominantly New England development.[26] Further and critically, it was the dominant model of collective solidarity, enshrined in the colonial center and not in competition with other, more traditional or primordial models of identity and solidarity.

The problems of identity in seventeenth-century New England went, as can be adduced, beyond those aspects shared with English Puritan society. For, beyond the breakdown of existing, primordial systems of solidarity, the New England emigrants faced the crucial aforementioned problem of Church affiliation and were in constant tension with English civil and ecclesiastical authorities, as well as with Puritans in England, as to the proper definition of their Church organization. The problem of separatism was central in all the religious debates of the period. Today, it is perhaps difficult to assess the enormity of emotion that went into the separatist question in those years. But in the seventeenth century, not yet recovered from the schism of the Reformation, to be deemed a separatist or schematic was tantamount to being thrust beyond the borders of common humanity. In a society undergoing a process of change and transformation, the Church provided the major focus of collective solidarity and to break from it was, for many, an unthinkable proposition, evoking associations of antinomianism (in 1630, the specter of Munster was still very much alive).[27] The particularities of the New England Way, as their unique experiment at theocracy was termed, however, set them from the beginning against the Church of England. Hence, from the first decade of settlement, the Congregational clerical elites were engaged in a constant attempt to justify their ways and practices in relation to the English Reformation tradition.[28]

The Foundation of Authority

The reassertion within the Puritan communities of the charismatic dimension in novel symbolic and organizational forms was, as we have seen, dependent on its prior disembedment from the sacramental orders of the Church. Whereas this resulted in a transformation of the existing spatial and temporal categories through which it was conceived ("freeing" it, as it were, to enter different institutional realms) and allowing for the emergence of a this-worldly soteriology directed at the construction of new institutional spheres, it affected as well the analytic characteristics of charisma. For, with the disjunction effected between the sacrament and the sacred and as part of the overall rejection of existing and institutionalized rituals, hierarchies, offices, and roles by the Puritans, the mode of its symbolization was transformed. Devoid of its entrenchment in and symbolization through the institutional frameworks of the Church, it was rearticulated as an instance of what Weber termed *pure* or *genuine* charisma, that is to say, as a quality existing outside the realm of everyday routine and profane experience—connecting those sharing in its "call" to the ultimate principles of meaning and order.[29]

Accordingly, the New England Puritans introduced a number of organizational practices that exemplify the noninstitutionalized, immediate, unattenuated, and shared nature of their connection to the ultimate principles of meaning and cosmic ordering. The two realms where this reorganization of social life was felt most strongly were those of authority and membership in the collectivity. Within New England Congregationalism, both realms were explicitly linked in a manner that defined the uniqueness of their experiment in building a godly

Commonwealth. The practices upon which this experiment were based were the abjuration of ordination from England, lay ordination, and contractual versus sacerdotal conception of ministry.

Abjuration of Ordination from England

Upon arrival in New England, many of the leading ministerial elites renounced the ordination they had received at the hands of the English church and underwent a ritual of reordination.[30] In so doing, ministers of the stature of John Cotton, John Williams, George Phillips, and John Davenport repudiated the validity of the institutional framework of the Church in England in granting authority to the minister. To this they opposed a new set of practices.

Lay Ordination

In line with their conception of the bond between minister and a particular Church—as the root of the former's authority—many ministers underwent, as part of their reordination, ordination at the hands of laymen.[31] This practice, involving the "laying on of hands," was, while debated by some (notably James Noyes), accepted by the majority of ministers in New England in the early years of settlement.[32] Many churches, such as those "gathered" in Concord in 1637, founded the calling of the ministry "entirely on grace" and "vested their clerical status on the call of the gracious, whose sainthood endowed them with the unique prerogative of raising a fellow saint to the status of minister."[33] Interestingly enough, even those ministers, such as Richard Mather, who viewed lay ordination as inessential to the making of the ministry, declared that it was nevertheless "a comely and convenient rite . . . not to be neglected when it may be had in God's way."[34]

The principle of lay ordination and the practice of the laying on of hands both expressed the Puritan insistence on the close ties of minister to particular congregations, and the locus of ministerial authority in these ties. Such a connection, in its immediacy and intimacy, free from the attenuations of office, represents an attempt to articulate authority and the connection between figures of authority and those subject to it in terms of an undifferentiated, nonhierarchical union (akin to that of the primitive apostolic Church, which was indeed their

58   Innerworldly Individualism

express model). Both practices as well as the Puritan repudiation of the ordination from England, were part of a new conception of the ministry, which indeed stated this principle more explicitly.

Contractual vs. Sacerdotal Conception of Ministry

In their attempt to construct a new basis for the Church polity, the Puritans redefined the nature of the ministry as contractual.[35] As opposed to what was termed the sacerdotal conception, holding that the office of the minister was handed down from Christ, the Puritans held that the status of the minister rested on the "mutual engagement" of minister and congregation, the "body of the Church."[36] This conception, which tied the minister to one particular congregation and which stood apart from the practice of many English Puritans, was at the root of what was termed the *New England Way*. Itself based on the notion of the Church covenant of the gathered saints, the contractual understanding of the ministry affirmed in principle the direct and immediate connection of minister to a particular body of congregants. Thus, for example, John Cotton explained his refusal to carry out his ministerial functions (of administering the rite of baptism) while at sea, due "not for want of fresh water," but "1, because they had no settled congregation there; 2, because a minister hath no power to give the seals but in his own congregation."[37]

The principles and practices reviewed above, tending as they did to a reassertion of a nonhierarchical basis for Church polity, involved a change in the dominant modes of authority and membership within the Puritan communities, a fact that was not lost on their English contemporaries, who were critical of the seeming dependence of ministerial authority on the community of covenanted saints.[38] And, indeed, the problems raised by the English critics went to the heart of the contradictions inherent in New England church policy.[39] For the practices of lay sermonizing, popular preaching, prophecy, and lay ordination —usurping the prerogatives of the minister—all called into question the status and special character of the ministry. The essence of this form of Church organization was defined close to half a century later by John Norton, who affirmed "that all of the Church were a Royal Priesthood, all of them Prophets, and taught of God's Spirit, and that a few words from the heart were worth a great deal: intimating the Benefit of Bretherens prophesying."[40] This notion of the Church and the concrete practices it involved effectively represented a relatively open, undifferentiated, noninstitutionalized mode of social ordering, involving a new, more direct link between the ministers and congregants and, in essence, between community and the sources of cosmic meaning and authority. (This, of course, is the meaning of lay prophecy.)

The creative link forged between minister and congregation in mutual pursuit of divine purpose was, however, one which carried with it severe consequences for the construction of ordered and institutionalized models of social action. For, inherent in New England practice, in the very intimate interweaving of structures of authority with the basis of collective identity, were the seeds of an unresolvable conflict. The working out in the following decades of the tensions inherent in any social order between "structure" and "communitas," between genuine and routinized charisma, took the form of a tension or conflict between authority and community in New England.

The locus of the new link between authority and community with its incumbent tensions was in the covenant, which afforded a new "contractual" understanding of the relation between man and God, as well as between ministers and congregants. In such a manner, it provided new models of collective membership and of the boundaries of the collective, through the concept of the gathered Church of covenanted saints, and of legitimation of authority, through the contractual notion of ministerial authority. Both conceptions were, moreover, linked, based as they were on the conception of a shared unattenuated, egalitarian, and immediate connection to the ultimate source of meaning.[41] Finally, this charismatic moment was articulated symbolically in the historical visions of the settlers, who saw in the covenanting together of disparate individual wills the means to hasten the redemptive moment in history.

The Organization of Collective Meaning

Any understanding of the concrete practice of the New England Way (as defined by the covenant, the particular terms of Church membership and participation in the civil and ecclesiastical orders) must be secured within the context of the New England Puritans' attempt to build a godly Commonwealth. This served as an important ordering principle, or set of principles, which defined not only collective goals and this-worldly institutions (as working in the pursuit of the most

60   Innerworldly Individualism

transcendental of aims), the nature of the political order so that, in Edward Johnson's words, they may create "a new Heaven and a new earth in new Churches and a new Commonwealth together," but also and crucially for our purposes, the principles of collective meaning and identity.[42]

Tracing the outlines of any notion of collective meaning is, however, by its very nature a difficult endeavor and one that—as we shall see—changes over time. Comprising something more than the sum of individual meanings, collective meaning points to their embedment in those institutional spheres relevant to all members of the society. In the world of early seventeenth-century New England Puritanism, these can most easily be found in the motives for the emigration itself and the organization of Congregational church policy. Both, moreover, were interwoven and heavily invested with soteriological meanings.

Providential History

In the broadest of terms and with a richness that we cannot even begin to reproduce here, these meanings were tied to the Puritan view of history—or more properly of providential history.[43] For, as noted above, by breaking with the Augustinian dualism of this- and otherworldly spheres, the Puritans sought to infuse history and more especially their own undertaking with soteriological efficacy. With grace freed from its ritual embedment, it was, we may suppose, free to enter historical activity in the world, in fact and in certain periods in the early seventeenth century, to make of history itself, sacred history, *Heilsgeschichte*. (This of course has been a much studied theme of English Puritan historiography forming the core of the debates over English Puritan millennialism and of the place of millennial orientations among Puritan emigrants to the New World).[44] And though the radical articulation of their role in providential history would change over the course of the seventeenth century (though reappearing in certain forms in the jeremiad sermons of the last third of the century) the original impulse to settlement (and organizational forms thereof) were infused with an imagery and set of meanings that would resonate well into the eighteenth century.

For, drawing on long-standing English apocalyptic traditions, but coming, by the end of the first decades of the seventeenth century, to dismiss England's role in the history of salvation, the New England

Puritans saw their emigration (and hence "separation" from the Church of England) as infused with a transcendent meaning of hastening the Kingdom of Christ on earth.[45] As Thomas Hooker argued:

> For these are the times drawing on, wherein Prophecies are to attain their performances: and its a received rule and I suppose most sane, when Prophecies are fulfilled they are best interpreted, the accomplishment of them is the best commentary....
>
> ... These are the times, when the knowledge of the Lord shall cover the earth as the waters the Sea: and these waters of the Sanctuary shall encrease from the ankles unto the knees, thence unto the loins, and thence become a river that cannot be passed.[46]

It was to play their own role in the fulfillment of biblical prophecies (most especially of the eschatological scenario laid out in the Book of Revelation) that New England Puritans moved to the New World to construct their own models of ecclesiastical and civil polities.

Following the earlier traditions of John Bale, John Fox, and more especially Thomas Brightman, the leaders of the Puritan emigration reasoned their move in terms taken from the Book of Revelation.[47] Viewing themselves as actors in the apocalyptic scenario outlined by John of Patmos, they identified the English church and its policy with the "lukewarm Laodicea" and sought, through the establishment of the proper organization of civil and ecclesiastical orders, to bring about the "beginnings of Christ's glorious Reformation."[48]

Going forth into the New England wilderness, "To carrye the gospel into these parts of the world and to rayse a bullwarke against the Kingdom of Anti-Christ," the leaders of the migration asked if perhaps "God hathe provided this place [Massachusetts] to be a refuge for many whom he meanes to save out of the general destruction."[49] Indeed, as attested to by Edward Johnson in his *Wonder Working Providence of Sions Saviour in New England* the terms of the emigration itself were those of apocalyptic destruction and cosmic regeneration:

> When England began to decline in Religion, like luke-warm Laodicea, and instead of purging out Popery, a farther compliance was sought not onely in vaine Idolatrous Ceremonies, but also in prophaning the Sabbath, and by Proclamation throughout their Parish churches, exasperating lewd and prophane persons to celebrate a Sabbath like the Heathen to Venus, Baccus and Ceres; in so much that the multitude of irreligious lascivious and

popish affected persons spred the whole land like Grashoppers, in this very time Christ the glorious King of his Churches, raises an Army out of our English Nation, for freeing his people from their long servitude under usurping Prelacy; and because every corner of England was filled with the fury of malignant adversaries, Christ creates a New England to muster up the first of his Forces in; Whose low condition, little number and remotenesse of place made these adversaries triumph, despising this day of small things, but in this hight of their pride the Lord Christ brought sudden, and unexpected destruction upon them. Thus have you a touch of the time when this worke began.[50]

It is, furthermore, in this context that the "wilderness" was viewed by the Puritan emigrants. Again following the "holy Brightman," they interpreted the wilderness of the Book of Revelation with that of the New England forest where the faithful, those who hold to the true religion and "who cannot come together to worship God in publike assemblies because (of) the iniquities of the times," could repair in peace to worship and construct "the Temple." The wilderness in this interpretation was that place where "the poore handsome of the Elect lurke, where that Innumerable company lived, that posessed the holy city."[51]

Possession of "the holy city" implied, however, not simply the possession of "inner light," but the proper organization of Church and State in line with the Puritan conception of the early Christian church. "Called to be the faithful Soldeirs of Christ . . . to assist in building up his Churches . . . in pulling downe the Kingdome of Anti-Christ," the emigrants were likewise called upon to build a community that would be a "Cittie vpon a Hill."[52]

Indeed, in the thought of leading New England divines, the theme of proper Church organization and practice was linked to their view of providential history. An apocalyptic scenario of the future was often part and parcel of their belief in the ultimate justification of their own Church practice. Thus, for example, John Cotton reasoned that the great conflagration, which would

> raise such an earthquake . . . that if any City rise up against them fall it must, and stop unto them, and at length Rome it selfe fall, and all the Cities of the Nations that cleave unto her, and every mountain shall be rooted up, and all their consecrated places shall lie level with the common soile

would not cease until "men once begin clearely to see which is the true Church of God, that it is not Cathedrall, nor Provincial, nor Diocesan, but congregationall only, the officers whereof are godly Pastors, and Teachers and ruling Elders and Deacons."[53]

In such a manner, drawing on the apocalyptic traditions of the English Reformation, the Puritans explained to themselves and to the world both the very fact of their "errand into the wilderness" and the specific form of social life they established there—the singular meanings of which can be unraveled through analysis of the terms of membership held by the community.

Covenanted Communities

The major model of collective identity in Puritan New England— though its practice would change after the first decade of settlement —was the covenant. The covenant was first of all a mechanism providing borders between the pure and the impure. Deeming their own civil covenant as coexistent with the covenant of grace between God and mankind at the time of Christ, the settlers admitted into membership only those visible saints—the regenerate elect.[54] This drawing of clearly demarcated boundaries between and among collective members was, I would maintain, an ordering device of supreme magnitude. Positing basic divisions between those in covenant and those outside, the Puritans attempted a reordering of their shared symbolic and social universe in line with their particular cosmic visions.

Through the practice of covenanting together, a new definition of the model community, in township as in Church, was established.[55] This model community of the elect, of those who had undergone the experience of regeneration and presumably of sanctification, served as the fundamental referent of collective solidarity as a whole.[56]

This covenanting of communal members was itself, moreover, informed with strong providential meanings, which found expression in the different theological tracts expounding on the nature of the covenant. So, for example, one of the central texts of covenant theology, Thomas Hooker's *Survey of the Summe of Church Discipline,* sees expounding on "The order and manner, how the government of his kingdome is managed outwardly in his Churches" as one of the two most important subjects of inquiry "for this last age of the world."[57]

Innerworldly Individualism

For Thomas Hooker and for others, pursuing the pure form of Church organization, based on the covenanted congregations of visible saints was, in those times of "the shakings of heaven and earth," the central means to build the "kingdome of God."[58] In a less eschatological vein, but nevertheless stressing the transcendental aims of settlement, Winthrop aboard the *Arbella* stressed the aim of settlement as being

> to improue our liues to doe more seruice to the Lord the comforte and encrease of the body of christe whereof wee are members that our selues and posterity may be the better perseued from the Common corrupcions of this euill world to serue the Lord and worke out our Salvacion vnder the powr and purity of his holy Ordinances.[59]

The social (and symbolic) mechanism through which these goals were pursued was that of the covenant drawn up between the congregants.[60]

In light of our own earlier discussion of the role of covenantal theology in restructuring the parameters of the sacred in Puritanism, it is important to note the congruence between the covenant as the new locus of the sacred, of the social center, and as a definition of its contents. For while the covenant was, on the one hand, an ordering device marking off the boundaries of the center and participation and inclusion within it, it was also the central symbol of the social order, containing the referents to the ultimate loci of cosmic meaning and ordering. As such it played an important role in constituting the relations between civil and ecclesiastical orders.

The Theocratic Ideal

The connection between the overriding meanings attributed to the Puritan errand into the wilderness and the political principles of settlement were expressed most crucially in the particular Puritan notions of theocracy.[61]

In fact, it is not possible to understand the legitimation of either political or ecclesiastical authority in New England without viewing their roots in the uniquely Puritan concept of theocracy. For, true to Calvin—but interpreted after their own manner—the emigrants sought not only to construct the model of the "true Church" of regenerate saints, but to establish a Christian or godly Commonwealth. As Edward Johnson declared: "We chose not the place for the land, but for the government, that our Lord Christ might raigne over us, both in Church and Commonwealth."[62]

As implied in Johnson's dictum, the basis of the political order in New England was on a particular cooperation of civil and ecclesiastical institutions, existing "in co-ordinate state, in the same place reaching forth help mutually each to other for the welfare of both according to God."[63] Implying neither the unification nor opposition of civil and ecclesiastical spheres, the Puritans maintained that "God's institutions (such as the government of Church and of commonwealth) may be close and compact, and co-ordinate one to another, and yet not confounded."[64] The bases of this coordination were the covenants drawn up in civil and social realms "to profess and practice one truth according to that most perfect rule, the foundation whereof is everlasting love."[65] For the Puritans founded their social venture on two distinct forms of the covenant. One was the Church covenant, governing the ordering of the religious realm, while the other was the social or federal covenant, drawn up before the foundation of town or Church and intended as the basis of civil society.[66] The coordination of both covenants and their respective realms provided the basis of the Puritan notion of theocracy, a

> Form of Government where 1. the people that have the power of chusing their Governours are in Covenant with God 2. Wherein the men chosen by them are godly men, and fitted with a spirit of government: 3. In which the Laws they rule by are the Laws of God: 4. Wherein Laws are executed, Inheritances alloted, and civil differences are composed, according to Gods appointment: 5. In which men of God are consulted with in all hard cases, and in matters of Religion.... The form which was received and established among the people of Israel whil'st the Lord God was their Governour ... and is the same that which we plead for.[67]

This form of government, which kept the ungodly from participation in the political realm and limited both election to office as well as the right to "chuse among themselves magistrates and officers" to the company of the saints was, therefore, a theocracy only in a very special sense of the term. For, rather than the establishment of a sacerdotal order, under the rule of the ministers, it was an attempt to constitute a pure social order, untainted by the corruption of history. This conception with its radical implications of reformulating the fundamental terms of social existence was explicitly argued in Winthrop's letter to

66   Innerworldly Individualism

Viscount Say and Sele, where he argued that: "Whereas the way of God hath always beene to gather his churches out of the world; now the world, or civill state, must be raised out of the churches."[68]

The gathering of the civil state out of the churches and of civil society out of the community of saints presumed the coming of a new dimension of history, one in which the hitherto contradictory spheres of nature and grace would be united under a new dispensation.

The realization of this union in the sphere of the polity was in the particular mode of godly civil government instituted by the early settlers. It was, moreover, through the practice of this form of social organization that the emigrants saw themselves as participating in the great work of redemption, which would culminate in the establishment of Christ's kingdom. In the words that Edward Johnson put into the mouth of one of the "Souldiers of Christ," "taking their last farwell of ... Native Country, Kindred, Friends and Acquaintance":

> I am now prest for the service of our Lord Christ, to re-build the most glorious Edifice of Mount Sion in a Wildernesse, and as John Baptist, I must cry, Prepare yee the way of the Lord, make his paths strait, for behold hee is comming againe, hee is comming to destroy Antichrist, and give the whore double to drinke the very dregs of his wrath. Then my deare friend unfold thy hands, for thou and I have much worke to doe, I [ay] and all Christian Souldiers the World throughout.[69]

Central to the Puritan participation in this great and final instauration was the mode of civil government established in the New England colonies. Rule by holy ministers and sainted magistrates ensured the proper exercise of God's ordinances and so the establishment of a social order under the direct auspices of God's authority.

Summing up the above, it can be said that Puritan society in New England was a very particular social formation where the problems of maintenance of boundaries of communal membership, legitimation of authority, and anchoring collective existence in a cosmic order achieved a particular solution. First, the major model of organized communal life was that of the covenant entered upon by the regenerate saints. Second, the primary boundary maintaining mechanism was the Church itself, which symbolized, both to those in covenant and those without, the boundaries of the ideal community. Third, regulating the boundaries of membership (through the ritual of "owning the covenant"), the Church also embodied the ideal moral community of visible saints.

Moreover, in line with the propensity in the early years of settlement to define the nature of authority as being directly rooted in community, the covenant provided the major model for legitimizing authority and its organizational frameworks by anchoring them in a transcendental and finite cosmic order.[70] Exerted solely through those chosen from among the regenerate, the frameworks of authority in Church and civil polity were, as we have seen, rooted in the same categories of meaning as were those of community. The mechanisms through which authority was exerted (and acceptance evoked) were thus those through which communal identity was articulated as well. Membership in the Church of covenanted saints provided not only the locus of community, but also a bastion of authority, albeit one that was to exist in "coordinate state" with such lay structures as the general court, the courts of assistants, and the magistrature in imposing a particular set of definitions of social and cultural order.[71]

Notes

1. T. H. Breen, *Puritans and Adventurers: Change and Persistence in Early America* (New York: Oxford University Press, 1980), 46–62.
2. Michael Watts, *The Dissenters,* (Oxford: Oxford University Press, 1978), 62.
3. The roots of the Puritan migration to New England in terms of their anticeremonialism is discussed by Bozeman, *To Live Ancient Lives,* 102–14.
4. George Haskins, *Law and Authority in Early Massachusetts* (Hamden: Archon Books, 1960), 29.
5. John Davenport, *A Discourse about Civil Government in a Plantation whose Design is Religion* (Cambridge, 1663), 16.
6. We will return to a greater exploration of these themes in the final chapter.
7. See note 12 in chapter 1.
8. A similar insight into the this-worldly aspects of Anabaptist rule was offered by Karl Mannheim, *Ideology and Utopia* (New York: Harcourt Brace and Jonavitz, 1936), 212. The "reorganization of society in Munster" (Cohn, "The Pursuit of the Millennium," 294) was exemplified in such actions as the promulgation of a new legal code, the abolition of private ownership of money, the institution of a communism of goods, and polygamy. All of these were among the means instituted by Jan Bockelson to bring about a new social order. On the Anabaptists in Munster see also George Williams, *The Radical Reformation* (Philadelphia: Westminster Press, 1962), 362–86.
9. Seymor M. Lipset, *The First New Nation* (London: Heineman, 1963).
10. Peter Bulkeley, *The Gospel Covenant* (London, 1646), 425.
11. Bruce Kapfere, ed., *Transaction and Meaning: Directions in the Anthropology of Exchange and Symbolic Behavior* (Philadelphia: Institute for the Study of Human Issues, 1976), 15.

12. For studies of sectarian groups in New England, see Philip Gura, "The Contagion of Corrupt Opinion in Puritan Massachussets: The Case of William Pynchon," *William and Mary Quarterly* 39 (1982): 469–91; idem, "The Radical Ideology of Samuel Gorton," *William and Mary Quarterly* 36 (1979): 78–100; idem, *A Glimpse of Sion's Glory: Puritan Radicalism in New England 1620–1660* (Middletown, CT: Wesleyan University Press, 1984); and David Lovejoy, *Religious Enthusiasm in the New World, Heresy to Revolution* (Cambridge: Harvard University Press, 1985). For a study of New England's relations with England at this time, see Avihu Zakai, "Exile and Kingdom: Reformation, Separation and Millennial Quest in the Formation of Massachusetts and its Relation with England 1628–1660" (Ph.D. diss., Johns Hopkins University, 1982). On the changing relations of ministers and congregants, see Paul Lucas, *Valley of Discord: Church and Society Along the Connecticut River 1636–1662* (Middletown, CT: Wesleyan University Press, 1968); Emory Elliot, *Power and Pulpit in Puritan New England* (Princeton: Princeton University Press, 1975); and for the eighteenth century, Donald Scott, *From Office to Profession: The New England Ministry 1750–1850* (Philadelphia: University of Pennsylvania Press, 1970). In recent years work has been done in analyzing the role of the family in seventeenth-century New England beyond Edmund Morgan, *The Puritan Family, Religion and Domestic Relations in Seventeenth Century New England* (New York: Harper and Row, 1966) and the even earlier work of Arthur Calhoun, *A Social History of the American Family from Colonial Times to the Present* (New York: Barnes and Noble, 1945), vol. 1. Philip Greven's study entitled *The Protestant Temperament: Patterns of Child Rearing, Religous Experience and the Self in Early America* (New York: New American Library, 1977) is an important contribution to this much neglected field, as is the more interpretive work of David Leverenz, *The Language of Puritan Feeling, an Exploration in Literature, Psychology and Social History* (New Brunswick, NJ: Rutgers University Press, 1980). See also Daniel Smith, "The Study of the Family in Early America—Trends, Problems and Perspectives," *William and Mary Quarterly* 39 (1982): 3–28. The best study of the rise of the mercantile elite remains that of Bernard Bailyn, *The New England Merchants in the Seventeenth Century* (Cambridge: Harvard University Press, 1955).
13. Early histories of New England that deal with these problems are those by John Winthrop, *The History of New England from 1630 to 1649,* ed. John Savage (Boston, 1853) and Thomas Hutchinson, *The History of the Colony and Province of Massachussets Bay,* ed. L. S. Mayo (Boston, 1963). A good perspective on the English background of the settlers is provided by Breen, *Puritans and Adventurers,* 4–67, and T. Breen and S. Foster, "Moving to the New World: The Character of Early Massachusetts Immigration," *William and Mary Quarterly* 30 (1973): 189–222. See also Keith Sprunger, "William Ames and the Settlement of Massachussets Bay," *New England Quarterly* 39 (1966): 66–79.
14. This position was taken in 1648, the year he published *The Way of the Congregational Churches Cleared*. Although the New England Puritans denied any connection with the separatism of Robert Browne, they were undoubtedly at least the "spiritual heirs" of his vision of a "reformation without tarrying for anie." On these perspectives, see Watts, *The Dissenters,* 26–34. A good exposition on the

whole debate around the separatist question can be found in David Hall, *The Faithful Shepherd: A History of the New England Ministry in the Seventeenth Century* (New York: Norton, 1972), 3–47.
15. Davenport, *A Discourse,* 73.
16. Perry Miller, *Orthodoxy in Massachusetts* (Boston: Beacon Press, 1959), 73–102.
17. See Edmund Morgan, *Visible Saints: The History of a Puritan Idea* (Ithaca: Cornell University Press, 1975), 65.
18. Lazer Ziff, ed., *John Cotton on the Churches of New England,* (Cambridge, 1968), 186–95.
19. See Hall, *The Faithful Shepherd,* 79. This debate notwithstanding, the very rejection by the New England Puritans of the English *Book of Common Prayer* belies any protestations to nonseparatism.
20. Ibid., 88–92; Lazer Ziff, *Puritanism in America: New Culture in a New World* (New York: Vintage Press, 1973), 27–48.
21. Zakai, "Exile and Kingdom," 211–27.
22. Ibid., 226.
23. Quoted in Michael Zuckerman, "The Fabrication of Identity in Early America," *William and Mary Quarterly* 34 (1977): 191.
24. Indeed, the connection established in the lives of the emigrants between the break with primordial identities and ties on the one hand, and the establishment of a pure Church practice on the other, was explicitly stated by John Allin, the first minister of the Dedham congregation, who reminded his congregants that "only 'the hope of enjoying Christ in his ordinances' could have persuaded the emigrants to 'forsake dearest relations, parents, brethren, sisters, Christian friends and acquaintances.'" Kenneth Lockridge, *A New England Town, the First Hundred Years* (New York: Norton, 1970), 23.
25. On the differences between these Puritan settlements, see Watts, *The Dissenters,* 26–76 and Tolmie, "The Triumph of the Saints." A contemporary description of the separatist colony at Plymouth is provided by William Bradford, *Of Plymouth Plantation* (New York: 1979) and analyzed by Jesper Rosenmeier, "With My Own Eyes: William Bradford's *Of Plymouth Plantation*," in *The American Puritan,* ed. S. Bercovitz, 77–104. Further material on the colony at Plymouth can be found in John Demos, *A Little Commonwealth* (Oxford: Oxford University Press, 1970) and J. Bumstead, "A Well-Bounded Toleration: Church and State in the Plymouth Colony," *Journal of Church and State* 10 (1968): 265–79.
26. In attempting such a move the New England Puritans were tackling what was the prime difficulty in Calvinist practice—the building of the "godly society" in a community larger and more diversified than that of a city.
27. See, for example, the reference to the Anabaptists in *The Book of General Lauues and Libertyes,* (Cambridge, 1648), 1.
28. This problem of the place of the New England church system within the English Reformation tradition forms the subject of E. Morgan's masterful study entitled *Visible Saints*. The emigration was not solely a clerical venture. The importance of the laity in the emigration has been analyzed by Zakai, "The Gospel of Reformation," 584–602.
29. Weber, *Economy and Society,* 241–45.

70 Innerworldly Individualism

30. L. Ziff, ed., *John Cotton*, 41–3; Thomas Hooker, *A Survey of the Summe of Church Discipline* (London, 1648), 11, 41.
31. A description of this practice can be found in Winslow, "Meetinghouse Hill," 22–23.
32. On James Noyes, see Hall, *The Faithful Shepherd*, 105.
33. Steven Foster, "New England and the Challenge of Heresy, 1630–1660: The Puritan Crises in Transatlantic Perspective," *William and Mary Quarterly* 38 (1981): 655.
34. Quoted in Hall, *The Faithful Shepherd*, 105.
35. For an interesting attempt to argue the basis of the contractualism of the ministry in terms of their social position, see Zaret, "The Heavenly Contract."
36. Hall, *The Faithful Shepherd*, 102.
37. Winthrop, *History of New England*, vol. 1, 131.
38. See Hall, *The Faithful Shepherd*, 103. On other aspects of New England theology in respect to English doctrine, see Richard Burg, "The Ideology of Richard Mather and its Relationship to English Puritanism Prior to 1660," *Journal of Church and State* 9 (1967): 364–77.
39. One example of the attempt to deal with English criticisms of the New England Way was John Allin and Thomas Shepherd's *A Defense of the Answers Made to Nine Questions or Propositions* (London, 1648), which carried on a debate begun in 1637 over New England church policy. Further evidence of English Puritan concern over developments in New England is evinced in A. Forbes, ed., *The Winthrop Papers*, vol. 3 (Boston: Massachusetts Historical Society, 1929–1947), 54, 100.
40. Related by Samuel Sewall, *The Diary of Samuel Sewall 1674–1729*, vol. 1, ed. M. Halsey Thomas (New York, 1973), 37.
41. John Cotton, *The Way of the Congregational Churches Cleared* London, 1648), 4.
42. Edward Johnson, *Wonder Working Providence of Sions Saviour in New England*, ed. J. F. Jameson (London, 1654; New York: Scribner, 1952), 25.
43. Zakai, "Exile and Kingdom," 156–206
44. The role of millennial orientations among Puritans on both sides of the Atlantic has of course been a continuing and heated subject for scholarly debate. Some of the more well-known contributions to this debate on the English side include: Bryan Ball, *A Great Expectation: Eschatological Thought in English Protestantism to 1660* (Leiden: E.J. Brill, 1975); Bernard Capp, *The Fifth Monarchy Men: A Study in Seventeenth Century English Millennarianism* (London: Faber and Faber, 1972); idem, "The Millennium and Eschatology in England," *Past and Present* 52 (1972): 106–17; Christopher Hill, *Anti-Christ in Seventeenth Century England* (London: Oxford University Press, 1971); idem, *The World Turned Upside Down: Radical Ideas During the English Revolution* (Harmondsworth: Penguin, 1975); idem, *Puritanism and Revolution: Studies in Interpretation of the English Revolution of the Seventeenth Century* (London: Mercury Books, 1962); William Lamont, *Richard Baxter and the Millennium: Protestant Imperialism and the English Revolution* (London: Helm Books, 1979); Tai Liu, *Discord in Zion: The Puritan Divines and the Puritan Revolution* (The Hague: M. Nijhoff, 1973); Leo Solt, " The Fifth Monarchy Men: Politics and the Millennium," *Church History* 30 (1961):

314–24; Charles Webster, *The Great Insaturation: Science, Medic and Reform 1626–1660* (London: Duckworth, 1975). On the American side, see Sacvan Bercovitz, *The Puritan Origins of the American Self* (New Haven, CT: Yale University Press, 1975); Clark Gilpin, *The Millenarian Piety of Roger Williams* (Chicago: University of Chicago Press, 1979); A. Gilsdorf, "The Puritan Apocalypse: New England Eschatology in the Seventeenth Century" (Ph.D. diss., Yale University, 1965); Alan Heimart, *Religion and the American Mind* (Cambridge: Harvard University Press, 1966); John F. MacClear, "New England and the Fifth Monarchy: The Quest for the Millennium in Early American Puritanism," *William and Mary Quarterly* 32 (1975): 223–60; idem, "The Republic and the Millennium," in *Religion in American History*, ed. J. Millder and J. Wilson (Englewood Cliffs, NJ: Prentice Hall), 181–99; Ernest Tuveson, *Redeemer Nation: The Idea of America's Millennial Role* (Chicago: University of Chicago Press, 1968). A general, if somewhat dated, bibliography of these and other perspectives on millennialism can be found in Hillel Swartz, "The End of the Beginning: Millennarian Studies," *Religious Studies Review* 2/3 (1976): 1–15.
45. This interpretation has most recently been contested by Theodore Bozeman in *To Live Ancient Lives,* 193–262.
46. Hooker, *A Survey of the Summe*.
47. For the contemporary sources of the emigrants' eschatology, see John Foxe, *Acts and Monuments of These Latter and Perilous Days* (London, 1563); Thomas Brightman, *The Revelation Illustrated* (Leiden, 1616). The English tradition has been expounded on by William Haller, *Foxe's Book of Martyrs and the Elect Nation* (London: Jonathan Cape, 1963); Katherine Firth, *The Apocalyptic Tradition in Reformation Britain 1530–1645* (Oxford: Oxford University Press, 1979); Paul Christianson, *Reformers and Babylon: English Apocalyptical Visions from the Reformation to the Even of the Civil War* (Toronto: University of Toronto Press, 1978).
48. Johnson, *Wonder Working Providence,* 23, 49.
49. John Winthrop, *General Observations for the Plantation of New England,* vol. 2, ed. A. Forbes (Boston, 1929), 114.
50. Johnson, *Wonder Working Providence,* 23.
51. Thomas Brightman, "The Revelation Illustrated," 133. For further perspectives on the wilderness see Peter Caroll, *Puritanism and the Wilderness* (New York: Columbia University Press, 1969); Alan Heimart, "Puritanism, the Wilderness and the Frontier," *New England Quarterly* 26 (1953): 61–82.
52. Johnson, *Wonder Working Providence,* 30; John Winthrop, in *The Puritans,* ed. Miller and Johnson (1630), 199.
53. John Cotton, *The Pouring Out of the Seven Vials* (London, 1642), 16. (The numbering of this edition begins again with the explication of each "vial." This number refers to the last, seventh vial.)
54. See Mosse, "The Holy Pretense," 91.
55. For a history of one such community that stresses the covenantal element, see Kenneth Lockridge, "The History of a Puritan Church 1636–1766," *New England Quarterly* 40 (1967): 399–424.
56. A good description of the covenanting together of Church members and its cen-

72   Innerworldly Individualism

trality in the lives of the congregation is provided by Winslow, *Meetinghouse Hill,* 18–35.

57. Hooker, *A Survey of the Summe,* a2.
58. On Thomas Hooker, see Clinton Rossiter, "Thomas Hooker," *New England Quarterly* 25 (1952): 409–88.
59. Winthrop, (1630) in Miller and Johnson, eds., *The Puritans,* 197.
60. For a concise statement of the role of the covenant in organizing social life, see A. Forbes, ed., *The Winthrop Papers,* vol. 4 (1944), 170–71.
61. On theocracy, see Zakai, "Exile and Kingdom," (1992), 231–52.
62. Johnson, *Wonder Working Providence,* 46.
63. Davenport, *A Discourse about Civill Govenment,* 6–8.
64. John Cotton, (1636) in Miller and Johnson, eds., *The Puritans,* 209.
65. Lockridge, *A New England Town,* 4–5.
66. Discussion of the different Church and civil covenants can be found in Lockridge, ibid., 24–30. It must be noted that often the Church covenant preceded that of the town.
67. Davenport, *A Discourse About Civill Govenment,* 14–15, 45.
68. John Winthrop, "A Reply to an Answer Made to a Declaration," in *Collection of Papers Relative to the History of the Colony of Massachusetts Bay,* vol. 1, compiled by T. Hutchinson (Boston, 1865), 100–101.
69. Johnson, *Wonder Working Providence,* 52.
70. It is important to note that in the early years of settlement, this notion of the "ideal community" was more than just a symbolic model. There existed among the early settlers an expectation that sooner or later all members of the community would join the Church. (P. Miller, *The New England Mind,* 80; D. Hall, *Faithful Shepherd,* 97; K. Lockridge, *New England Town,* 36.) The failure of this mass conversion to take place was, as we shall see, central to the developing dynamics of authority and community in seventeenth-century New England.
71. Davenport, *A Discourse About Civill Govenment,* 8.

3

Protest and Collective Boundaries

The problems posed by the institutionalization of the original conceptions of social ordering into long-lasting patterns of social action were great. For, following the first flowering of the charismatic impulse in the early years of settlement (as marked by a series of conversions), the settlers of the Massachusetts Colony were forced to admit the inherently finite nature of a genuinely charismatic definition of social existence. The falling off in Church membership, the drop in the number of initiates into the community of saints, together with the growth of alternative loci of communal identification and of authority—such as among the followers of Anne Hutchinson—threatened the very basis and meaning of the communal venture.

The Hutchinson affair, or the Antinomian crisis, was, it will be argued, a major, if typical development, stemming from the original premises of settlement in New England. The continuity of certain themes of protest, first raised during the Hutchinson affair, in the preaching and practice of Samuel Gorton, as well as among New England's Quakers, illustrates the perduring nature of those tensions first brought to light during the Antinomian crisis.

These themes centered on the indwelling of the Holy Spirit and consequently on the freedom of the "true Christian," of those under the "law of grace" for abiding by the "moral law."[1] This doctrine, with its salient derivatives in terms of obedience to authority and acceptance of the given terms of community, was inherent in the very definition of the social order in New England—as a community of shared grace. The tension, existent within this doctrine, toward a particular and individualistic articulation of grace, beyond the purview of community and authority, emerged in full force with the very institutionalization of this particular definition of the social order.

In this chapter we shall analyze the Antinomian crisis as an instance of the dynamics of institutionalization. That is to say, given the original symbolic premises of settlement, the emergence of Anne's "heretical" ideas and the resonant echo they found among many of the settlers was in a sense mandated or "overdetermined" by the development of those social roles, statuses, and organizational structures that make up the fabric of social life.

It is no mere coincidence that the years of the Antinomian crisis fall within a period marked by legal codification and the construction of organizational frameworks for local political rule.[2] As we shall explore in the following two chapters, the relation between both developments was no accident of history. The Antinomian crisis not only furthered the organizational differentiation of authority from community, but was also a particular response to a growing crisis in the ideal models of community. Similarly, while the formalization and codification of principles of authority and social ordering only culminated in the period following the banishment of Anne, its origins preceded her preaching.

Inherent in the attempt to make the principle of grace the symbolic basis of social ordering, both developments registered the inherent contradiction of such a conception. This contradiction, as well as the solutions posited in early seventeenth-century New England, were of great importance to the later development of social life.

The Emergent Tensions

The original impetus to settlement, as well as its early years in the first decade, were characterized by a shared experience of grace, or, at the very least, an expectation of such an experience. This experience provided an immediate connection of communal members to the ultimate matrixes of meaning and cosmic order. United together by strongly felt, shared ideological ties and divesting themselves (at least in part) of established kinship and other more primordial links, these communities were organized under the "stewardship" of ministers and magistrates professing an immediate relation both to their congregants and to the loci of ultimate authority and cosmic meaning. While frameworks of authority were constituted in the form of magistrates, ministers and the body of the general court and the courts of assistants, the ideal model of authority—at least in the Church—rested on its intimate links to the community of covenanted saints. Furthermore, the limiting of the body of electors to Church members was itself an affirmation not only of the fundamental models of community, rooted in the covenant, but of the nature of authority—in this case, civil authority—as rooted in this sainted community.

Having rearticulated the nature of social life in terms of a community of sainted individuals sharing in divine grace, the Puritans faced the particular problems inherent in the institutionalization of this conception within the social order. The course of institutionalization, which would eventually lead to the transformation of the matrixes of social existence from the Church to the world, was structured by the major tensions existing with the symbolic definitions of the social order and the concrete dynamics of enacting these symbolic premises in worldly affairs.

The major tension within the symbolic premises of New England Congregational Puritanism was between the structural and organizational imperatives of institution building, of building the "Cittie upon the Hill," and the highly "liminal," antistructural nature of the broad definitions of meaning and order. That is to say, on the one hand, there existed an overriding concern with constructing a system of meanings and identities, which led in turn to a salient concern with the posting of boundaries, with the delineation of the parameters of order, and with the positing of a totalistic, tightly structured system of cultural and social ordering based on the covenanted Church of visible saints. On the other hand, the very terms in which these definitions were posited of regeneration and the experience of grace—tended toward more open, diffuse, and undifferentiated modes of interpreting the social order—as was indeed manifest in the growth of different protest groups articulating a doctrine of free grace and impinging on the Puritan social and religious center. This trend toward, following Mary Douglas, a more "effervescent" mode of symbolizing the social order stood in tension with the construction of more ordered and institutionalized modes of social interaction.[3] The locus of this tension was in the potential for a genuinely charismatic experience to lead to both the building of a social order and the diffusion of institutional arrangements. So, for example, the selfsame direct experience of charisma as an infusion of grace, the same "outpouring of the spirit" that led to

John Cotton's "harvest" (conversion) of sixty-three new Church members in 1633 (thus strengthening the building of a "Godly Commonwealth"), led as well to the Antinomian crisis three years later (which threatened the very basis of social life).[4]

Related to this tension, which was inherent in the attempted articulation of community and authority in terms of a shared experience of grace and still on the symbolic level, was the ultimately circumscribed nature of this experience. The expectations of continuous conversions, and hence the inclusion of most, if not all, members of the community within the Church of visible saints—which had characterized the first years of settlement—was soon disappointed. Hence, together with the growth of the age-old dichotomy between the Church and the world within Puritan New England, arrangements had to be made to accommodate both realms and to bring them into a unitary frame of meaning. This was attempted through the codification and enactment of civil and ecclesiastic legislation, for which agitation had begun as early as 1635 and which culminated in 1648 with *The Cambridge Platform of Church Discipline* on the one hand and *The Book of General Lawes and Liberties* on the other. However, and legislation notwithstanding, a tension remained between the existence and, indeed, the growth of a populace beyond the confines of the Church and the ideal models of community and authority rooted in the Church of covenanted saints.

More concretely, these tensions were felt in the growth of different forms of protest to the social and religious centers of collective life. So, for example, the Antinomian crisis of 1636–37 impressed on all participants the problematic nature of basing the principles of community and authority on free grace, as did the protest of "Vanists," Grotonians, and, later, Quakers and Baptists. In a similar manner, Robert Child's petition to the Massachusetts General Court in 1646 to enlarge Church membership and so broaden the basis of the electorate, exemplified the problems of enforcing a Holy Commonwealth on an increasingly "profane" body of communicants.

The institutionalization of the original terms of settlement into longlasting patterns of social order was structured by the above noted factors, of concrete historical action as informed by the symbolic visions of the social actors involved. The long-term trajectory of institutionalization was marked by a reformulation of the original locus of collective existence, by its transformation and changing arena, from the Church of covenanted saints to the world beyond the Church.

In slightly more concrete terms, this transformation was felt in the changing set of relations between and within the definitions of authority and models of community over the first hundred years of settlement. The first thirty years of settlement were characterized by the growth of a strongly felt tension within the polity between the agencies of authority and the definitions of community. Rooted in the selfsame models of cosmic ordering noted above and enacted in similar organizational mechanisms of covenanted churches, at the start of settlement, the process of their divergence began almost immediately. The period from 1630 to 1660 was thus marked by an asymptotic development of a codification (attempted institutionalization) of models of social order by those in positions of authority and the growing articulation of alternate models—of both authority and community—by different protest groups within society. Analysis of this process, through two case studies, of the Antinomian crisis as exemplifying the forces of protest and the codification of laws in the decade of the 1640s, will allow us to define the developing tensions and problems inherent in the process of institutionalization.

The Antinomian Crisis

Protest and the Contradictions in the Social Order

The fragility of the social order, defined by the set of tensions noted above, was made almost immediately apparent in the growing struggles between different groups in the polity over the proper understanding of New England's errand. Within six years of settlement, the contradictions implied in building a social order on the principles of grace made themselves apparent. These were manifest in the positive reception accorded the doctrines of different groups among the emigrants to the Massachusetts Bay Colony, whose interpretation of Puritan doctrine set them in opposition to the magistrates and ministers of the still infant social center. Groups of "Hutchinsonians," "Vanists," and Grotonians (and later Quakers and Baptists) preached, in the first decades of settlement, a doctrine of "inner grace" and spirituality, which brought upon them the opprobrium and wrath of the powers at large.[5]

To understand the extent of intolerance granted these groups and the place of "Toleration of divers Religions," along with "The standing of the Apocrypha in the Bible, Forrainers dwelling in my Country," and "Alchymized coines" as those four things "naturally detested" by Nathanial Ward, it is imperative to analyze the nature of these conflicting world visions as well as their sociological concomitants in the context of the attempt to institutionalize the original premises of settlement.[6]

The struggle carried out against the various protesting groups in the first half of the seventeenth century in New England was in a sense over the fundamental and defining tenets of communal life—over the definitions of communal identity, membership, and solidarity and over the legitimation of authority. The extent of repression (banishment, hangings, whippings) meted out to "Hutchinsonians," Grotonians, and Quakers can only be understood in the overall context of the struggle to define the social parameters of the godly Commonwealth, the course of which revealed the growing chasm between authority and community as it developed in the first generation of settlement.

In the past, different attempts have been made to explain the nature of these conflicts. Some studies, such as those by Emory Battis, have concentrated on the Antinomian crisis from the perspective of power relations within the Boston community, while others have focused on the theological elements in the debate.[7] These have been supplemented by the important work of Kai Erikson, on the Hutchinsonians in particular (but also on other groups), from the perspective of deviance—seeking to explain the reasons for their repression by the powers of magistrate and ministers in terms of the defense of the moral boundaries of the community.[8]

My own treatment of the problem of tolerance in New England will place it in the perspective of the developing tensions between definitions of community and the terms of authority, tensions which marked the first phase of institution building in seventeenth-century New England.

The Antinomian crisis was in many ways a test case of the New England Way. And although the protagonists and many historians have vindicated the outcome, in that it allowed for the further strengthening of communal ties and the continued building of the "Cittie Upon the Hill," free of the "American Jezebel," I would propose a somewhat different interpretation. For, in essence, the course of the controversy showed up the fundamental, built-in contradiction at the heart of New England's errand. Seeking to build a social order on a shared experience of grace, which dictated an immediate, direct, and relatively undifferentiated connection between authority and community, the leaders of the Bay Colony and, indeed, Connecticut were forced in its wake to institute a slow separation of realms, to posit a distance between community and authority. Consequently, authority began, soon after the end of the crisis, to seek institutional mechanisms for maintaining its prerogatives.

Moreover, they soon learned that seeking to base civil and ecclesiastical authority on the labile concept of free grace opened up a void of uncertainty, indefinition, and chaos, as a host of self-proclaimed saints could not only decree their own salvation, but question, in so doing, the very fabric of society's laws and institutions.[9] Building their social order on a promise of the imminent conversion of all communal members and the no less imminent realization of grace within the orders of the world, they soon learned that the "spirit," as John Bossy once remarked, "bloweth where it listeth."[10] And, it should be added, in so blowing, opened up the possibility for alternative systems of meaning and order to be advanced in opposition to the original tenets of the communal venture.

The Theological Terms of the Conflict

Implicit to the process of institution building is a problem of ordering. This is felt in a heightened concern to order mundane existence and bring it in line with the major principles of cosmic order. It is therefore not surprising that most of the struggles carried out between different groups of social elites in this period revolved around the proper application of divine principles to the mundane sphere of social organization. This was, in essence, the crux of the argument surrounding the Hutchinson affair, as well as of the pervasive controversies between the Puritan authorities and other groups, such as the Quakers and Baptists. The theological controversy over nature and grace, over the efficacy of the "covenant of grace" as opposed to the "covenant of works," was, in essence, over the fundamental and ruling premises of Puritan life. As such, it touched the nerve center of social life—the conceptions of authority and community.

Puritan theology, it is remembered, rested on a doctrine of the two covenants: the covenant of works concluded between God and Adam, which promised mankind everlasting life in return for obedience to divine law; and the covenant of grace, which replaced it after the Fall. The covenant of works, which concluded with Adam, was essentially the law of nature, that moral law implanted in the heart of "uncorrupted" man, naturally known to man whose being was so constructed to allow the unaided performance of the duties and obligations of the covenant. Adam's failure to keep the covenant—the Fall—brought about not only just punishment, but the establishment of a new covenant (first with Abraham and renewed with Jesus Christ) that took account of man's inability to fulfill the law or indeed any possibility of agency in upholding the terms of the covenant. Given man's now corrupt and fallen state, God demands (in the new covenant) "not a deed but a belief, a simple faith in Christ the mediator."[11] And in return for this belief, God undertakes not only to save the believer and provide the strength for belief but also to provide that grace necessary to fulfill the terms of the new covenant.

In explicating the difference between the covenants of works and grace, Peter Bulkeley in *The Gospel Covenant or the Covenant of Grace Opened* noted the following:

> The first one requires doing, the other believing; the one workes, the other faith; the one faith, Doe this and live, the other faith, Believe and thou shalt be saved . . . the Covenant of works is made without a Mediator, to mediate between God and man. But in the covenant of grace there is a mediator coming between, to unite God and man together, to make them one. . . . In the Covenant of workes, a man is left to himselse, to stand by his own strength; But in the Covenant of grace, God undertakes for us, to keep us through faith. . . . In the covenant of works, Gods highest end is the glorifying of his justice; In the Covenant of grace, it is to glorifie his Grace: In the Covenant of works, God reveals himselse a just God, rewarding good and punishing evil, condemning sin; but in the Covenant of grace, he shews himselse a God gracious and mercifull, forgiving iniquity. . . . In the Covenant of workes, God deals alike with all, that are alike in themsleves . . . grace deales diversly with men that are equall in themselves. . . . That the Covenant of works (if it be accomplished and fulfilled) leaves in man matter of glorying and boasting in himselse; in the covenant of grace excludes all glorying in a mans self, and leaves him nothing of his owne to boast of, but in the grace of God. . . . The Covenant of workes is impossible to be fulfilled by us, in this state of corruption;

But the Covenant of grace by the helpe of grace is possible to be fulfilled.... The Covenant of workes was made with man in the state of Innocency before his fall; but the Covenant of grace was made afterwards, when he had fallen; for before the fall, there was no impossibilitie, but man was able to have fulfilled the Law, and therefore God might justly require such obedience of him: then man stood in no need of a Covenant of grace, he might have had life by the Covenant of workes; but after the fall, then he became impotent, unable to fulfill the Law which God had given him, and then without a new Covenant of grace he could not live, and therefore now God enters into a Covenant of grace with him. [In sum] The Covenant of works is revealed by the light of Naturel but the covenant of grace is revealed by a supernaturall light from above.[12]

Now it must be added that the potential tension between these two covenants often manifested itself in the religious thought of certain Puritans in both New and old England. For the fulfillment of the terms of the covenant of grace bespoke, in Peter Bulkeley's thought, a new dispensation, a new birth where man, reconciled to God, "lays down all weapons of defiance and submits in love ... making these subjects happy that are free in his Kingdom." Binding the saint to the Lord, grace

makes the soul lament its bondage unto other Lords ... and ... see the blessing of the Lord's government, the Laws of God which were before counted as cords and bonds, fitter for bondslaves than for freemen, are now esteemed holy and just and good.[13]

To John Cotton and the Hutchinsonians, this state of grace (in, it may be added, direct opposition to the intentions of the author) implied a break with the covenant of works and with the ontological order of creation it represented. Thus, John Cotton, in his own *Treatise of the Covenant of Grace* (1652) makes much use of that "Christian liberty" that appears in the New Testament as the work of God, through Christ redeeming mankind of their created nature by "taking it" upon himself:[14]

Even from a state of bondage, unto Christian liberty; this is found in all redemption properly so called: It findeth us in bondage, and setteth us in a state of liberty .... He took our nature upon him, that he might deliver them, who through fear of death were all their lifetime made subject to bondage. . . . In a state of Bondage we were under the Law and the curse of God, but Christ hath redeemed us from the curse of the law (Galatians 3:13) and now sin shall no more have dominion over us, for we are not under the law (Romans 6:14) that is not under the Covenant of the Law, though we lie under the Commandment of it in Christ: we were sometime under the bondage of sin, under the guilt and strength of sin; but by Christ we have redemption, even the forgiveness of our sin: and as the Law was the strength of sin; so sin was the strength and sting of death (l Corinthians 15:56) but now O death where is thy sting! O grave, where is thy victory! the Lord hath delivered us from him that hath the power of death . . . and from this evil world . . . and from the wrath to come.[15]

In contrast to the mainstream of Puritan thought, represented by such divines as William Ames, John Preston, and Richard Sibbes in England and Thomas Shepard and Peter Bulkeley in New England, John Cotton's conception saw the covenant of grace as effectively replacing the covenant of works and "the continuity of the ontological and moral orders established at creation."[16] This doctrine, viewing the covenants of works and grace as mutually exclusive, was understandably viewed with apprehension, if not outright fear, by the leaders of the Bay Colony (as well as by divines in England), who saw in the repudiation of the covenant of works a rejection of "the order of being and morality that compose the substance and rule of earthly life."[17] The road opened by such an interpretation led, in their eyes, directly to a negation of all morality and respect for magistracy. And so they constantly emphasized that although the covenant of grace replaced the covenant of works as "the instrument of God's salvific government . . . it does not free the faithful from the law as a rule."[18] In consequence, and as "the doctrine of the covenant [became] the scaffolding and the framework for the whole edifice of theology . . . the essence of their program of salvation," it was necessary to emphasize the continuity of nature (as the covenant of works) and grace (the covenant of grace) as "mutually implying each other."[19] Within the mainstream of Puritan thought, a synthesis between the two was therefore posited. In William Stoever's words, the process of regeneration was in Puritanism "approached through a dialectic of nature and grace that preserve[d] the integrity of the one and the efficiency of the other."[20]

However, Protestant thought in general and New England practice in particular was, through its stress on grace, more than partial to the

Antinomian pole of the tension between nature and grace.²¹ This "Antinomian bent," which was manifested in the particular unity sought between models of community and authority, as well as in the view of providential history of the settlers, was nevertheless constantly held in check by the pervading belief in the continuity of the moral law. These checks, which ultimately made social order possible, as developed by Reformation divines of sixteenth- and seventeenth-century England, revolved in the main around the process of regeneration itself. Positing a "sweet concurrence between divine grace and natural human activity," the Puritan theologians saw regeneration as progressing through natural human capacities (empowered to perform holy actions), a doctrine which implied, on the one hand, the need (if not the sole efficacy) of institutions such as the Church and its ordinances and officers (and, in New England, the very construction of the Godly Commonwealth) and, on the other, the ability of individuals to perceive evidence of their "justification" in the workings of a sanctified life.²²

It was precisely this doctrine, which Anne opposed with a vehemence, that turned the covenant of works into a synonym of degeneration and damnation. Denouncing the ministers for preaching a covenant of works, she accused them of fooling the people into thinking they were saved "because they see some worke of Sanctification in them." In place of this "legalistic" doctrine of works and duties, Anne sought the immediate indwelling of the Holy Spirit. In her own words:

> Here is a great stirre about graces and looking into hearts, but give mee Christ, I seeke not for graces, but for Christ, I seeke not for promises, but for Christ, I seeke not for sanctification, but for Christ, tell not mee of meditation and duties, but tell mee of Christ.²³

What Anne and her followers preached was, therefore, a doctrine easily characterized by those in positions of authority as Aantinomian—a negation of the moral law and of the social norms and institutions that rested upon it. Indeed, it was precisely this positing of the believer beyond the moral order or boundaries of the community and its authority that Anne's opponents stressed as the prime danger of her teachings:

> For if a man need not be troubled by the Law, before faith, but may step to Christ so easily; and then, if his faith be no going out of himselfe to take

Christ, but onely a discerning that Christ is his owne already, and is onely an act of the Spirit upon him, no act of his owne done by him; and if he, for his part, must see nothing in himselfe, have nothing, doe nothing, onely he is to stand still and waite for Christ to doe all for him. And then if after faith, the Law no rule to walke by, no sorrow or repentance for sinne; he must not be pressed to duties, and need never pray, unlesse moved by the Spirit: And if he fals into sinne, his is never the more disliked of God, nor his condition never the worse. And for his assurance, it being given him by the Spirit, he must never let it goe, but abide in the height of comfort, though he fals into the grossest sinnes that he can. Then their way to life was made easie, is so no marvell so many like of it. . . . Oh, it pleaseth nature well to have Heaven, and their lusts too.[24]

The accusations that Anne and her followers sought "Heaven, and their lusts too" was based on the two major theological points in dispute in the Antinomian controversy. These were: "1) That the person of the Holy Ghost dwells in a justified person, 2) That no sanctification can help to evidence to us our justification."[25]

That these doctrines and the principled points that Anne Hutchinson and her followers derived from them led to the single most threatening event in the first years of settlement can only be explained by placing them in the meaning-giving context of Puritan belief. Given the prevailing definitions of the symbolic order, the threat perceived by ministers and magistrates in these doctrines was of the dissolution of their own moral authority and, in essence, of the breakdown of the moral bonds of community. For, as noted above, the basis of the Puritan social experiment was that it was possible to build a Church and Commonwealth of the visible saints, that is, to construct a holy community out of those persons who, having undergone regeneration, could see evidence of their salvation in the daily conduct of their lives and in the proper working of their social institutions. This evidence, termed *sanctification,* provided, in terms of Puritan doctrine, evidence of their "justification," "In which God, in virtue of Christ's righteousness believed in, absolves the person from the guilt of sin and from his debt to obedience to the moral law."[26]

The problem of assurance, that is, of the believers finding evidence of saving grace, the most central element of the Puritan world view, was, if not solved in the doctrine of a sanctified life, at least somewhat mitigated. And although different Puritan divines attributed more or less optimistic interpretations to the nature of the correlation between outward sanctification (the leading of a proper moral life) and inward justification (salvation), it served for all as a model to ease somewhat the awful tension caused by constant preoccupation with the problem of salvation and damnation that stood at the core of Puritan doctrine.

Taking her rejection of the doctrine of sanctification to its logical conclusion Anne Hutchinson was led, through the internal logic of her own position, to reject the doctrine of works and to "traduce" the ministers for preaching a "Covenant of Works." Given the context of Puritan belief, this attack on the ministers went beyond a question of their own authority or legitimacy; it led, by its internal dynamic, to a questioning of the very basis of communal meaning and the boundaries of the normative order. For by questioning the doctrine of works, Anne brought into question the whole purpose of the collective endeavor. If "works" in the mundane world was not a soteriological arena, then the whole basis for the construction of the Holy Commonwealth was lost.

This questioning of the legitimacy, and indeed, transcendent meaning of collective life was best exemplified in the reaction of the leaders of the Bay Colony to the mortalist doctrine and the spiritualist eschatology of the followers of Anne Hutchinson. For one of the crucial reasons for the wrath of the officials incurred on the Hutchinsons and their followers was their implicit attack on the soteriological premises of the collective endeavor. As pointed out by Fulton MacClear, the acceptance by the Antinomians of the mortalist heresy, linked, as it was, to a "realized and spiritualized eschatology," struck at the basis of the fundamental meaning-giving framework of collective life.[27] Denying the final judgment, Anne was indeed led to question the Last Day, "insisting that some Resurrection prophecies of Scripture applied not to a future rising but to the present experience of the saints in their union with Christ."[28] This belief, which interpreted the Kingdom of Christ in terms of spiritualized grace and not in terms of concrete historical processes, stood in direct opposition to the dominant Puritan belief that Christ's Kingdom was not just a model for individual salvation but implied as well the very real redemption of the world also. It was, after all, to contribute to the building of this perfection and to gain the "inheritance" that they had moved to the New England wilderness.[29] The view as expounded by Anne (and the other sects, for that matter, especially the followers of Roger Williams and the Quakers), which saw in the regeneration process a total break with nature and created order, broke as well the necessary link between the actions of the godly and the hastening of the Kingdom of Christ. Ascribing salvation solely to the inner working of the Holy Spirit, it also denied the efficiency of constructing a godly Commonwealth as a stage in the realization of history's telos.

The threat involved to the concrete process of institution building and ordering of social life by a spiritualized eschatology had its complement, as Jesper Rosenmeier has pointedly analyzed, in the debate between Thomas Shepard and John Cotton on the image of Adam and the image of Christ in man's salvation.[30] In his analysis of the conflicting views of man's image in both theologians, Rosenmeier convincingly shows how Shepard's vision stressed the soteriological efficacy of action in the mundane world while Cotton's denied that human activity had any contributory role in the history of redemption. In terms of our analysis, the difference between the two interpretations is striking. The first legitimized the construction of the Holy Commonwealth as a "moment" in the coming of the Kingdom of Christ, while the second removed the coming of the Kingdom from any connection to the world of man. The questionable status of John Cotton's doctrine, which stressed the indwelling of the Holy Spirit among divines such as Thomas Shepard, John Wilson, and magistrates such as John Winthrop, was therefore understandable.[31]

The Symbolic and Structural Context

The doctrine of the "inner light" and the indwelling of the Holy Spirit, which had always been the "shibolleth" of "enthusiastic" religion, coincided in early seventeenth-century New England with a very particular set of social circumstances. Among the most important of these were threats, both external and internal, to the as yet infant colony. Of the former, the most salient were the sustained attempts in England to revoke the charter of the Massachusetts Bay Company (especially in 1633–34) and the beginnings of the hostilities with the Native Americans that culminated in the Pequot War of 1636–37. Of the latter, the most salient were the growing movement of freemen for an institutionalized role in governing communal affairs, an increase of immigration bringing heterogeneous elements into the colony, and the relocation of townships, first within and then beyond the original boundaries of the colony.[32] All these developments tended to intensify the need to posit boundaries and maintain them against internal and external threats.

To these factors must be added another, more difficult to substantiate but nonetheless crucial to the understanding of the importance of the Antinomian crisis in the history of New England: the personal refraction of these communal experiences in the lives of the settlers. Puritanism revolves around the problem of assurance, around the need to find signs of saving grace. This need and its inherent anxiety, the source of so much modern sociological theory, was also the source of less constructive ventures. For with the drop in new membership following the revival of 1633 (membership, in fact, continued to increase through 1634) and the concomitant lack of personal and communal testaments to saving grace, many of the settlers experienced an acute religious anxiety.[33] The depth of this anxiety was recorded in John Winthrop's *History of New England,* where he tells of

> a woman of Boston congregation, having been in much trouble of mind about her spiritual estate, at length grew into utter desperation, and could not endure to hear of any comfort, etc., so as one day she took her little infant and threw it into a well, and then came into the house and said, now she was sure she should be damned, for she had drowned her child.

A year earlier he had told this sad story:

> A man of Weymouth (but not of the church) fell into some trouble of mind, and in the night cried out, "Art thou come, Lord Jesus?" and with that leaped out of his bed in his shirt, and, breaking from his wife, leaped out at a high window into the snow, and ran about seven miles off, and being traced in the snow, was found dead next morning. They might perceive, that he had kneeled down to prayer in divers places.[34]

The "spiritual depression" of 1635–36 was, and this is a crucial point, of both a personal and communal nature.[35] For in its nature, New England Puritanism united both. In Perry Miller's words, "the Puritan philosophy demanded that in society all men, at least all regenerate men, be marshalled into one united array."[36] The very Church covenant that formed the basis of their public lives was, in Lazer Ziff's words, "the solace of their private moments as well."[37]

Indeed, the unity of personal and communal entities found its expression in the uniquely Puritan doctrine of the "test of relation," that is, in the public recounting by the communicant of his or her conversionary experience.[38] For whereas prior to the 1633 revival, entrance into the Church covenant was contingent solely upon soundness of doctrine and proper behavior, the outpouring of conversionary testaments during the revival encouraged some preachers (in the expectations of continual "harvests") to make the test of relation a necessary prerequisite for admittance into the Church covenant.[39] The course of this change was registered some seventy years later by Cotton Mather in the *Magnalia Christi Americana*:

> the first Churches of New England began only with a Profession of Assent and Consent unto the Confession of Faith and the Covenant of Communion. Afterwards, they that sought for the Communion, were but privately examined about a Work of Grace in their Souls, by the Elders, and then publickly propounded unto the Congregation, only that so if there were any scandal in their Lives, it might be objected and considered. But in the year 1634, one of the Brethren having leave to hear the Examinations of the Elders, magnified so much the Advantage of being present at such an Exercise, that many others desired and obtained the like leave to be present at it; until at length, to gratifie this useful Curiosity, the whole Church always expected the Liberty of being thus particularly acquainted with the Religious Dispositions of those with whom they were afterwards to sit at the Table of the Lord; and that Church which began this way was quickly imitated by most of the rest.[40]

The move from private examination to public confession was one of the single most defining characteristics of the New England Way. And although it was disputed by many ministers and congregations, it seems that by 1636 it had become instituted as the central ritual of collective membership.[41] Those seeking to join the Church covenant were told "that such as were to join should make confession of their faith, and declare what work of grace the Lord had wrought in them."[42] In that year, the very proceedings of covenanting a new Church in Dorchester were stopped by Thomas Shepard, who declared that those wishing to enter into covenant could not provide a satisfactory confession of saving grace:

> The reason was for most of them (Mr. Mather and one more excepted) had built their comfort of salvation upon unsound grounds, viz., some upon dreams and ravishes of spirit by fits; others upon the reformation of their lives; others upon duties and performances, etc., wherein they discovered three special errors: 1. That they had not come to hate sin, because it was filthy, but only left it, because it was hurtful, 2. That, by reason of this they had never truly closed with Christ, (or rather Christ with them,) but had made use of him only to help the imperfection of their sanctification and duties, and not made him their sanctification, wisdom, etc. 3. They expected to believe by some power of their own, and not only and wholly from Christ.[43]

This attempt to institute the public confession went so far that the general court in 1636 enacted a law stating explicitly

> that all persons are to take notice that this Court doeth not, nor will hereafter, approve of any such companyes of men as shall henceforth joyne in any pretended way of church fellowship, without they shall first acquainte the magistrates and the elders of the greater parte of the churches in this jurisdiccion, with their intencions, and have their approbacion herein. And further, it is ordered, that noe person, being a member of any churche which shall hereafter be gathered without the approbacion of the magistrates, and the greater parte of the said churches, shal be admitted to the freedome of this commonwealthe.[44]

The law of 1636, tying the "Joyning of Church fellowship" to the approval of magistrates and ministers, brings, into broad relief the importance of the test of relation as a central mechanism, ordering participation and membership in the moral community of believers. It served as the ritual locus where the realms of authority, community, and collective meaning came together.[45]

The Bonds of Community and the Role of Protest

The importance of the ritual of relation for an understanding of the Antinomian crisis and the further course of New England Congregational history is great. For, while the Church of the Visible Saints was the ideal model of membership and social identity, the ritual of joining the Church was the primary boundary-maintaining device, regulating participation in the moral community of the saints. Communicants seeking admittance to the Church were accordingly asked: "How it pleased God to work in them, to bring them home to Christ... how the Lord hath wonne them to deny themselves and their owne righteousness and to rely on the righteousness of Christ."[46] When assured of the workings of grace in their soul, they entered into the covenant, whose terms, as can be seen below, posited a model of purity for both the individual and the collective.

> Since it hath pleased God to move you brethren to hold forth the right hand of fellowship, It is your part, and that which I am to require of you in the name of the Lord, and of his church, before you can be admitted thereunto, whether you be willing to enter a holy Covenant with God and with them and by the grace and helpe of Christ be willing to deny your selve and all your former polutions, and corruptions, wherein in any sort you have walked, and so to give up yourself to the Lord Jesus making him your onely priest and attonement, your onely profit, your onely guide and King and Lawgiver and to walke before him in all professed subjections unto all his Holy Ordinances, according to the rule of the Gospel and to walke together with his Church and the members thereof in brotherly love and mutualle edification and succor according to God; then do I also promise unto you in the name of this Church that by the helpe of Christ we likewise will walke towards you in all brotherly love and holy watchfulnesse to the mutuall building up one of another in the fellowship of the Lord Jesus, Amen, Amen.[47]

In enacting the bonds of the covenant as a public ritual, we can observe not only the enactment of the bond between the individual and the community, but the locus of ordering and meaning rooted in the tightly woven nature of this bond. Here too, although representatives of collective authority (magistrates, ministers, and church elders) were present at the ceremony (indeed their presence decreed by law), what gave meaning to the proceedings was its collective nature, the participation of the whole community of covenanted saints. In this, the test of relation was very much like the Church confession (in terms of its sociological functions), akin to Tertullian's *agere poenitentiam,* to that change of mind "whose successful completion resulted in the restoration [here inclusion] of the individual to the sacramental life of the Church and inclusion in the routine life of family and community."[48] As a cathartic device, confession not only integrated a single individual into the community, but bound society as a whole around its central value system. As a ritual of inclusion, or of social closure, the test of relation asserted not only the ideal models of social identity, but the boundaries of membership and the basis of social solidarity as well.[49]

The importance of these functions becomes even clearer when placed within the context of the meaning-giving framework wherein they were exerted, returning, that is, to the problem of assurance, which was the crux of Puritan spiritual life and of the Antinomian crisis as well. For giving testimony to saving grace was the ultimate expression of this assurance, beyond the commonplaces of proper behavior and consent to the "Confession of Faith." Moreover, as a communal ritual, public testimony to assurance or saving grace asserted not only the salvific position of the individual, but of the collective (in its relation to the cosmos) as well. For, in the Puritan conception, "what [was] enacted in the microcosm of each man's soul [was] a perfect reflection of God's work in the macrocosm."[50]

However, and this is the crux of the issue, in the period between the winter of 1633 and the autumn of 1636, there was, as noted, a marked decline in piety, a falling off of new Church members and a concomitant falling off of those very collective rituals of communal assurance. The Antinomian conflict burst out in this mood of despair and the collective anxiety it engendered (complicated by other, more structural factors, as outlined above). Offering a way out of that anxiety, the doctrine preached by Anne and her followers did so at the expense of established orders and channels of grace.

In fact, in terms of the major analytic model we have been using, what Anne offered was a new locus of meaning and of social identity to her followers and to the collective at large. With the failure of the existing basis of meaning and order (in the institutionalized rituals of Church membership), experienced as the collectively felt failure of assurance, Anne presented in her doctrine (as in her person) an alternative to the institutionalized channels of grace, through the Church. Answering the needs of some (in fact, the majority of the Boston congregants, as well as members of the churches in Salem, Newberry, Roxbury, Ipswich, and Charlestowne) and threatening others (ministers and magistrates), her twice-weekly gatherings, assuming a public or semipublic character, came to be perceived as threatening the primary model of community as articulated through membership in the gathered Church.

Similarly, her very talks were seen, in the eyes of both supporters and opponents, as threatening the ministerial sermon. The occasion "was the only regular weekly occasion on which the settlers would meet together under one roof and therefore was a moment of solidarity, a crucial means of psychological reassurance of the sanity of an arduous life in the wilderness," and as such it was condemned in the Newtown synod of 1637:[51]

> 1. That though women might meet (some few together) to pray and edify one another; yet such a set assembly, (as was then in practice in Boston,) where sixty or more did meet every week, and one woman (in a prophetical way, by resolving questions of doctrine, and expounding scripture) took upon her the whole exercise, was agreed to be disorderly and without rule.[52]

These threats to community received even more explicit expression in John Wheelwright's Fast Day sermon of 1637. In this sermon, which was the cause of his sedition trial, Wheelwright, like the other followers of Anne Hutchinson, effectively divided the community into two groups, those under the covenant of works and those under the covenant of grace.[53] His distinctions, moreover, were made with a vengeance that threatened the basic solidarity of the community. For he preached that those under the covenant of works,

> the more holy they are, the greater enemies they are to Christ.... It maketh no matter how seemingly holy men be according to the Law; if they do not know the worke of grace and the wayes of God, they are such as trust to their owne righteousness, they shall dye sayth the Lord... therefore if men be so holy and so strict and zealous, and trust to themselves and their righteousness, and knoweth not the wayes of grace, but oppose free grace; such as these, have not the Lord Jesus Christ, therefore set upon such with the sword of the Spiritt, the word of God.[54]

Those under the covenant of grace, he enjoined to

> prepare for a spirituall combate, we must put on the whole armour of God, and must have our loynes girt and be redy to fight; ... [to] prepare for battle and come out against the enimyes of the Lord, and if we do not strive, those under a covenant of works will prevaile.... The battle betweene Michaell and his Angells, the battle between Gods people and those that are not, those battles of Christians must be burning; and what is

it, but the burning of the word of God accompanied by the Holy Ghost, this is prophesied of in Malachi 4.1. the day shall come that shall burne like an oven and all that do wickedly shall be stubble, and this is the terrible day of the Lord, when the gospell is thus held forth, this is a terrible day to all those that do not obey the Gospell of Christ; Brethren, we know that the whore must be burnt, Revelation 18.8, it is not shaving her head and paring her nayles and changing her rayment, that will serve the turne, but this whore must be burnt.[55]

Although, as Wheelwright throughout makes clear, the battle is of a spiritual nature ("for the weapons of our warfare are not carrnell but spiritual"), his speech was sufficiently inflammatory to frighten Winthrop and the majority of magistrates and ministers of the Bay Colony.[56] They saw it as ample testimony to the paths of disunity that opened with the acceptance of the doctrine of free grace.

Indeed, as the case of Dorchester made perfectly clear, the elders were only willing to admit testimony to saving grace when it was given to some form of control by ministers, magistrates, and congregants. The doctrine of the Hutchinsons, however, placed them and their adherents beyond the parameters of regulation by Church institutions.[57]

Through their idiosyncratic interpretations of grace, the different sectarian groups attacked the very basis of the social order and the fundamental ordering principles of society. In addition to calling into question the primary boundary-maintaining devices of society (entrance into the community through the test of relation), these groups also attacked the basis of authority in the colony, as was made clear in the only formal charge brought against Anne—that of violating the third commandment, honor thy father and thy mother—and by the constant preoccupation of her accusers with her disrespectful attitude.[58] In Anne's case, as in that of the other sectaries as well, a direct derivative of the doctrine of free grace was a salient concern with the spiritual equality of all believers, which led them to attacks on authority, both in its legitimizing functions and in its very person.

Having perhaps sinned excessively in positing the terms of the Antinomian controversy in our own categories of thought and not in those of the participants, it would be only fitting to end with a more "emic" designation. Thus, we should remember that the above noted threat to communal identity was conceived within a framework of divine justice and promise, and, as such, was ingrained within the collective memory of New England. For there, as represented in John Winthrop's *A Short History of the Rise, Reign and Ruine of the Antinomians,* Anne's tragic pregnancy of 1638 and abortion of a hydatidiform mole, as well as her subsequent murder by Indians in 1643, were interpreted as divine retribution for her sins.

> Mistris Hutchinson being big with child, and growing towards the time of her labor, as other women doe, she brought forth not one (as Mistris Dier did) but (which was more strange to amazement) 30. monstrous births, or thereabouts, at once; some of them bigger, some lesser, some one shape, some of another; few of any perfect shape, none at all of them (as farre as I could ever learne) of humane shape.... And see how the wisdom of God fitted this judgement to her sinne every way, for looke as she had vented mishapen opinions, so she must bring forth deformed monsters.... But Mistris Hutchinson being weary of the Iland, or rather Lland weary of her, departed from thence with all her family ... to live under the Dutch.... There the Indians set upon them, and slew her and all her family, her daughter, and her daughters husband and all their children, save one that escaped.... I have never heard that the Indians in those parts did ever before this, commit the like outrage upon any one family or families and therefore Gods hand is more apparently seene herein.[59]

As an antistrophe to these signs of divine wrath, it is important to note how, in the postscript to Thomas Weld's 1644 London preface to John Winthrop's history of the Antinomian crisis, he brings a promise of divine fulfillment. For, after bowing his knees to God for having "heard our groanes to heaven, and freed us from this great and sore affliction...," he adds

> That two Sagamores, (or Indian Princes) with all their men, women and children, have voluntarily submitted themselves to the will and law of our God, with expressed desires to be taught the same; ... which morning-peepe of mercy to them (faith he) is a great meane to awaken the spirit of prayer and faith for them in all the Churches.[60]

Given the meaning attached to the conversion of infidels as hastening the Second Coming, we see here a vindication, not only of the New England Way but of the course of providential history itself.

In sum, what Anne's meetings and preaching threatened and what the leaders of the Bay Colony sought to reassert in her banishment were the particular principles of communal membership, basis of authority, and terms of meaning upon which their social order was based. The matrix of these facets of social ordering was the particular models of Church membership based on the experience of regeneration and ritualized in the testimony given before the community of saving grace.

The falling off in this ritual activity (with the decline in conversions) may have been as we suggested, an important factor in attracting followers to Anne's weekly meetings. For Anne's meetings posited what was, in fact, an alternative model of community to that of the covenanted Church.

Interestingly, these meetings can be characterized as well by what Victor Turner termed *communitas,* that is, by a breaking down of social hierarchies leading to "undifferentiated, egalitarian, direct, extant, nonrational, existential, I-Thou relationships."[61] Indeed, that moment of communitas, existing "in and out of secular social structure," revealing however fleetingly some recognition of a "generalized social bond," has been connected by Turner to rites of passage—which were, of course, precisely what the rite of the testimony of assurance was about, delineating the passage of the communicant from unregenerate sinner to regenerate saint and full member of the community. This moment, argues Turner, "emerges recognizably in the liminal period, is of society as an unstructured or rudimentary structured and relatively undifferentiated 'comitatus,' community, or even communion of equal individuals who submit together to the general authority of the ritual elders."[62] It is, he argues, the recognition given in that moment to "an essential and generic human bond" that makes society possible at all. As such, the purely existential or spontaneous communitas is often "organized into a perduring social system," taking the form of what Turner calls "normative communitas."[63] It was precisely this structured moment of communitas that Anne's biweekly meetings so threatened. That communitas previously institutionalized in the test of relation was here transplanted to Anne's public exposition of doctrine. For in Anne's house, people of different social statuses joined together in a communal pursuit of grace that saw no social distinctions or differentiations. Similarly, her preaching to men and women together, thus breaking down one of primary ordering categories of collective life (the inferior position of women in respect to men) can be viewed—as, indeed, it was by her prosecutors, who laid it as a charge against her—as an attempt to constitute a new basis of social order through the positing of a new locus of communal identity.[64]

96   Innerworldly Individualism

As we will see in the following chapter, the search for new loci of communal identity and social solidarity did not cease with the banishment of Anne Hutchinson, but continued throughout the next decades of settlement. Indeed, the very process of institutionalization in the 1640s and 1650s was marked by a parallel search by many people for alternative models of social identity and meaning—constantly calling into question the fundamental tenets of the New England Congregational Way. The continuing dialectic between the process of institutionalization and the problems it called forth form the subject of the following chapter.

Notes

1. On these aspects of Samuel Gorton's thought, see Gura, "The Radical Ideology," and his *A Glimpse of Sion's Glory,* 291–300. Gorton's thought on the image of Christ in man, are worked out in, among other works, his *Simplicities Defense Against Seven-Headed Policy* (1646).
2. Haskins, *Law and Authority,* 25–42.
3. For the use of this Durkheimian term as a way of classifying a system of social order, see Mary Douglas, *Natural Symbols: Explorations in Cosmology* (New York: Random House, 1973), 104.
4. Winthrop, *History of New England,* 144.
5. In addition to the writing of Gura and Lovejoy, on the followers of Anne Hutchinson, see Emery Battis, *Saints and Sectaries: Anne Hutchinson and the Antinomian Controversy in the Massachusetts Bay Colony* (Chapel Hill: University of North Carolina Press, 1963). Further social aspects of the conflict are explored by Marilyn Westerkamp, "Anne Hutchinson, Sectarian Mysticism and the Puritan Order," *Church History* 59 (December 1990): 482–96.
6. Nathanial Ward, *The Simple Cobbler of Aggwam in America* (London, 1647), 5.
7. J. F. MacClear, "Anne Hutchinson and the Mortalist Controversy," *New England Quarterly* 54 (1981): 74–103; W. Stoever, *A Faire and Easie Way to Heaven: Covenant Theology and Antinomianism in Early Massachusetts* (Middletown: Wesleyan University Press, 1978). For additional perspectives on the Antinomian crisis, see Ronald Cohen, "Church and State in Seventeenth Century Massachussets," *Journal of Church and State* 12 (1970): 475–94; Amy Lang, "Antinomianism and the Americanization of Doctrine," *New England Quarterly* 54 (1981): 225–42.
8. Kai Erikson, *Wayward Puritans* (New York: John Wiley, 1966).
9. For a study of these different groups in terms of their articulation of the "mystical element" in Puritan religious thought, see J. F. MacClear, "The Heart of New England Rent: The Mystical Element in New England Puritanism," *Mississippi Valley Historical Review* 42 (1956): 621–52.
10. Bossy, *Christianity in the West,* 108. On the expectation of mass conversions, see

Miller, *Errand into the Wilderness,* 36; Hall, *The Faithful Shepherd,* 97; Lockridge, *A New England Town,* 36.
11. Miller, *Errand into the Wilderness,* 62.
12. Bulkeley, *The Gospel Covenant,* 57, 61, 81, 83, 88, 86, 102, 106, 162.
13. Ibid.
14. John Cotton's *A Treatise of the Covenant of Grace* was preached in the mid 1630s but not published until 1652 in London. See Phyllis Jones and Nicholas Jones, eds., *Salvation in New England—Selections from the Sermons of the First Preachers* (Austin: University of Texas Press, 1977), 45.
15. Ibid., 49.
16. Stoever, *A Faire and Easie Way,* 11. William Ames's *The Marrow of Sacred Divinity* (1642) and Richard Hooker's *Laws of Ecclesiastical Polity* (1850) were to a large extent the pillars of English Puritan thought. For good insights into the lived, experienced world of Thomas Shepard's Puritanism, see his *Journal and Autobiography* (1972).
17. Stoever, *A Faire and Easie Way,* 180.
18. Ibid., 93.
19. Miller, *Errand into the Wilderness,* 60.
20. Stoever, *A Faire and Easie Way,* 8. The tension between these two interpretations and the never fully resolved contradiction between nature and grace which ran through the heart of Puritan theology runs, of course through the heart of the Christian tradition as a whole, existing, as it does, in a tension between legalism and antinomianism, between the belief that religion, taking its impetus from revelation, through reason achieves forms and laws which are essential to the aiding of weak human nature and to the continuity of divine law upon earth; and the belief that since man's relation to God is super-rational, consisting as it does of the Lord's gift of grace to the individual believer, laws and rituals are dead except insofar as they are directly informed by the Holy Spirit acting through the individual believer. (Ziff, "Literary Consequences," 34)
21. This "partiality" was expressed in part by the very different terms of Puritan piety discussed by Jerald Brauer, "Types of Puritan Piety," *Church History* 56 (1987): 39–58. Brauer presents a topology of piety including the "nomistic," "evangelical," "rationalistic," and "mystical (spiritual)," the last of which is closest to the phenomena of antinomianism.
22. For an analysis of the relation between "conversion" and "grace" in Puritan thought, see C. J. Sommerville, "Conversion vs. the Early Puritan Covenant of Grace," *Journal of the Presbyterian Historical Society* 44 (1966): 178–97.
23. In David Hall, ed., *The Antinomian Controversy: A Documentary History* (Middletown: Wesleyan University Press, 1968), 17–18.
24. Thomas Weld, Preface to John Winthrop, *A Short History of the Rise, Reign and Ruine of the Antinomians, Familists and Libertines* (1644), (appears in Winthrop, *A History of the Rise,* 74).
25. Ibid., 239.
26. Stoever, *A Faire and Easie Way,* 123.
27. MacClear, "Anne Hutchinson," 74–103. The mortalist heresy was the belief in the

death of the soul, or "soul-sleep" with the death of the physical body. This heresy, of long heritage in Christianity, was upheld by many (especially among the radical sects) in seventeenth-century England—one of its most famous proponents was John Milton. For a history of this heresy in English Protestant thought, see Norman Burns, *Christian Mortalism from Tyndale to Milton* (Cambridge: Harvard University Press, 1972).

28. MacClear, "Anne Hutchinson," 87.
29. Jesper Rosenmeier, "New England's Perfection: The Image of Adam and the Image of Christ in the Antinomian Crises," *William and Mary Quarterly* 27 (1970): 438.
30. Ibid., 435–59.
31. It is therefore important to state clearly that it was not John Cotton's millennialism per se that set him against the ministers such as Bulkeley, Shepard, and Eliot. They, too, anchored their visions of the social order in a millennial imagery. John Eliot's missionary activity among the Native Americans to raise "the Kingdome of Christ among them" and his millennialist tract, *The Christian Commonwealth* (1659), were infused with a millennialism no less vital than that of John Cotton. The point of contention was thus not the millennial expectations, shared by all, but the "spiritualized" form it took in John Cotton's sermons, which, like the doctrine of his errant followers, threatened to undermine the foundations of a social order built on an imminent and yet unrealized conception of the eschaton.
32. For some perspectives on these pressures, see Katherine Brown, "Freemanship in Puritan Massachusetts," *American Historical Review* 59 (1954): 865–83; idem, "Puritan Democracy in Dedham Massachusetts," *William and Mary Quarterly* 24 (1967): 378–96; Michael Zuckerman, "The Social Context of Democracy in Massachusetts," *William and Mary Quarterly* 25 (1968): 521–54; K. Lockridge and A. Krieder, "The Evolution of Massachusetts Town Government 1640–1740," *William and Mary Quarterly* 23 (1966): 549–74; Richard Simmons, "Freemanship in Early Massachusetts: Some Suggestions and a Case Study," *William and Mary Quarterly* 19 (1962): 422–28; idem, "Godliness, Property and the Franchise in Puritan Massachussets: An Interpretation," *Journal of American History* 55 (1968): 495–511.
33. See Battis, *Saints and Sectaries,* 330–44 for a list of Church members in Boston of the 1630s.
34. Winthrop, *A History,* 281–82, 255.
35. On the use of these terms, see Hall, *The Antinomian Crises,* 15.
36. P. Miller, *Errand into the Wilderness,* 143.
37. Lazer Ziff, "The Social Bond of the Church Covenant," *American Quarterly* 10 (1958): 462.
38. On this aspect of Puritan religiosity, see Charles Cohen, *God's Caress: The Psychology of Puritan Religious Experience* (Oxford: Oxford University Press, 1986), 137–61.
39. This is discussed in Hall, "The Antinomian Crises," 14.
40. Cotton Mather, *Magnalia Christi Americana,* vol. 5 (New York: Russell and Russell, 1967), 43, reproduction of the edition of 1862.

41. Among the opponents of this practice were James Noyes, Nathanial Ward, and Thomas Shepard (Hall, "The Faithful Shepherd," 110–11).
42. Winthrop, *A History,* vol. 1, 215.
43. Ibid., 219.
44. Quoted in Morgan, *Visible Saints,* 101.
45. Some examples (albeit of a later date) of the formula used can be found in Mary Rhinelander McCarl, "Thomas Shepard's Record of Relations of Religious Experience 1648–1649," *William and Mary Quarterly* 48X (1991): 433–66.
46. John Cotton, *A Copy of A Letter of Mr. Cotton of Boston in New England . . . With the Questions Propounded to Such as are Admitted to the Church Fellowship and Covenant It Selfe* (London, 1641), 5.
47. Ibid., 6. For another example of a Church covenant, see *The Winthrop Papers,* vol. 3 (1943), 223–25.
48. H. Hepworth and B. Turner, eds., *Confession: Studies in Deviance and Religion* (London: Routledge and Kegan Paul, 1982), 43.
49. See, for example, Winslow, *Meetinghouse Hill,* 42–49.
50. Rosenmeier, "New England's Perfection," 423.
51. Ziff, *Puritanism In America,* 53.
52. Winthrop, *A History,* vol. 1, 286.
53. On the later-day correspondence between Cotton and Wheelwright where they discuss their past disagreements over the interpretation of the burning issues of the Antinomian crises, see Sargent Bush, Jr., "Revising What We have Done Amisse—John Cotton and John Wheelwright," *William and Mary Quarterly* 45 (1988): 733–50.
54. John Wheelwright, in Hall, ed., *The Antinomian Crises,* 164.
55. Ibid., 158, 165.
56. Ibid., 158.
57. The doctrine of free grace—termed *spiritualist*—was, of course, not the sole province of the so-called Antinomians, but was shared by other sectarian groups in New (and Old) England. Not surprisingly, the chief proponents of this doctrine—Roger Williams, Samuel Gorton, and of course the Quakers—met with a similar fate as the followers of Anne Hutchinson, and for much the same reasons.
58. This point has been noted by Erikson, *Wayward Puritans,* 58.
59. Weld, Preface, 93–94.
60. Ibid., 94.
61. Victor Turner, *The Ritual Process* (Harmondsworth: Penguin, 1974), 274.
62. Victor Turner, *Dramas, Fields and Metaphors* (Ithaca, NY: Cornell University Press, 1974), 82.
63. Ibid., 120.
64. For an illuminating discussion of the relation of enthusiasm to antistructure and communitas in general, see Heyd, "The Reaction to Enthusiasm," 258–80.

4

The Emergent Tensions of Institutionalization

Focusing on the attempt to institutionalize the original principles of social ordering, this chapter concentrates on the growing divergence between authority and community over the first generation of settlement. The divergence of both institutional realms was felt in a number of developments that characterized mid-century Puritanism. These were: (a) the continual growth of alternative loci of membership and authority among sectarian and protesting groups, such as Baptists and Quakers; (b) the development of tensions between ministers and their congregants and, indeed, a general crisis in authority; (c) a perceived (at least by the ministers) falling off in piety and religious sentiment; and (d) a questioning of the fundamental tenets of collective meaning and purpose.

All of these found expression in a reassessment of the basic tenets and premises of Congregational Puritanism, which led, among other developments, to the rearticulation of the relation between the religious principles of the settlers and the legal assumptions that they too brought over with them from England.

Against the background of structural changes in the New England communities and the growth of legal institutions there, what we will term the *retraction* of authority from its roots in the community is presented here as the underlying dynamic beneath the crisis in authority faced by the Puritan ministry in the mid-seventeenth century.

Codification

Whereas the Antinomian crisis posited the limits of building collective identity and constituting authority on the basis of a shared experience of grace, it was, in fact, but the first of many problems, all incumbent on the institutionalization of the original terms of settlement within collective life.

The crux of these problems was, I would argue, in the act of institutionalization itself. The very enactment of principles of social ordering, of definitions of the collectivity and of the duties and obligations toward authority engendered numerous problems and conflicts. While complicated and structured by such historical exigencies as the Civil War in England—whose millennial undercurrent brought many in New England to question their own collective "errand"—and the growth of townships and of trade—which was part of a large-scale process of social differentiation—it is to the internal dynamic of institutionalization that we must look to understand the changing nature of New England Puritanism.[1]

In both Church and State, the formalization of codes of conduct regulating social life began in the mid-1630s and 1640s. In the former case, this was evinced in the general meetings of ministers held at Cambridge in 1643, in the publication of Thomas Hooker's *Principles* in 1645, and finally, in the convening of the Cambridge Synod at alternate times from 1646 until 1648—which resulted in the publication of the *Cambridge Platform of Church Discipline* in 1648.[2] In the realm of civil society, the agitation of 1635 for a formal body of laws was met by the convening of various committees, which resulted first in the publication in 1642 of the *Body of Liberties* and, finally, in 1648 in the promulgation of *The Book of General Lawes and Liberties Concerning the Inhabitants of the Massachusetts*.[3]

The year 1648 thus marks the culmination of over a decade of attempts to formalize, codify, and, in fact, translate the general symbolic premises of settlement into concrete rules of conduct in both civil and ecclesiastical realms. The causes behind this formalization of rules of conduct were many and varied. The convening of the committees responsible for the promulgation of the *Body of Liberties* and the *General Lawes and Liberties* was in response to popular demand to delimit the power of the magistrates. The publication of Thomas Hooker's *Principles* in 1645 was at least partially in response to the

Westminster Assembly of Divines in England in 1643, where a more Presbyterian policy of Church organization was drawn up.[4] In all cases, however, the very codification of the principles of social ordering represented a first attempt to enact and institutionalize the original premises of settlement as ordering principles for social life.

The implications of these acts were felt in the modes of organizing social life, in both the churches and in the community at large. For the very process of codification led not to a resolution of the problems of meaning opened up by the Antinomian crisis, but to their intensification. For, whereas the given definitions of communal identity and authority were based on a shared connection of all members to the ultimate source of cosmic meaning, the very act of codification and institutionalization of models of authority and community tended to restrict the directly felt connection of Church members to the sources of the sacred. Moreover, beyond the realm of the Church proper, the implications of these acts were felt in the structuring of communal identity beyond that of Church members alone. Through the process of institutionalization, authority tended to develop by defining itself autonomously and beyond communal referents. The very act of codification and the process of social differentiation it entailed drove a wedge between hitherto unified models of authority and community based on the ideal model of community as one of shared grace. And while those in positions of authority continued to base their legitimacy on an immediately felt connection to community, in effect the structures of authority began to differentiate and distinguish themselves as autonomous entities.

The progress of institutionalization and the codification of the relations between ministers and congregants in early seventeenth-century New England can be traced by the development in the late 1630s of a number of new practices, all of which illustrate the increasing formalization of roles and organizational structures.

Thus, for example, this period saw the first institutionalization of tithes (in 1639) and the end to the period of questions and answers hitherto affixed to every period of sermonizing.[5] The first measure both denoted the beginnings of formal obligations of congregants to ministers and gave evidence of the weakening of informally felt and immediately perceived ties between the two. Similarly, the latter measure, a direct consequence of Anne's preaching, served to put a distance between the congregation and its ministers, furthering the former from participation in the *locus classicus* of Puritan solidarity and charisma—the sermon. It served to strengthen that view of the ministry advocated by John Eliot, for whom the ministers "are witnesses of Christ," a view that was strengthened even more in the growth of ministerial power and prerogative—as emphasized in the acceptance of the principles of the "negative voice" and of "special acts," both of which strengthened the ministry at the expense of the congregation.[6] The principles of the negative voice that the ministers adopted from the magistrates gave them, in essence, veto power over decisions made by the majority of the congregations.[7] Together with the concept of special acts, it combined to give the Church elders greater disciplinary power, especially in the calling of a Church together and in the critical sphere of participation, the very right to talk in Church:

> 8. The power which Christ has committed to the elders, is to feed and rule the church of God, and accordingly to call the church together upon any weighty occasion, when the members so called, without just cause may not refuse to come: nor when they are come, depart before they have been dismissed: nor speak in the church, before they have leave from the elders: nor continue so doing, when they require silence, nor may they oppose nor contradict the judgment or sentence of the Elders, without sufficient and weighty cause, because such practices are manifestly contrary unto order, and government and in-lets of disturbance and tend to confusion.[8]

Through these practices and, indeed, more explicit pronouncements, the nature of the relation between authority in the Church and the community of congregants was redefined:

> 7. Church-government, or rule is placed by Christ in the officers of the church, who are therefore called Rulers, while they rule with God: yet in case of mal-administration, they are subject to the power of the church, according as hath been said before. The Holy Ghost frequently, yea alwayes, where it mentioneth Church-Rule and church-government, ascribeth it to Elders: whereas the work and duty of the people is expressed in the phrase of obeying their Elders; and submitting themselves unto them in the Lord: so as it is manifest, that an organick or compleat church is a body politik, consisting of some that are Governor, and some that are governed, in the Lord.[9]

The move expressed in the above to a far less equal conception of the relation of ministers to congregants than had previously existed was furthered by the growing sacerdotal interpretation of the ministry, in both theory and practice. Thus, while the framers of the Cambridge Platform could not part with the concept of the covenant as the basis for ministerial authority, they managed, through a set of distinctions between the "virtual" and "formal" attributes of power, as well as between the holding of power and its execution, to effectively "deny that the congregation delegated authority to its ministers."[10] This retraction of authority from its source in the community was expressed not only in the organizational realm, but in the symbolic as well. For there, a sacerdotal tone worked its way into the text of the platform along with the existing contractual understanding of the Church:

> though officers be not absolutely necessary, to the simple being of churches, when they be called: yet ordinarily to their calling they are, and to their well being: and therefore Lord Jesus out of his tender compassion hath appointed, and ordained officers which he would not have done, if they had not been usefull and need full for the church; yea, being Ascended into heaven, he received gifts for men, and gave gifts to men, whereof officers for the church are Justly accounted no small parts; they being to continue to the end of the world, and for the perfecting of all the Saints.[11]

The ministry accepted lay ordination to an extent: "Church officers are not only to be chosen by the Church, but also to be ordeyned by Imposition of hands, and prayer."[12] But it also attempted to limit its use and circumscribe its practice to those in some position of authority:

> 3. In such Churches where there are Elders, Imposition of hands in ordination is to be performed by those Elders.
> 4. In such Churches where there are no Elders, Imposition of hands may be performed by some of the Brethren orderly chosen by the church therunto....
> 5. Nevertheless in such Churches where there are no Elders, and the Church so desire, wee see not why Imposition of hands may not be performed by the Elders of other Churches.[13]

The growing symbolic autonomy of ecclesiastical authority from its roots in the community of the covenant marked a slowly changing conception of the sacred and of the charismatic dimension as being rooted in the community of covenanted saints. Albeit slowly, a degree of mediation developed as charisma began more and more to be associated with particular statuses and roles of authority and less with the community as such. An indication of this development was Shepard and Allin's declaration that a minister could "administer the seals [that is, the sacraments] in another Congregation."[14] While they declared that this right was based not on a sacerdotal conception of the ministry (or in more etic terms, a charisma of office), but on their "being called thereunto by the desire of the Church," this notion was an important step toward the growing retraction of the ministry from particular congregations.[15]

Echoing this attitude was that clause in the Cambridge Platform's chapter on Church communion, which allowed for a Church with more than one minister to dispatch one of its ministers to another congregation in "needful season" to administer the sacraments.[16] While phrased in such a manner as to limit this prerogative to the extraordinary case of "an absent or sick" minister, it was essentially a declaration of the "power of a pastor to administer the sacrament to a congregation not his own," as Cotton Mather made clear close to half a century later.[17] Power, in this case, rested on an increasingly autonomous identification of the charismatic propensity, with the ministry as autonomous from a particular covenanted community.

A further and central aspect of the growing identification of the charismatic dimension with the Church authority at the expense of shared communality was in the realm of boundary maintenance, as exemplified in the changing rituals of membership. For, once again, following the Antinomian crisis, this ritual was moved out of the public realm and became a private rite of the initiates" profession of faith before the minister. While the text of the Cambridge Platform represented the private ceremony as only an alternative to the collective rite, in actual practice it became the accepted mode.[18] This move, by distancing the congregation from participating in the test of relation, at one and the same time restricted the function of social control over collective boundaries to the ministry alone and further attenuated the connection of most collective members to the ideal models of community and to the ultimate locus of cosmic meaning. Doing away with the rite of collective covenant owning distanced (in a most Durkheimian fashion) the collective from the source of the sacred, from the effervescent moment of *la vie serieuse.*

Finally, nothing registered this growing process of mediation and institutionalization more than the very act of codification of the principles of collective life in the Cambridge Platform of 1648, which, for the first time gave a formal structure to the Congregational Way. The formal enacting of the above measures led to a slow move back to a more sacerdotal interpretation of the ministry—at the expense of its "contractual" elements—and to a more centralized conception of Church affiliation, attenuating the discrete autonomy of each Church and subjecting them to some form of communal control through the formal institutionalization of synods and councils.[19]

Structural Constraints and the Crisis of Meaning

The attempt to centralize authority and institute formal symbolic and institutional prerogatives to the ministry—in essence, an attenuation of their tie to the community of "covenanted saints"—progressed against a background of both internal and external constraints. Externally, the single most important development was the English Civil Wars, which engendered, as is well known, a great degree of millennial speculation and expectation, touching New England and directing in its wake many ministers and congregants back to England to participate in the making of the millennial kingdom there.[20] Moreover, the course of revolution in England and the rise of the saints in the New Model Army and Barebones Parliament caused many in New England to doubt their own errand and role in providential history, thus leading to rising collective doubts as to the very framework of meaning within which their collective enterprise was carried out.

The growing questioning of collective meaning and the doubt raised as to the New England Way were exacerbated even further by those very internal factors that marked the material "success" of the errand. For the period until mid-century was one of marked economic growth, demographic change and structural diversification.[21] The growing specialization in crafts, the development of different trades, with sometimes conflicting interests among groups of fur traders, transatlantic merchants, the nascent clothing industry, and fisheries, were important elements in the "fragmentation" of communal life after the first decade of settlement. Growing differences in wealth, disparate property holdings, together with emergent competition among merchants bespoke the breakup of earlier modes of social solidarity centered on Church membership and, consequently, a weakening of the link between town and Church, each developing their own discrete spheres of authority that, moreover, tended to conflict (as, for example, in the opposition of free trade interests to the 1645 legislation against Anabaptists).[22]

These structural changes in the organizational realms of communal life provided an especially poignant backdrop to the problems of socializing the second generation to the founders' values. Given the rapid rate of change and diversification, the problem of ensuring continuity engendered a crisis of severe proportions in preserving communal values. For the emergence of new interest groups and, within them, new elites articulating different values, in both religious and political realms, led, together with the changing structures of organizational life, to a change in the meaning-giving orders or symbolic systems of the community.

On the level of social structure, it may be useful to conceptualize the changing framework as a move from what has been termed by Herman Schmalenbach a *Bund* type of solidarity to what he has termed a *community* type of solidarity.[23] More particularly, this change within each community saw the breakdown of a society characterized by intensive commitment to collective values; small size; social homogeneity with an absence of functional differentiation and institutionalization; and with a strong emphasis on overall collective solidarity and communality, denying legitimacy to subgroups and, while free of institutional restraints, marked by instability, latent tensions and ideological splits.[24] As we have seen, all these aspects of social life, however, began to change after the first decade of settlement. Change was itself part of the process of institutionalization and diversification, which marked a decline in overall solidarity as this was replaced by subgroup loyalties—to particular townships, to economic interest groups, and to status positions.[25]

These transformations in the structural conditions of social life led, moreover, to the growth of strife and to that "contention" for which mid-century New England was known—contention between different factions in one township, between townships, between ministers and congregations, fathers and sons, magistrates and people, employers and wage earners.[26] The rise of social strife, brought in its wake the enactment of new laws—there was, for instance, no specific punishment for theft until 1644—and a more rigorous definition of discrete spheres of authority, served to intensify even further the growing distance between the forces of authority and those of community in the colonies.[27] These, too, contributed to the collective crisis in meaning.

One arena where the interwoven problems of meaning and the split between authority and community was felt was in the developing relations between ministers and congregants, a relation that degenerated rapidly in mid-century.[28] The first stage in the changing role of the minister was already evinced in 1638 with the increasing difficulty in providing for ministers from voluntary contributions. The decline in the "maintenance system" of voluntary contributions—which, for ministers such as John Cotton and Richard Mather, approached the ideal of the early Church—and the necessity for the secular powers to intervene and legislate for the provision of ministers (1638), marked for some the impending decline of religion. In the period following the publishing of the Cambridge Platform, the process of institutionalization and formalization of duties was, however, to increase even more.

Together with the rising presbytery, centralization and authority of the ministry, and the increased symbolic distance posited between ministers and congregants, other factors attenuating the connection between them began to be felt. Thus, as the first ministers graduated from Harvard College, they were dispersed among newly incorporated towns and Churches in need of ministers and no longer shared the type of bond ministers had previously shared with specific congregations. The arbitrary connection between ministers and congregations was complicated even further by the sense of prestige and social status that began to be attributed to the ministry. As ministers became involved with local structures of prestige, status, and power, their tie to the whole of the congregation weakened. This fact was noted by many and attested to by the growing need to institute written contracts between ministers and congregations. A "cash nexus" was a far cry from the type of immediate and intimate bond that united the first generation of ministers to their congregations. Indeed, even these contracts were insufficient to prevent strife and wrangling between congregations and ministers over the terms of the latter's ministry.

The effect of this growing disjunction between ministers and congregations together with the factors noted above was to lead to a crisis in the fundamental meaning-giving orders of society—a crisis in modern sociological parlance of hegemony. This was felt in the decline in Church attendance, in new membership, and in family catechizing, which, together with the removal of ministers to England, all point to the growing inability of the major articulators of social order, authority, and meaning to effectively assert their control of social life.

This failure in social control was experienced by most of those in positions of authority—by magistrates, ministers, and even first-generation fathers facing the demands of their sons. Indeed, studies such as those carried out by Philip Greven and Emory Elliot have stressed the generational element in the mid-century crisis.[29] These studies have stressed the "isolationism, exclusivism and intolerance" that characterized the first generation of settlers in their unwillingness to share control or grant emotional or economic independence to the next generation.[30] And just as the structures of the Puritan family and of land-holdings provided no room for second-generation children to come into their own, so did participation in the community remain closed to them. The models of the community remained those of the visible church, its boundaries ordered and maintained through the test of relation. Evidence of assurance was, however, the one thing that few of the second generation could provide. Although they were children of Church members, those of the second generation who could not provide evidence of saving grace were thus excluded symbolically from full participation in the ideal community and, in Massachusetts, from participation in the political community as well. This development, as certain ministers (notably, Richard Mather, Peter Bulkeley, and George Philips) realized, seriously threatened their continuing role as articulators of collective models—as the community of their congregants threatened to dwindle to an insignificant fraction of the overall society.[31]

The Legitimation of Authority and the Continuity of Protest

In light of these developments, which set the stage for the Half-Way Synod of 1662 and the reworking of Congregational Puritanism, it would, I believe, be useful to analyze the developing tension of mid-century Puritanism in terms of the continuing tension between authority and community. It may, in fact, be said that what had taken place was that the ministerial elites had overstepped the limits of their authority. For while the principles of domination continued to rest on an immediate relation of authority to community, of ministers to congregants (through the covenantal notion of Church and ministry), the concrete structures of domination had effectively changed. They became more institutionalized, attenuated, mediated, and less immediate at precisely the same time as manifestations of shared grace as the symbolic locus of an authority rooted in community were disappearing (fewer and fewer congregants being capable of providing evidence of regeneration and, even when provided, being attested to in private).

An important indicator of the continued, felt need for these moments of community was in the continual support granted the different "enthusiastic" elites and sects that arose in the colony. As historians such as Stephen Forster and Philip Gura have argued, Puritanism, in its first decades in New England, was far from being of a homogeneous nature.[32] Nathanial Ward's very concern with "Familists, Libertines, Erastians, Anti-trinitarians, Anabaptists, Antiscripturalists, Manifestarians, Millinaries, Antinomians, Socinians, Arrians, Perfectists, Brownists, Mortalisms, Seekers and Enthusiasts," and with the "New-sprung Sect of Phrantasticks which would perswade themselves and others, that they had discovered the Nor-wests passage to Heaven" belie any notion of one, integral, "Puritan Mind."[33]

Indeed, protest against the "Congregational Way," whether of diverse sects or organized groups, never ceased to trouble the leaders of the colony, much protest arising, in fact, from the very centralizing tendencies of the Cambridge Platform. Thus, for example, the questioning of the covenant as the basis for redemptive history was evinced in 1639 when Ambrose Martin called the Church covenant "a stinking carryon and a humane invention, and saying he wondered at God's patience, feared it would end in the sharpe and said the ministers did dethrone Christ and set up themselves."[34] In a similar vein, William Dell in his tract, *The Tryal of Spirits,* inveighed against the growth of ministerial privilege in mid-century.[35]

Individuals, however troublesome they may have been, did not present the major threat to the communal venture. Those like Martin were fined and sent to be taught the proper doctrine. Those like Captain Underhill, who seduced virtuous matrons by recounting to them

> how he came to his assurance, and that was thus: He had lain under a spirit of bondage and a legal way five years, and could get no assurance, till at length he was taking a pipe of tobacco, the Spirit set home an absolute promise of free grace with such assurance and joy, as he never since doubted of his good estate,[36]

were summoned before the general court and their sins subjected to public scrutiny.

Innerworldly Individualism

The real threat, as evidenced in the body of laws passed against them, as well as in their physical repression, was that of the different organized groups of sectarians. Moreover, from Roger Williams through Anne Hutchinson, Samuel Gorton, the Anabaptists, Particular and General Baptists, and Quakers, a unitary line can be drawn, however different the doctrine and specific practice of each group. For all not only questioned the basis of the social order, of its authority and loci of community, but posited alternative loci of identity, membership, and solidarity. Doctrinally diverse, though united in their rejection of the Puritan doctrine, their interest lies in the very audience for their views and in its timing. The growth of the Baptists (in the 1640s) and of the Quakers (in the 1650s), as well as Gorton's return to New England in 1648, were after all in those decades that saw the codification of the principles governing collective life and the increasing autonomy of authority from communal referents. Protest developed in precisely that period when communal values were being shaken and when the structures of authority were being increasingly removed from their roots in the community. The growth of protest groups and the positive echo they gained in the lives of many was directly related to the growing divergence of authority and community and to the "retraction" of that moment of "communitas" that we have been studying.

A particularly salient example of the quest of many to retain their immediate connection to the ultimate sources of meaning can be found in the Baptist practice, begun in Rhode Island in 1656, of the laying on of hands as "necessary to all baptized persons," a practice that reminds us of the early forms of ministerial ordination practiced in the Congregational churches as an assertion of the communal bond.[37] Moreover, both Baptists and Quakers, through their acceptance of free grace, defined anew the boundaries of community. Rejecting paedobaptism, the very ritual of adult baptism provided an arena where individuals, as individuals and as a group, could reassert not only the indwelling of grace, but their communal ties, again, a ritual reminiscent, in theme if not in content, of the earlier and fallen off communal test of relation of the Congregational church. Equally important to understanding the social role of these groups was their advocation of "lay prophecy," a practice that had fallen into disfavor in the period following the Cambridge Platform. This practice, which expressed the immediate connection of the laity (and not those in authority, such as the ministers) to the source of the sacred in society, was, as some scholars maintain, one of the real reasons for their repression.[38] Representing an attempt to return to the original charismatic or "effervescent" type of social ordering, it was decidedly rejected by those holding offices and roles of authority now institutionalized and routinized.

Going one step further, the example of Quaker nudity (and the positive reception it gained) may point to a similar need on the part of many to reassert their connection with the source of the sacred, "to come into contact with the very essence of being, to go to the very roots of existence, of cosmic, social and cultural order, to what is given as sacred and fundamental."[39] Nakedness is, as Victor Turner noted, a "property" of liminality and so of that spontaneous communitas that stands at the root of religious experience.[40] That such a quest may indeed have been present is evidenced by the charge laid against the Baptists of indulging in lewd and obscene practices in the course of the ritual of baptism. Reminiscent of the charges brought against the early Church by the Romans and, indeed, against heretical sects, as well as Jews, during the course of Christianity, it points to the realization that the heresiarchs were indeed positing alternative loci of the sacred and so alternatives also to the centers of society, its moral boundaries, and systems of authority.

The Church and the World

What we have characterized as the disjunction opened up between the ideal models of community and the growing autonomy of authority from communal referents was, in effect, a consequence of the particular nature of charisma in society and the modes of its institutionalization. The charismatic locus of existence in New England in the 1630s and 1640s was, as we recall, intimately connected to the vision of a polity based on grace and the role to be played by this polity in the workings of providential history.[41] For New England Puritans this cosmic errand was predicated on the proper forms of Church (and civil) organization, ones which saw the interweaving of this-worldly and otherworldly action, or in other worlds, the mutual relevance of the Church and the world.

The mutual relevance of both realms was rooted in a complex dynamic that took account of the difference between the ultimate and penultimate "Ends" of each. As both the ecclesiastical and civil spheres have the same last End, viz. The Glory of God, yet they differ in their next Ends; for the next end of Civil Order and Administrations, is the Preservation of Humane Societies in outward Honour, justice and Peace: But the next Ends of Church Order and Administrations, are The Conversion, Edification and Salvation of Souls, Pardon of Sin, Power against Sin, Peace with God.[42]

The difference in "next Ends" dictated the need to keep separate the discrete exercise of authority in each realm. Crucial here is the stress on the separation of officers and holders of authority in both spheres and not the disjunction of polities as such. For while Davenport, in his *Discourse about Civil Government in a New Plantation Whose Design is Religion* (originally printed in 1638), warns of the dangers of placing civil power in the hands of Church officers, he is adamant on the need to place civil power in the hands of Church members who "are of all men fittest [to exercise such power], being sanctified and dedicated to God, to carry on all worldly and civil business to God's Ends."[43] It was, therefore, as can be seen, precisely their sanctified nature as members of the covenanted Churches, sharing in the covenant of grace, which allowed them to realize the "last End" of civil government—the greater glory of God.

The problems of organizing social life in accordance with this conception became clear, however, as soon as a considerable body of congregants developed who were not members of the Church and so not participants in the covenant of grace. The vision of two mutually supportive structures, of the Church and the Civil State with "God's Glory the last end of them both," ran afoul of the very frailty of human life and the failure of continuing coversions.[44] The falling off in conversions and the growth of a population without the covenant gave the lie to the interweaving of this-worldly and otherworldly spheres in New England Puritanism. It resulted as well in the emergent problems of reconciling the two realms of the Church and the world—conceived in coordinate state, but in fact increasingly going their separate ways.[45]

Different solutions to this problem were posited by different groups of congregants and ministers over the 1640s and 1650s. Thus, for example, many of the gathered churches in Connecticut, while maintaining the principle of "church purity" and restricted membership, in practice opened the doors of the Church to a much larger body of communicants than Massachusetts, thus bridging somewhat the chasm that had opened between sacred and secular orders.[46] A totally different solution to that of Samuel Stone in Connecticut was that posed by Roger Williams in Rhode Island. Rejecting the principle of mutual relevance between the Church and world, he split them totally asunder, maintaining a vision of purity in the Church even beyond that of the strict Congregationalists he separated from.[47] He did not, however, posit the Church as a model for the organization of civil society, nor grant the civil order any soteriological function. His famed religious freedom rested precisely on his denial "that the State had anything to do with religion, thus making it an association for purely temporal worldly purposes."[48]

Nothing, however, could have been further from the conception that reigned in the godly Commonwealth of Massachusetts, where civil power was legitimately seen to impinge on the religious realm.[49] The prerogative of the civil magistrate to decree the calling of Church Synods and the modes of communion between churches were direct derivatives of that conception that saw "the establishment of pure religion and the reformation of corrupt religions concern[s of] the civil peace."[50] In the wake of the Antinomian affair, the role of the civil magistrate was extended to the concrete regulation of communal boundaries. In a general court order of March 1636–37, admission of people to the commonwealth was restricted to the approval of the civil magistrate.[51] Bringing the civil magistrate into Church affairs, restricting the electorate to Church members, and placing the magistrate as the guardian of the "Godly Commonwealth" were all based on the principled interweaving of this-worldly and otherworldly spheres of the Church and the world in the godly Commonwealth.

This conception, legitimized in biblical precedent, served as the judicial basis of life in the Massachusetts colony. With it, the colonists tempered the principles of fundamental law that they brought with them from England.[52] As stated clearly in the opening sentences of the 1648 *Book of General Lawes and Liberties*: "So soon as God had set up Political Government among his people Israel he gave them a body of Lawes for judgement both in civil and criminal cases. These were brief and fundamental principles."[53] Fundamental laws were here rooted in godly commandments and human laws rooted in the Laws of God, for "God was said to be amongst them or neer to them because of his Ordinances established by himselfe and their Lawes righteous because himselfe was their Lawgiver."[54] Going one step further and modeling their commonwealth on the "Judicial laws of Moses," the leaders of the Massachusetts colony combined the notion of fundamental law, existing beyond any specific institution and common to all nations, with the covenant of grace (and so with their own models of Church organization) that they may "injoyne the special presence of God in the puritie and native simplicity of all his ordinances by which he is so near to his own people."[55] Basing their own ordinances on the "Lawes of God," they thus conceived of Church and Civil State as:

> planted and growne up (like two twinnes) together like that of Israel in the wilderness by which we were pit in minde (and had opportunitie put into our hands) not only to gather our Churches, and set up the Ordinances of Christ Jesus in them according to the Apostolick patterne by such light as the Lord graciously afforded us: but also withall to frame our civil Politie, and Lawes according to the rules of his most holy word whereby each do help and strengthen other (the Churches the civil Authoritie, and the civil Authoritie the Churches) and so both prosper the better without such aemulation and contention for priviledges or priority as have proved the misery (if not ruine) of both in so many other places.[56]

Authority in the world (in the form of the civil magistrate), no less than in the Church (in the form of ministers, elders, and deacons) was, therefore, rooted in a particular model of communal identity based on the covenanted church of visible saints. Submission to this authority was based on acceptance not only of the moral law of God (or the law of nature, common to all humanity), but of that positive law of God revealed first in the Mosaic injunctions of the Old Testament and later transformed by the covenant of grace at the time of Christ.[57] Consequently, as pointed out by John Norton in his *Sion the Outcast Healed of Her Wounds* (1661), the "Ministerial Judge" was, and remained, a fundamental component of the "order Divine."[58]

The organization of social life according to the later emanations of God's positive law (works plus grace) were in fact seen to define the peculiarities of the New England Way, with its unique calling of covenanted churches and definitions of the nature of the relations between the Church and the world. This is amply attested to in Shepard and Allin's defense of Congregational policy in 1648 where they declare:

civil societies and governments thereof is herein left to rules of human prudence by the Lord and Government of the Whole World; and therefore may admit various forms of Government, various Laws and Constitutions, . . . but here in the Kingdom of Christ we must attend to what kind of Churches he hath instituted, so we must cleave to such rules, priviledges and forms of government and administrations he hath ordained.[59]

As can be seen, a distinction is posited here between two laws—the law of nature, common to all societies, and the law of grace, the distinct province of New England. The fulfillment of the latter in addition to the former is, indeed, presented as the imperative of New England's divine mission, of realizing therein the Kingdom of Christ.

Characteristic of New England (in both Church and Commonwealth) was thus a particular interweaving of the moral law, or the covenant of works (what was in essence natural law doctrine) with the covenant of grace, imbuing the former with soteriological efficacy while rooting the latter in the structures and orders of the world. Existing as neither an ordered hierarchy nor in opposition (as in other communities of saints), this interweaving of natural law and godly ordinances served two purposes. It drew political authority and institutions into the salvational drama of New England's mission but, at the same time, maintained the autonomy of those institutions (and the law upon which they were based) from sacerdotal interference.

Within this symbolic order, the problem of institutionalizing charisma became acute as soon as the world grew apart from the Church and the covenant of grace no longer encompassed the majority of congregants. The ensuing tensions were felt in the perceived disjunction between the terms of communal identity and of authority in both Church and State.

The Terms of Community and the Practice of Authority in Mid-Seventeenth-Century New England

By the mid-seventeenth century, the particular concepts upheld in Puritan New England of the social order and of the sources of authority were losing their relevance for more and more people. The interwoven roots of civil and ecclesiastical authority in the community of saints and hence the soteriological significance attributed to civil authority became increasingly problematic as more and more congregants were excluded from membership in this community. As pointed out by Reinhard Bendix, "each system of domination remains 'valid' only within limits, and when these are ignored or exceeded for too long, the type of domination either changes form or loses its original authoritative character."[60]

This latter development took the form of what we have called the retraction of authority from community. The crisis in meaning and social ordering incumbent on this development must, however, be addressed. For, while it is clear that the genuinely charismatic experience can never be fully institutionalized as such, the question remains as to the particular venues taken by its institutionalization. Why, over the first generation of settlement, did the institutionalization of the charismatic propensity develop in terms of the increased isolation of authority from community?

Indeed, in terms taken from more classical sociological discussion, the social developments that we have been studying were an almost "paradigmatic" example of any process of institutionalization, that is, of the need to embody "the experience of the holy" in the routine frameworks and structures of daily life, or, in Weberian terms, of "social action."[61] This social dynamic, however, does not in and of itself imply the emergence of a fundamental crisis in collective meaning, nor a growing chasm between authority and community (as ideally conceived or as practically enacted). True, the need to ensure social regularity by the imposition of institutional structures inevitably leads, as sociologists have pointed out, to a number of specific and generalized developments. Thus, instead of an immediate response to the religious "call," there develops stable institutional matrixes of offices and roles, a change that, as A. N. Whitehead pointed out, fundamentally restructures religious activity from "an adventure of the spirit" to a "rule of safety."[62]

Furthermore, as part of this process, there develops also an objectification or "symbolic transformation" of the religious experience, which often takes the form of a concretization of the original religious message into definite rules, specific norms, and patterns of behavior restricted by legal formulations and controlled by institutional structures. While these developments, emerging from the contact of charisma with the more prosaic elements of daily life and especially with the power structure of society, have led to what has been termed by Talcott Parsons and others, *the dilemma of institutionalization,* this in

The Emergent Tensions of Institutionalization   119

itself is not sufficient to explain the course of developments in New England.[63] For, in this case, the growth of an institutional matrix of Church officers with clearly defined duties, of synods and councils, of centralized authority and patterned behavior with properly defined duties and obligations, of a "rule of safety," and of formalized, "bureaucratized" religious activity led not to a stable and perduring pattern of beliefs and actions, but to a centrifugal burst of protest and an immediate intensification of the problems of maintaining order, social control, authority, and moral boundaries.

Why, then, did this initial attempt at the routinization and institutionalization of charisma, which, after all, involves a retraction of its genuinely charismatic locus in community, engender in New England such a high degree of ideological fragmentation? The answer, I believe, is to be found in the dialectic of authority and community. For what happened was that while a process of institutionalization took place in the organizational and symbolic spheres of authority, it did not take place in the related sphere of community, which remained in a sense rooted in the premise of the "charismatic band" type of organization, typified by a "Bund"-like type of solidarity and symbolized in the covenanted Church of the regenerate saints.

The successful routinization of charisma involves its symbolization and systematization in terms of a broad frame of value referents. As pointed out by Liah Greenfeld, for genuine charisma to be institutionalized it must lead to the establishment of new values through "the successful internalization of symbolic constructs."[64] The "internalization of values and cognitions" is, she points out, a central aspect in the routinization of charisma. For, if not symbolized in terms of particular values, routinized and thereby transformed into an order based on "social action," the genuinely charismatic phenomenon remains necessarily transient.[65] It was precisely this aspect of routinization that developed in New England along two asymptotic trajectories. Authority, as we have seen, did undergo a process of systematization (in its very codification), routinization (in the exact criteria laid down for officeholders and their prerogatives in the Cambridge Platform), as well as a very particular mode of symbolization (in the increasingly sacerdotal conception of the ministry).[66] However, the pervasive definitions of community in the colony remained unchanged. Thus, instead of a broad "sanctification" of the collective, which, as Greenfeld, following Shils and Weber, points out, is often a necessary mode of sensitizing people to the charismatic center of society, increasingly more members were excluded from the "sanctified" community of visible saints due to their failure to live up to the terms of the test of relation.[67] Instead of bringing the wider collective into the "charismatic arena" the ministers and the models of community they articulated became increasingly less relevant for members of society as a whole.

In sum, the ultimate principles of validity, upon which authority rested and around which society was organized, were those of the covenanted Church whose initial premises, while accepted in principle, were denied in the practice that evolved following the process of codification that took place over the 1640s. More explicitly, the initial assumptions of authority, tied, as they were, to the ultimate source of meaning, were based on a genuinely or purely charismatic notion of the social order. This mode of symbolizing the social order implied a basic lack of differentiation between frameworks of authority and definitions of community, as well as an immediate connection between members of the community and the charismatic dimension of existence. With the process of institutionalization and routinization of charismatic authority begun in the 1640s, a greater differentiation evolved between authority and community as the latter was distanced from immediate participation in the "charismatic experience." This process, which implied a formalization of the moral boundaries of society, stood, however, in contrast to the explicitly articulated ideology of Congregational Puritanism based on the covenant and a polity founded on the experience of grace.[68] In short, the structural framework of society and its relations of authority were changing, while its symbolic premises effectively remained those of the 1630 gathered Church.

As a result of the inability to institutionalize charisma in terms of the originally perceived interweaving of the world and the Church there did not develop any concrete broadening, systematization, and symbolization of the charismatic dimension in different institutional spheres, especially those related to the realm of community and the basic terms of solidarity, primarily the Church and the family.[69] Such a development, had it occurred, may have opened up access to the charismatic center for the collective as a whole (in Shils's terms, *the periphery*).[70] The failure of this opening up of the center and the concomitant distancing of "community" from the sources of the sacred in society was, in fact, the focal point of the crisis in the mid-seventeenth century and the core of the dissonance that emerged between structures of authority and models of community.

Moreover, as we have seen in our study of the Antinomian crises, the terms in which community itself was defined and constituted were important factors in the developing dualism between community and authority. As a community of shared grace, there existed a continual propensity to oppose the workings of grace to the ordered patterns of social action and institutions. The pull toward an individual articulation of grace, beyond its communal referents and independent of authority, continually questioned the premises of collective meaning, the validity of social authority, and (through the proliferation of other "deviant" groups) the loci of cosmic meaning and definitions of the boundaries of the collective. However, in a community dedicated to the holy work of reformation and cosmic redemption, grace remained that fulcrum upon which definitions of membership and participation hinged. The problems faced by mid-century Puritanism, as a meaning-giving system, turned therefore on the construction of definitions of community, which, while remaining rooted in grace, would nevertheless insure the continual working of the social order.

The Antinomian crises, as well as the doctrine of Grotonists and Quakers, highlighted the centrifugal potentiality of a community defined in terms of a "genuinely charismatic" experience of grace. Similarly, the early stages of institutionalization emphasized the increasing isolation of models of community from the felt experience of most collective members. In many ways this dilemma, and the particular solutions posited to it by the ministerial elite of Congregational Puritanism, structured the further progress of institutionalization over the next two generations of social life. The decisions taken by the Reforming Synod of 1662 and the implementation of the Half-Way Covenant (in concert with other factors to be studied below) in response to this dilemma represented a unique solution to the problems of communal identity, first opened up in the Hutchinson Affair.

Notes

1. The effect of developments in England on New England is noted in *The Winthrop Papers,* vol. 4, 205.
2. Williston Walker, ed., *The Creeds and Platforms of Congregationalism* (Boston: The Pilgrim Press, 1960), 132–48, 157–237.

122   Innerworldly Individualism

3. Thomas Barnes, ed., *The Book of the General Lawes and Libertyes Concerning the Inhabitants of Massachusetts* (San Marino: The Huntington Library, 1975), 5–10.
4. Walker, ed., *Creeds and Platforms,* 139–43.
5. Hall, *The Faithful Shepherd,* 111.
6. Darrett Rutman, *Winthrop's Boston* (New York: Norton, 1965), 125.
7. Hall, *The Faithful Shepherd,* 112.
8. Walker, ed., *Creeds and Platforms,* 219.
9. Ibid.
10. Hall, *The Faithful Shepherd,* 113.
11. Walker, ed., *Creeds and Platforms,* 210.
12. Ibid., 215.
13. Ibid., 216.
14. Thomas Shepard and John Allin, *A Defence of an Answer* (London, 1648), 134.
15. Ibid.
16. Walker, ed., *Creeds and Platforms,* 232.
17. Mather, *Magnalia Christi Americana,* vol. 2, Book 5, 237.
18. Walker, ed., *Creeds and Platforms,* 223; Hall, *The Faithful Shepherd,* 101.
19. Walker, ed., *Creeds and Platforms,* 229–34.
20. Among the most prestigious of the returning ministers were Hugh Peter, Giles Firmin, and William Aspinwall. As pointed out by William Sachse the importance of migration back to England was not so much in the number of returning colonists, but their quality, comprising "seven of the nine graduates of Harvard's first class" and by 1656 fully a third of all graduates. Quoted in Avihu Zakai, *Exile and Kingdom,* (1982), 392. On Harvard College, see Samuel Morrison, *The Founding of Harvard College* (Cambridge: Harvard University Press, 1939).
21. On these developments see especially Bailyn, "The New England Merchants."
22. In this context it would be well to subject to more rigorous inquiry L. Ziff's (1973:75) suggestion of the attraction of free grace to mercantile elites whose "affinity" to more individualistic religious values would be greater than that of other segments of the population.
23. Herman Schmalenbach, "The Sociological Category of Communion," in *Theories of Society,* ed. T. Parsons et al. (New York: The Free Press, 1961), 331–47.
24. A very similar process of change and differentiation (in the context of the Israeli kibbutz) was studied by Erik Cohen (1982:123–46). The analytic scheme developed in that study (of a more modern "community of grace") has informed my perception of change in the no less ideological communities of seventeenth-century New England.
25. On the local level, marked evidence of these tensions were felt in such developments as the growing struggle over seating arrangements within the different churches. The very appointment of "seating committees" to properly administer the "positioning" of different members in the congregation, as well as the continual difficulties of such regulation, has been noted by Ola Winslow (1972:142–46). Further and hitherto neglected insights into the construction of symbols of prestige in seventeenth-century New England are provided by Norman Dawes, "Titles as Symbols of Prestige in Seventeenth Century New England," *William and*

Mary Quarterly 6 (1949): 69–84.
26. Winthrop, *A History of New England,* vol. 2, 216.
27. Ibid., 203. On law in general, see Haskins, *Law and Authority*; George Billies, ed., *Selected Essays: Law and Authority in Colonial America* (New York: Dover, 1965), especially the contribution by Darrett Rutman (149–67). On discipline in the early Puritan colonies, see Emile Obelholzer, *Delinquent Saints: Disciplinary Action in the Early Congregational Churches of Massachusetts* (New York: Columbia University Press, 1956).
28. The following summary of the relations between ministers and congregants is taken in the main from Hall, "The Faithful Shepherd," 187–96.
29. Elliot, *Power and Pulpit*; Philip Greven, *Four Generations: Population, Land and Family in Colonial America* (Ithaca, NY: Cornell University Press, 1970). See also John Waters, "Family, Inheritance and Migration in Colonial New England: The Evidence from Guilford Connecticut," *William and Mary Quarterly* 39 (1982): 64–86.
30. Elliot, *Power and Pulpit,* 27.
31. Walker, ed., *Creeds and Platforms,* 307; Robert Pope, *The Half Way Covenant: Church Membership in Puritan New England* (Princeton: Princeton University Press, 1969), 14.
32. Foster, "New England and the Challenge," 624–60; Gura, *A Glimpse of Sion's.*
33. Ward, *A Simple Cobbler,* 11, 18. The term *Puritan Mind* is, of course, taken from the title of Perry Miller's (1953) classic study of Puritanism.
34. Quoted in Gura, *A Glimpse of Sion's,* 69.
35. Ibid., 72.
36. Winthrop, *A History of New England,* vol. 1, 321.
37. Gura, *A Glimpse of Sion's,* 113.
38. Lovejoy, *Religious Enthusiasm,* 59.
39. S. N. Eisenstadt, "Comparative Liminality," 322.
40. Turner, *The Ritual Process,* 92–93.
41. Indeed, in line with this role, the early 1640s saw an increase in millennial speculation on the part of a number of prominent ministers in New England, a development that was, of course, intimately connected with the course of the Puritan revolution in England. These were the years of John Cotton's *An Exposition on the Thirteenth Chapter of Revelation, the Pouring Out of the Seven Vials* (1642), of Thomas Lechford's speculations on the coming of the millennium as well as such speculation among the less illustrious (such as among the inhabitants of Rhode Island). Among Congregational Puritans, however, and John Cotton is a case in point, this speculation was intimately tied to the doctrine of the Congregational church—as testified in his works of 1644, *The Keyes of the Kingdome of Heaven* and *The Way of the Congregational Churches Cleared* (1648). In these writings, however, and in retreat from his earlier position in the Antinomian affair, he tied a millennial interpretation of history to a particular model of social order—that of the Covenanted churches of visible saints. In a similar vein, Thomas Shepard and John Allin, in the 1648 *Defense of an Answer to Nine Questions or Positions,* defended the basic principles of the New England Way as the fulcrum of reform in "these times of light and of the consumption of the AntiChrist." So too, John

124   Innerworldly Individualism

Eliot, in *The Holy Commonwealth,* included in his program for the millennial kingdom, the fundamental criteria of membership as applied in the godly Commonwealth of Massachusetts. This very mode of membership was, however, the crux of the problem. For, as we have seen, this particular model of the social order, this "Congregational Way," had with time excluded more and more people from the fundamental models of participation and inclusion in the collective through their failure to join the covenanted churches.

42. Davenport, *A Discourse,* 7.
43. Ibid.
44. Ibid., 6.
45. Here, too, the Antinomian crisis marked a watershed in the attempt to reconcile the world and the Church. Thus, John Winthrop's defense of the autonomy of the civil magistracy (in the wake of the Wheelwright affair and popular demands that the Church elders censor the governor for his condemnation of Wheelwright) is characterized by a marked leaning toward the separation of this-worldly from otherworldly realms. Such statements as "Christs kingdome is not of this world, therefore his officers in this kingdome cannot Juditially enq[uire] into affairs of this world" (*Winthrop Papers,* vol. 3, 505–6) indicate a tendency to separate the interwoven realms of the Church and the world.
46. Lucas, *Valley of Discord,* 34–39.
47. On Roger Williams's vision of history, see Gilpin, *The Millenarian Piety.* On his conceptions of Church-State relations, see Edmund Morgan, *Roger Williams: The Church and the State* (New York: Harcourt Brace and World, 1967).
48. Edmund Morgan, *The Puritan Dilemma: The Story of John Winthrop* (Boston: Little Brown, 1958), 131.
49. Winthrop, *A History of New England,* vol. 2, 255.
50. John Cotton in Ziff, *John Cotton on the Churches,* 153.
51. For Winthrop's defense of this measure, see *Winthrop Papers,* vol. 3, 422–26, 463–76.
52. On the relation of biblical law to English law among the New England Puritans, see Haskins, *Law and Authority,* 1–8, 141–62.
53. *Body of Lawes* (1648), A2.
54. Ibid.
55. Ibid.
56. Ibid.
57. On these distinctions, see Haskins, *Law and Authority,* 158–62.
58. John Norton, *Sion the Outcast Healed of Her Wounds* (Boston, 1664), 8.
59. Shepard and Allin, *A Defence,* 86.
60. Reinhard Bendix, "Max Weber's Sociology Today," *International Social Science Journal* 17 (1965): 19.
61. The classic study of this experience is of course William James, *The Varieties of Religious Experience* (Glasgow: Fontana, 1960). On the concept of the "holy," see Rudolph Otto, *The Idea of the Holy* (Oxford: Oxford University Press, 1950).
62. Quoted in Thomas O'Dea, "Sociological Dilemmas: Five Paradoxes of Institutionalization," in *Sociological Theory, Values and Socio-cultural Change,* ed. E. Tiryakian (New York: Harper and Row, 1963), 76.

63. Ibid., 71–89.
64. Greenfeld, "Two Charismas," 125–28.
65. Ibid., 128.
66. This symbolization took place, as can be seen, only in the realm related to authority and did not affect the community as a whole. It was, therefore, not of the same order as that dimension of symbolization of the charismatic discussed by Edward Shils (1975:3–16) in his notion of the symbolization of the charismatic center.
67. Greenfeld, "Two Charismas," 129; Shils, *Center and Periphery*, 3–16.
68. It would be interesting in this context of the maintenance of moral boundaries to speculate on the rise of sexual deviance, or, at the very least, an increasing concern with it in precisely those years of increased millennial agitation. The concern of Winthrop and others in authority with bestiality, rape, sodomy, or just plain fornication and adultery in the same period is tantalizing in its implications (see, for example, John Winthrop, *A History of New England,* vol. 2, pp. 11, 34, 45, 51, 54, 57, 78, 110). For if, on the one hand, a rise in such behavior did indeed occur immediately following the codification of the Cambridge Platform, it would seem to indicate a growing feeling of anomie in the wake of the growing routinization of authority and the loss of its tie to the community, a feeling that must have been only intensified by a millennial expectation that excluded many from the salvational collective. If, on the other hand, what we see is but an increasing concern with boundary maintenance, it would seem to point to the need of authority to extend the organizational implications of its systematization into the realms of everyday life.
69. On the role of the family in maintaining solidarity, see Morgan, *The Puritan Family,* and G. Moran and Vinouvskis, "Puritan Family and Religion," *William and Mary Quarterly* 39 (1982): 291–363.
70. Shils, *Center and Periphery,* 3–16.

5

The Half Way Covenant and the Jeremiad Sermon

Just as the attempt to institutionalize the original terms of social life in the first thirty years of settlement led to a widening gap between structures of authority and models of community, so the following decades saw various attempts to reintegrate both facets of collective meaning and social ordering. This was carried out through the implementation of a number of measures, whose consequences, while not always foreseen, led to a major transformation of both models of community and notions of authority. The two primary factors in the reworking of Congregational Puritanism as a meaning-giving framework of collective life were the Half Way Covenant and the jeremiad sermon—the first an organizational innovation and the second a renovation of existing forms of symbolic rhetoric, developed in the period of the 1660s to the 1690s. Their effects went far beyond those envisioned by either the ministers who gathered in Boston's First Church in March 1662 at the opening of the "Half Way" Synod, or by those ministerial "jeremiahs" who, in an often apocalyptic rhetoric, castigated their congregations for their decline in religion and piety. For, as was to be witnessed by the last decades of the century, the direct, if unintended, consequences of these acts were to lead, in Church as in polity, to a new synthesis of manners and mores. The rise of Stoddard's system of Church membership, of Cotton Mather's revival societies, and of mass covenant revivals, together with religious tolerance and the growth of ritualism in religion, all exemplified a major change in the basic terms of communal life.

In the following, we will analyze this change as a transformation of the fundamental ordering premises of social existence, which allowed the eventual reintegration of community and authority in the second half of the seventeenth and the first third of the eighteenth century in New England. This transformation of ordering premises constituted what may, in fact, be characterized as the institutionalization of charisma in social life. The particularities of this institutionalization, characterized by a unique reformulation of the relation between the Church and the world and the formation of a particular model of collective identity, were structured by the contradictions in the symbolic universe of New England Puritanism studied above. Analysis of this process will concentrate on three major changes in the organizational and symbolic realms of social life: (a) a redefinition of the ideal moral boundaries of the collective; (b) a transformation in the modes of legitimizing authority and in defining distinct spheres of its enactment; and (c) a reconstituting of the sense of collective meaning. Taken together, these changes (and the particular social mechanisms through which they were effected) represent a unique solution to that problem, of institutionalizing a definition of community in terms of shared grace and virtuosi religion first broached in the preaching and practice of Anne Hutchinson.

The Half Way Covenant

The Historical Background

In March 1662 the Massachusetts General Court issued a call for a church synod to discuss an issue that had with each passing year become more pressing—the issue of baptism and Church membership. As we recall, the early Congregationalists upheld the view that "regenerate membership was an absolute essential to the properly constituted Church."[1] Only one category of people were excluded from the need to covenant with God and their fellow men to be become Church members—the children of already regenerate saints. These children of regenerate members were seen to be Church members (and as such were baptized) through partaking in the covenant of their parents. With the maturity of this generation, however, there arose the serious problem of their own progeny. Could these children of Church members who had not undergone regeneration be admitted into baptism? Could this third generation be incorporated into the Church, and, if so, on what basis? Ministerial concern with this problem of what essentially the boundaries of the community were and the terms of membership therein progressed throughout the 1650s. In fact, the serious dissensions among ministers and Churches over a narrow or broad definition of collective membership (that is, over the inclusion or exclusion of this third generation from Church membership) resulted first in the Ministerial Assembly of 1657 and later in the Half Way Synod of 1662.[2]

As has been recognized by many scholars (and, indeed, as feared by its albeit few ministerial opponents), the Half Way Covenant bespoke a fundamental reorientation in the nature of New England Congregationalism.[3] In reworking (and broadening) the terms of entrance to the Covenant, the Synod of 1662 effectively transformed the ideal model of community, a move that, in conjunction with other developments, led to a repositioning of the borders of membership as well as the basic terms of membership in the collective.

As noted, the problem faced by the conveners of the Synod was how to ensure the continuity of Church membership tied, as this was, to the experience of regeneration. For the continuing practice of New England orthodoxy "was predicated on the hereditary growth of faith."[4] Entering the life of the Church and the community with infant baptism, the individual was expected to: learn the catechism; follow obediently the strictures of parents and elders; experience edification through the Word as preached by the minister; lead an exemplary life; and, at some time, undergo the experience of regeneration upon which he or she was made a full member in the Church and allowed to partake of the Lord's Supper. As more and more people could not provide evidence of "saving grace," could not pass the "test of relation," and so could not participate fully in the religious and hence political life of the community, the ideal model of communal solidarity was called into question. Moreover, besides the questions hovering over the proper status of these individuals, the ultimate issue was the question of their children. Born to parents who had not undergone regeneration, could these children be baptized? Did the unregenerate status of the parents terminate the covenant relation? Such a possibility, far from the thoughts of those who founded the Bay Colony in 1630, was, by mid-century, a pressing question, one whose implications ran much deeper than the fate of any particular child or family. For a termination of the covenant relation implied the end of New

England's mission, indeed, of its very raison d'etre. New England was, after all, founded to advance the Kingdom of Christ and, as Jonathan Mitchell wrote to Increase Mather in 1667, "It was never heard of in the world, from Abraham to this day . . . that a people did continue for any length of Time to be Religious, who were either all, or in great part of them uncircumcised or unbaptized."[5]

The failure of the following generation to follow in the ways of their parents threatened the very continuity of the social order. The collective failure to give evidence of saving grace meant nothing less than the withdrawal of God's providential favor, threatening the very foundations of collective meaning; the "premature" truncation of the covenant threatened as well the very existing definitions or models of community and of authority. For the terms of their meaning and power were intensely interwoven with the very covenantal definition of the social order. Moreover, it must be remembered that a consistent falling off of full Church members brought fewer and fewer people into that symbolic arena whose authoritative locus was the minister.

The Half Way Covenant addressed itself in the main to the interrelated problems of extending Church discipline and models of community to increasingly distanced members of the congregation and, in so doing, to reconstituting the increasingly attenuated links between the authority of ministers and magistrates, which rested on the covenanted community of saints and the community at large. And although ministers such as Richard Mather, Peter Bulkeley, Thomas Allen, and George Phillips had, since the 1640s, been seeking ways to maintain the primacy of the Church as a model for community (through broadening the terms of membership therein in the wake of the decline of regenerate members), it was not until the fifth or sixth decades of the century that such a "revisionist" attitude became popular among the majority of the ministers.[6] Seeking to include within the Church children of parents who had not undergone the regenerative process, the participants in the 1662 Synod hammered out a compromise position, between their total exclusion, on the one hand, or full communion, on the other. The crux of this, what eighteenth-century critics would call Half Way Synod, was found in proposition five of the program:[7]

> Church Members who were admitted in minority, understanding the Doctrine of Faith, and publickly professing their assent thereto; not scandalous in life, and solemnly owning the Covenant before the Church, wherein

they give up themselves and their Children to the Lord, and subject themselves to the Government of Christ in Church, their children are to be Baptised.[8]

Henceforth, parents (themselves offspring of regenerate members) would have only to "own" their own baptismal covenant, that is, *intellectually* to assert their adherence to the principles of Congregational policy, in order to present their own children for baptism and hence continue membership in the Church.

The result of the Synod of 1662 did not, however, settle the matter, for it left the implications of its decisions to the individual churches. As a result, the progressive acceptance of the Synod's decisions was a slow, halting, strife-ridden process. This led, in such places as Hartford and Windsor, to the fragmentation of churches, the establishment of dual ministries, and the formation of new churches from the dissenting membership of existing ones.[9]

Thus far, little work has been done in documenting the process of instituting the decisions of the 1662 Synod in particular churches. One of the few attempts to trace this process was carried out by Robert Pope who studied the Third Church Boston and the churches of Roxbury, Charlestown, and Dorchester in depth and charted more schematically the progress of the Half Way resolution in other New England communities. Despite the differences in all congregations (Dorchester being actively opposed to its implementation and the Third Church Boston splitting from the First Church precisely over the latter's acceptance of the Half Way Covenant), Pope found full acceptance and use of the Covenant in New England churches only by the end of the 1670s and beginning of the 1680s.[10] Indeed, what Pope found in the majority of cases was what past scholars have consistently pointed to—the mass rejection of the Half Way scheme by the majority of the congregants. For while the ministers perceived the need to extend baptism, fearing a situation in which their churches would contain less than half the population of New England, the majority of the congregants in both Massachusetts and Connecticut were, until the late 1670s, actively opposed to halfway membership.[11] Opposition expressed itself both in principle, leading to the fragmentation of churches in such places as Boston, Windsor, and Hartford, and in practice. For, as Pope's studies show, even where the principle of halfway membership was accepted, its practice took over a decade to gain acceptance. Consequently, one result of the Half Way Covenant —implemented to sustain ministerial power and hegemony within the community at large—was, paradoxically, a greater tension between ministers and congregants opposing the implementation of the Half Way Covenant.

The Half Way Covenant and Collective Boundaries

Whereas in some cases, such as in Hartford, opposition to the Half Way Covenant rested not on the widening scope of baptism, but on the voting privileges within the Church that went with it, there is little evidence to suggest that in all cases, resistance to its proposals were based on such *Realfaktoren*.[12] This point is important to note in analyzing the Half Way Covenant. For, although historians continue to debate the relation of the Half Way Covenant to the franchise, nowhere is this issue raised in the contemporary debates around the Half Way Covenant. In fact, any direct connection between the implementation of the Half Way Covenant and the mechanisms of political participation is doubtful. In Connecticut (which merged with the New Haven Colony in 1665) and Plymouth, membership in the Church was never a prerequisite for freemanship. In Massachusetts, where freemanship was limited to Church members, the general court of 1636 made it clear that voting privilege in the town would only be granted to members "in full communion." Thus, here, too, the Half Way Covenant (which did not grant full communion) did not affect the actual workings of political participation. What it did affect, however, were the broader terms of conceiving the social order, the principles of its organization, and the basis of membership. It is from this perspective that we will analyze its importance in paving the way for more concrete changes (such as the granting of religious toleration) at a later date.[13]

Thus, as continually attested to in Pope's study, as well as in the work of David Hall, debates around the Synod's decisions, by both dissenting participants and later by the congregations at large, rested on the broader implications of the Half Way Covenant on the concepts of Church and State in Puritan New England, that is, on the fundamental premises of organized social life, as practiced in the first decades of settlement. Supporters of the Synod's proposals did their utmost to argue that the innovations of the Synod were, in fact, no innovations at all. Increase Mather's *The First Principles of New England* (1675) was, in fact, a long, drawn-out polemic filled with letters and quotations from the most prominent divines, dating back to 1634, arguing that the Half Way Covenant was "no Apostacy from the first principles of New England, nor yet any declension from the Congregational way."[14] The defense of the Synod's proposals by such ministers as Increase Mather and Jonathan Mitchell as well as by John Allin in his *Animadversions upon the Antisynodalia Americana* (1664) centered on proving that the halfway doctrine was not "a Novel Innovation, differing from first and primitive principles,"[15] for in the eyes of its critics, the Half Way Covenant constituted a fundamental break with Congregational policy. Condemning it as "[t]hat practice that exsposeth the blood of Christ to contempt, and baptism to profanation, the Church to pollution and the Commonwealth to confusion,"[16] the ministers saw it (in their *Answers of the Dissenting Ministers of the Synod* [1662]) as opening the way to withdrawal of divine favor from the colonies. Indeed, in the pamphlet literature surrounding the controversy, in Charles Chauncy's *Anti-Synodalia Scripta Americana* (1662), John Davenport's *Another Essay for the Investigation of the Truth in Answer to Two Questions* (1663), as well as in the *Answer of the Dissenting Ministers of the Synod* (1662), opponents claimed that the halfway solution opened the dam to "apostasy" and "corruption."[17] This view found eloquent expression in an addendum to the church register in Dorchester after the baptism of a nonmember's child: "a Corruption creeping in as an harbinger to old England's practice viz to make all members (which God prevent in mercy)."[18]

In fact, the opponents of the Synod understood very well the significance of the Half Way Covenant and precisely what in the New England Way it threatened. This knowledge was evinced in John Davenport's polemics, where he claimed that the only way apostasy and irreligion could be prevented was to have "the Porter look well to the Doors of the Lord's house."[19] This matter of doors and porters was the crux of the issue.

For what the Half Way Covenant did, in essence, was break down, or at the very least, seriously attenuate the fundamental ordering categories of collective life, that is, that distinction between the visible saints and the as yet unregenerate members of the community. The line drawn between these groups represented the boundaries of the ideal community. Full membership in the Church, with its attendant political privileges (of the franchise in Massachusetts) as well as obligations (for the full force of Church discipline extended only to regenerate members), bespoke participation in that community and so membership in the *ecumene* in the salvational collective. The Half Way Covenant, however, through the internal logic of its own position, seriously compromised the existing boundaries of the ideal community. By breaking down the very purity of the gathered church, it considerably weakened the primary boundary maintaining device within society. It is thus no wonder that critics of the proposals were concerned with the resulting defilement of the Church and the Lord's Supper that would result. Indeed, the "pollution" of the community of congregants was a theme that emerged in the Preface to the *Answers of the Dissenting Ministers of the Synod*: "It is apparant unto all what a corrupt mass of unbelievers... shall throng into the communion of God's people: and the children of strangers uncircumscised in heart shall bee brought into God's sanctuary to pollute it."[20] The themes of pollution, defilement, and the transgression of borders all betray a salient concern with the eradication of the moral boundaries of the community.[21] This concern with moral boundaries and the threat the halfway solution posed to existing arrangements stood, as John Davenport's dictum shows, at the heart of the opposition to the decisions of the Synod of 1662.[22]

The concern with the breakdown of moral boundaries and the break implied in the halfway compromise with existing religious practice contained a number of elements. Of primary importance was the very concern with the fundamental terms of institutionally ordering collective membership. For, in addition to what has been mentioned above, it is important to note that the halfway proposals involved a negation of the basic ordering mechanisms of society. By opening up halfway membership to children of the unregenerate, it seriously limited the importance of the "test of relation" as an ordering mechanism, capable of regulating membership in the community. Whereas the ultimate referent for admittance into the moral community was once the experience of saving grace, with the halfway solution this was no longer the case. Attestation to saving grace could no longer be the primary border-regulating mechanism once baptism was opened to all. And, in fact, it was replaced with the "owning of the covenant," a ceremony or ritual that dissenters such as Davenport rejected, pointing out that "when some of them having publickly said they own it, being afterward asked in private, what is the Covenant which you owned? answered, I do not know."[23] Although, with the growing acceptance of the halfway solution (from the mid 1670s to the 1690s), the collective ritual of covenant owning would become an important locus of the new terms of collective membership; in the first years of its practice it was viewed as but a meager substitute for the original rite—the testimony of saving grace.[24]

In comparing both rituals, two important elements stand out as portents of the changing times. The first was the aforementioned emphasis on reason and understanding that was implied in owning the covenant, an attestation to one's acceptance of the covenant on cognitive and not affective grounds.[25] The latter mode was the case in the test of relation, which marked the work of regeneration within the individual, that is, a felt change in one's emotional state and not a declaration of faith. The second important difference was that the ritual of covenant owning, while an affirmation of community, was less a rite of social closure than the "test of relation." In the latter case, membership was asserted in a rite of passage that clearly involved the crossing over to a new state of being—that of regenerate, visible sainthood. Entering this state and the community of saints marked a major passage, a break from the past and, by implication, a break from those not sharing in divine grace. The owning of the covenant, however, involved no such break, no such passage, and no such negation. By its very nature, it stressed continuity, and reaffirmation of doctrines learned and of one's original communal tie made at the time of baptism. As a mechanism ordering membership and participation in the community, the rite of "owning the covenant" carried with it a very different set of assumptions than the earlier ritual. We shall return to this in our forthcoming discussion of the overall change in the terms of community that marked the turn of the century.

Beyond this change in ordering mechanisms, the very breakdown of existing principles of social ordering threatened the ideal model of community and, in so doing, threatened as well the very terms of collective meaning, a meaning which, as we recall, was constituted through God's special relation to New England as sustained by the covenant. In the eyes of the Synod's opponents, the Half Way Covenant implied a departure from the original terms of the covenant and so a removal from their special place in providential history. As the fundamental meaning of the collective endeavor was predicated (at least ideally) on this special covenantal relation, any alteration in the terms of the covenant threatened the overarching sense of meaning within which collective life was structured.

This theme of a "reneging" on the original covenant and the danger to the collective mission that it contained was evinced even in the more moderate attacks on the Half Way Covenant such as those by William Stoughton. In his *New England's True Interest Not to Lie* (1670), Stoughton is at pains to show the necessity of cleaving to the original forms, to "the first ways of walking with God." Thus, he claims that

> when God doth in a more than ordinary way of Providence form a people, and settle them to be a people to himself, there is ever that which is eminent in the primitive frame of things amongst them, which God expects that they should keep to, and never make defection from[26]

adding that "David has his first wayes . . . and so Churches have their first wayes when they newly come out of the forming hand of God: Now the Lord expresseth not only great disappointment when these first wayes are neglected, or quite altered, and cast off."[27] Falling off from original practices brought, for him, the possibility that the terms of the covenant, the "engagement of grace," would be "broken and made void." "God," Stoughton reminded his hearers, "threatens to remove the Candlesticks . . . and often hath he done it."[28] He, too, emphasized the dangers of "mixtures and corruptions, . . . of false Doctrines and false Worship," stressing that:

> There is nor Error in Doctrine, or in Worship and Ordinances, but it tends some way or other to alter, pervert, and corrupt the Lord's Covenant with his people. By this we are to judge of the danger of Errors and erronoaus practices, and answerably to watch against the infection of them.[29]

The danger of these, what Stoughton termed *lies,* is not only in the abrogation of the covenant, but in a very loss of self, in a loss of identity, leading him to cry: "Alas! how is New England in danger this day to be lost even in New England? to be buried in its own ruins? How sadly may we lament it that All are not Israel that are now of Israel."[30]

As noted, the articulate dissenting clergy were not the only opponents of the Half Way Covenant. The very slow course of its institutionalization, the fact that it often took up to twenty years for congregations to accept its practice, points to the congregations sharing in the dissenting ministers' feeling that the halfway compromise undermined the institutional foundations of social life. Despite its slow adoption, in the face of both lay and clerical opposition, by the 1680s the Half Way Covenant became "the new Orthodoxy" and as such it must be addressed.[31] For while its final adoption rested, no doubt, at least in part on the crises of the 1670s and 1680s—King Philip's Wars and the Andros Revolt—its final acceptance bespoke a change in the terms of community, that is, in the model of the ideal community and in the mechanisms of maintaining it.[32] For what the acceptance of the halfway solution illustrated was a slow transfer of these models. By opening the channels of communion between the churches and the congregations at large (through the widening of baptism), the model of the gathered Church of visible saints began to lose its saliency as the locus of the social order. No longer "pure" or inviolable, extended membership began to obscure those very defining borders that had accorded Church membership its uniquely focal role in communal life. Charisma, in terms of a relation with ultimate principles, began slowly to leave the exclusive province of the Church.

This fundamental restructuring of the models of community occasioned by the opening up of the terms of membership was one of the most crucial developments toward the construction of a perduring institutional framework for social interaction in seventeenth-century New England. In itself, however, it would not have been sufficient to occasion the crystallization of a stable set of social relations in general, or of a reintegration of authority and community in particular. For if the gathered Church of regenerate saints lost its locus as the social center, what took its place? How can we explain the dynamic of the process that saw the test of relation lose its saliency as a boundary maintaining mechanism and ordering device (as, by the last decade of the century, most Church members were admitted under the halfway solution) and its replacement by the owning of the covenant? Moreover, if the Half Way Covenant implied a threat to collective meaning and an undermining of collective identity, then how did a sense of shared collective identity nevertheless crystallize? And, finally, if the Half Way Covenant implied a breakdown of existing ordering principles, what took their place? Any answer to these queries must of necessity be hesitant, circumspect, and qualified by the need for further research. Yet the developments in mid-century, of new social forms and novel organizational practices, as well as of new symbolic constructs, allow some indication of how New England Puritanism as an ideology or meaning-giving system was reconstituted by the end of the seventeenth century. These were developed in what has been called the jeremiad sermon, which, in giving new life to an old symbolic form, was a major element in the eventual reintegration of the New England polity, although again, like the Half Way Covenant, not necessarily in ways intended by its proponents.

The Jeremiad Sermon

While the Half Way Covenant attempted, on the organizational level, to maintain the continuity of the social order in New England, the evolution of the jeremiad sermon represented a similar attempt on the symbolic level. Endeavoring to recall the sense of cosmic errand in increasingly worldly oriented communities, its message was both a lament and a call to a mission, which, through a shaping of new symbols and a reshaping of old ones, forged a new basis for collective identity. The general form of the jeremiad—a sermon that at one and the same time castigated the people for their backsliding and celebrated with prophetic assurance God's promise to his covenanted people—both antedated and postdated the period in question.[33]

The jeremiad's roots were in the Puritan emphasis on the preaching of the word of God, and its continuity, according to some, can be found in eighteenth- and nineteenth-century American prose. Yet, even those, such as Sacvan Bercovitz, who argue for the pervasiveness of the jeremiad as a literary genre inherent in American culture, admit its saliency in the last quarter of the seventeenth century.[34] For it was in this period that the "classical" form of the jeremiad took shape in the sermons of dozens of ministers. In this period ministers such as Samuel Danforth, Urian Oakes, William Stoughton, Samuel Torrey, John Norton, Jonathan Mitchell, John Higginson, and Increase Mather, among others, developed a rhetoric that included both an exhortation to reformation and a promise of divine fulfillment.[35] As argued convincingly by Sacvan Bercovitz, they facilitated, in this manner, that "backing into modernity" with which Perry Miller characterized the transition of New England from religious theocracy to "a middle class empirical enterprising society."[36] The precise manner of this transformation, besides providing, in Bercovitz's words, "a system of sacred-secular symbols," has remained, however, unanalyzed.[37] In the following, I will attempt to overcome this lacuna and show the beginning crystallization of a sense of national identity by positing the development and underlying symbolic logic of the jeremiad in terms of a general reworking of the symbolic terms of collective life.

Above all, in relocating New England within the overall providential design of history, the jeremiad reasserted a sense of cosmic meaning and purpose to collective life. This was effected in the main by recalling the special relation of God with the people of New England. Like the earlier Israelites, Urian Oakes reminded his congregants in 1673:

> God hath sequestred you from the rest of the World, allured you into this Wilderness, and brought you into these parts of the Earth . . . that you might set up his way and worship in the purity and Gospel-glory of it. This was the refreshing mercy of God to his people when he first brought them over, and that which sweetned to them many a bitter Cup, and supported them under the burdensome inconveniences of a Wilderness condition.[38]

In a similar vein, Stoughton recalled to the people their special relation with God:

> The name and Interest of God, and Covenant-relation to him, it hath been written upon us in Capital Letters from the beginning. God had his Creatures in this Wilderness before we came, and his Rational Creatures too, a multitude of them; but as to Sons and Children that are Covenant born unto God, Are we not the first in such a Relation? in this respect we are surely the Lord's first-born in this Wilderness . . . we have been from the beginning, and we are the Lord's.[39]

However, as the ministers consistently reminded their congregants, the special relation with God rested on the particular terms of New England's errand, on the soteriological premises of their settlement. This was, as John Higginson reminded the populace of Boston in 1663, the true *Cause of God and His People in New England:* "New England is originally a plantation of Religion, not a plantation of trade."⁴⁰ As such, and as conceived by Higginson, "our cause is, not barely, a Reformation, but a progress in reformation; it was the charge of our Saviour to the Church of Philadelphia, hold fast what thou hast, it is also the duty of the people of God to go unto perfection."⁴¹ This fact of cosmic errand was brought home time and time again. In one of the most famous of the jeremiads, Samuel Danforth's *A Brief Recognition of New England's Errand into the Wilderness,* (1670) the people are reminded constantly:

> To what purpose did the children of Israel leave their cities and houses in Egypt, and go forth into the wilderness? . . . To what purpose did the children of the captivity upon Cyrus his proclamation, leave their houses which they had built and their vineyards and oliveyards which they had planted in the province of Babylon and return to Judea and Jerusalem, which were now become a wilderness? Was it not that they might build the house of God at Jerusalem and set up the temple-worship?⁴²

Taking Israel for a "type" of their contemporary errand, Danforth further elucidated:⁴³

> To what purpose then came we into the wilderness and what expectation drew us hither? Was it not the expectation of the pure and faithful dispensation of the Gospel and kingdom of God? The times were such that we could not enjoy it in our own land, and therefore having obtained liberty and a gracious patent from our Sovereign, we left our country, kindred and father's houses, and came into these wild woods and deserts where the Lord hath planted us and made us "dwell in a place of our own, that we might move no more and that the children of wickedness might not afflict us any more." What is it that distinguishes New England from other colonies and plantations in America? Not our transportation over the Atlantic Ocean, but the ministry of God's faithful prophets and the fruition of his holy ordinances. Did not the Lord bring "the Philistines from Caphtor, and the Assyrians from Kir" as well as "Israel from the land of Egypt"? But "by a prophet the Lord brought Israel out of Egypt, and by a prophet was he preserved." What is, the price and esteem of god's prophets and their faithful dispensations now fallen in our hearts?⁴⁴

Four years later, Samuel Torrey and Increase Mather both sought to remind their hearers of the principle cause of their communal venture and to recall to them:

our first New England interest; that is that Interest upon which this People and these Churches were first founded, as to their Religious Constitucion, which is God and Religion: that is the onely uniting Interest, our very hearts and Souls will cleave and unite most intirely, in Love with Peace and Union in our God and our Religion; this Interest will make a people of one heart and of one Soul.[45]

It was this interest of New England in religion that Increase Mather stressed "did distinguish us from other English Plantations, they were built upon a Worldly design, but we upon a Religious design."[46]

Crucially, this true interest and New England's special place in God's affections was tied to the proper fulfillment of the terms of the covenant. For,

when the Lord enters into Covenant with any people, this Covenant of his is a Covenant with Conditions. . . . hence there are the Laws, as well as the Promises of the Covenant. As the Lord obligeth himself to us, so he requires something from us, and thus the Commandments or Statutes of God are frequently called his Covenant.[47]

Here, however, the ministers took pains to castigate the people on their failure and backsliding. As Increase Mather asks ruefully:

And is there not woeful Covenant-breaking amongst us? Men when they come into the Church, enter into the solemneth covenant that can be; They promise in the presence of God, angels and Saints, that they will watch over one anothers Souls: But how little is that Christian and Brotherly Watchfulness attended ever after? indeed, if men fall out one with another, then they can watch for Haltings, and prosecute to the utmost which is to serve themselves and their own vile lusts and passions, upon Christ and his Holy Ordinances; but otherwise there are too many that can see one another sin, and never attend the Rules of Christ appointed for the healing of every sinning offending Brother. This is lamentable! As for the Children of the Covenant, as the Scripture calls them, are not they lamentably neglected?[48]

Or, as Samuel Torrey entreats, "O Christians it is your work to uphold Gods covenant in the life, spirit and power of it and unto all the spiritual and saving ends of it, as a Covenant of life in these Churches."[49] Living without the covenant was, for the ministers, the chief sign of the apostasy of the times:

> This is the sad Apostacy that many in New England are guilty of. A visible decay of, and declension from the practice of piety and pose of Godliness seizing upon a very considerable part of the professing party of these Plantations as to personal holiness and zeal for the precious interest of Jesus Christ among us.[50]

This apostasy would lead ultimately to a situation in which

> Church and Commonwealth will be neglected, all sink and the Tree will be chopt down or fall whilest men are busily building and feathering their several Nests in the Branches of it, unless the Lord shew mercy. Sad is it, that many good men have so far forgotten their great errand into this Wilderness.[51]

Indeed, concurrent with recalling the people to their errand and divine purpose, the jeremiad was at the same time an "unending monotonous wail," a lamentation, "a long threnody" over the corruption of religion and the sins of the second generation.[52] Pleading "for the life of a dying religion," Samuel Torrey exhorts the people to "Take heed that we do not exchange our Religion for the World" and warns of the dangers of the current decline in religion: "O let us then be Admonished to take heed that we do not destroy our Religion, and so destroy our own Life, destroy our selves utterly and most miserably, be destroying our Religion."[53] Borrowing from the text of the Book of Revelation, he describes the situation in almost apocalyptic terms:

> And we are the more concerned to give most diligent and earnest heed to such an Admonition and Warning; because our Lord Jesus seems to speak to these Churches as to the Church of Sardis. I know thy works, that thou hast a name that thou livest and art dead. That there hath been a vital decay, a decay upon the very Vitals of Religion, be a deep declension in the Life, and Power of it; that there is already a great Death upon Religion, little more left than a name to live; that the things which remain are ready to dye.[54]

Samuel Torrey named "Declension in Grace, Holiness and the Power of Godliness" along with "Hypocracy and Apostasie" as the cause of "the general Degeneracy."[55] These were in addition to Urian Oakes's list of more social faults, these being, among others: "A Fond and Foolish Admiration of Self, Pride of Parts, Gifts, Graces, Priviledges, Haughtiness."[56] Michael Wigglesworth prophesied

"The Day of Doom" in a poem that sold 1,800 copies within a year of its publication in 1662:[57]

> All filthy facts, and secret acts, however closly done,
> And long conceal'd, are there reveal's before the midday Sun.
> Deeds of the night shunning the light, which darkest corners sought,
> To fearful blame, and endless shame, are there most justly brought.[58]

Part of the popularity of Wigglesworth's poem rested upon its apocalyptical imagery and its intimations of final times, when the wheat would be separated from the chaff and when those

> Whom having brought, as they are taught, unto the brink of Hell
> (That dismal place far from Christ's face, where Death and Darkness dwell:
> Where Gods fierce ire kindleth the fire, and vengeance feeds the flame
> With piles of Wood and Brimstone Flood, that none can quench the same)[59]

were compared to those of an earlier time:

> For there the Saints are perfect Saints, and holy ones indeed,
> From all the sin that dwelt within their mortal bodies freed;
> Made Kings and Priests to God through Christs dear loves transcendency,
> There to remain, and there to reign with him eternally.[60]

The eschatological tension found in Wigglesworth's writing is not a solitary phenomenon (as noted in the references by John Higginson and Samuel Torrey to the churches of Philadelphia and Sardis), but reappears in many of the jeremiads of the late seventeenth century. One example is Jonathan Mitchell's call to the people to "give Account for our speaking, and of our hearing and doing" in anticipation of the day when "all worldly interests shall be worth nothing; when Estates, and Friends, yea Crowns and Kingdomes shall appear to be but pebbles of stone, compar'd with one good look from Christ Jesus."[61] Another instance is William Stoughton's reminder to his listeners that:

> It is not long before the Lord will finish his great works in the world: Antichrist shall be destroyed, Israel shall be saved; Zion shall be redeemed with judgement, and her converts with rightousness; though the Lord bear long with his Elect, yet he will avenge them speedily.[62]

Yet another occurrence is in Increase Mather's strict councils: "The Lord hath been whetting his sword for a long time, we have heard a noise and a dismall din that been in our ears, but now the sword seems to be facing and marching directly towards us.⁶³ It appears as well in Cotton Mather's *Magnalia Christi Americana,* that great work recording the history of New England as "a specimen or a little model of the Kingdom of Christ upon Earth."⁶⁴ The very title page of this work explicated its purpose of documenting the building of a new heaven and new earth upon the American Strand: "TANTE MOLIS EART, PRO CHRISTO CONDERE GENTEM" [So mighty was the work to found Christ's Empire here].⁶⁵

The apocalyptic imagery and millennial intimations found in the jeremiad were integral to their general purpose of recalling the sons of the second generation to the holy work of reformation. In attempting to reassert the divine purpose of the settlement and so its ultimate referent of meaning and order, the millennial rhetoric of the preachers were central. In tying together expectations of final things with a call for collective reform and a reminder of New England's special relation with God, they sought to reunite the realms of community and grace in an attempt to ensure cultural continuity. As with much else, and as will be discussed in the following, the continuity was ensured, but in terms quite different from the expectations of the New England "jeremiahs."

One of the most interesting aspects of the jeremiad sermon as a symbolic and communicative device was the different levels of meaning that it addressed. We have noted above its importance as an attempt to reassert the basis of collective meaning in religious terms, as well as its overriding concern with declension and decline in religion. This concern was often intermingled with the concern of the ministers over the loss of their own authority, as was brought out clearly by Urian Oakes:

> I considered also that there may be too many, even in the Bosome of New English Churches that have lived long in that great sin of confronting the faithful Ministers of Christ and gloried in their Rebellion against the Authority of Christ in his Churches.... Time was when the Messengers of Christ the Masters of Assemblies were precious and welcome, (even when they came with the rod) and their Feet beautifull and their words very acceptable... but now they are become the Enemies of some men, because they tell them the Truth.⁶⁶

The Half Way Covenant and the Jeremiad Sermon 145

The concern with authority of ministers and magistrates forms, in fact, one of the major threads of the jeremiad sermon, recurring here as a lament and there as a call for reform:

> Maintain a Reverand and High Esteem of godly Leaders, Civil and Spiritual Guides, and be subject to them in the Lord. Account regular subjection to be an excellent thing; and that a pliableness and yieldablness in this carries an excellency of spirit along with it.[67]

Or, as with Torrey, as a hymn to New England's uniqueness:

> A religious Reforming Magistracy hath hitherunto been our Crowning Mercy: if God Sit you over us in Mercy he will make you such a Magistracy. And therefore our Prayers for you shall ever be, That he that is the Light of Israel will be Light unto you, that you may be as the Light of Israel unto us.[68]

In the jeremiads, the people are called upon to heed the ministers who perform their "holy duty . . . not for low and sensual ends, but that God might have glory by his mercy to us and by the more abundant and fruitful service from us."[69] In such a manner, the people were reminded of the ultimate source and cosmic anchoring of the ministry.

Not surprisingly, this concern with a falling off in authority was matched with a concern with the growing "contention" and (what were essentially) changes in the terms of social solidarity. With economic and demographic expansion and the rise of a merchant class, new manners and mores grew in the colonies. Whether they were as calamitous as the latter day jeremiahs professed is perhaps doubtful. Yet, in the year of the drought (1662) Michael Wigglesworth asked in his *God's Controversy with New England*:

> Whence cometh it, that Pride and Luxurie
>   Debate, Deceit, Contention, and Strife,
> False-dealing, Covetousness, Hypocrisie
>   (With such like Crimes) amongst them are so rife,
> That one of them doth over-reach another?
>   And that an honest man can hardly trust his Brother.[70]

By doing so, he inferred the existence of an earlier time when:

> Such bright-beam'd, glist'ring, sun-like starrs I placed,
> As by their influence did all things cheere,
> As by their light blind ignorance defaced,
> As errours into lurking holes did fray,
> As turn'd the late dark night into a lightsome day?[71]

And even more forcefully, Increase Mather called for unity in the face of King Philip's Wars and the outbreak of fever and smallpox that plagued life in the 1670s:

> These are not times for us to be contending one against another but rather to be praying one with another and one for another. Shall we be worse than dumb and brute and savage Creatures have sometimes been? It is a memorable Passage which some Historians make mention of, That once in Somersetshire in England, when there was a sudden Flood, wherein many men were drowned, the dumb Creatures ran to the top of an Hill, that so they might escape the fury and destruction of the Flood, and there such Creatures as had an Antipathy in their Natures even Dogs and hares, yea Cats and Mice, could sit quietly together, and never offer to molest one another. Why behold, there is a Flood coming in upon us. And shall we not now live quietly by one another? Shall we not at such a time as this lay aside our Animosities and Variances about matters which its great pity that ever a contention should be upheld amongst good men about such small differences? Naturalists write concerning the Stone Tyrrhensus, that if it be cast upon the water whole, it will swim, but if it be broken it will sink presently. Would we sink or would we swim in this sea of trouble that is a coming? If we break we shall sink, if we divide we perish and are like to be an undone people. But if we be whole, if we unite, we shall swim our heads will then be above water, let what troubles can come: yea and we shall then be a burthensome stone to all that shall burthen themselves with us. If we do but become one with god and one another, as we ought to be, we need not fear all the world. Oh that our Divisions and other Evils that are amongst us, might be repented of, and then I dare speak it boldly before all this Congregation, God will make New England a burthensome stone, yea though all the Nations of the Earth should be gathered together against it they shall be broken in pieces.[72]

While Increase Mather and his fellow ministers called on their congregations to return to earlier practices and principles and so reestablish harmony, it was, ironically, the jeremiad itself that provided the basis for the much sought after integration of communal life. It did so, moreover, in a manner quite unintended. For one of the major tensions expressed in the jeremiad sermon was that between generations, between past practices and current ways. The sermons of the ministers are, in fact, full of (uncomplimentary) comparisons of present to past generations. Samuel Torrey exhorts the people to: "Do the first works: which signifie Reformation in the proper act of it, positive, practical Reformation. Remember from whence thou art fallen, repent and do the first works," and reminds them that "thou art fallen; thou hast left thy first love, thou hast lost thy first life, thou hast deserted they first works."[73] Concern with the original purity of the churches and the commonwealth became in the jeremiad an elegy to the fathers, to the founding generation:

> O let us keep and cleave unto naked Ordinances, simple Ordinances; the Crytalline purity of the waters of the Sanctuary, which are, as they arise and flow from the Fountain of divine Intuition clear as Crystal.... Preserve purity of Administration.... Preserve pure and holy order.... It was God's design and work, not only to set up his Worship in New England, but to set it up in the purity of it, by a purging, refining Reformation.... We must labor to recover our first holy Care and Watchfulness against all Will-worship, corrupt Worship and Corruptions in Worship.[74]

To these men who in covenant with God laid the foundations of the current edifice, Oakes writes,

> All this is not come to pass, either by the meer counsel of man or by chance and accident. They were wise and sober and industrious and good men that laid our Foundations and did what men could do ... but there all along appeared more of God than of man in it.[75]

According to Increase Mather, the passing of this generation was an "ominous sign":

> The taking away of the Ancient is mentioned as an ominous sign. Methuselah was the oldest man in the old world and he died the year before the Flood came. Inasmuch as many of our Methuselahs are lately gone, and that so near together, we may fear that a Flood is coming.[76]

Yet, this generation has

148   Innerworldly Individualism

> a living Memory and a lasting Monument in every godly heart, who hath experienced the converting, quicking, comforting presence and power of the Spirit in their Ministration. They are departed and we have wept over their faces with that Lamentation.[77]

It is this generation of passing saints that Stoughton directly addresses in an almost worshipful manner:

> Unto those who are yet abiding with us of the first generation of the Lords faithful Servants, those Plants of Renown wherewith God set his Garden here at the first. Let me speak a few words unto you Fathers, because you have known that which was from the beginning; you may take up the Apostle John's expressions and say, That which was from the beginning, which we have heard, which we have seen with our eyes, which we have looked upon, and our hands have handled of the Cause and [ ] of God in this Wilderness. You have had a long and large Experience of things; you have seen all the great works which the Lord hath done for his people; you have been long rooted and satiated in the House of the Lord: as you ought to be, and are so we esteem you and account you to be as a Crown and an Honour in the midst of us: Trials you have seen, and trials you may further see, but your Triumph is now at hand.[78]

The past, presented both symbolically as pure Church practice and more concretely in the persons of the founding generation, was a critical component of the jeremiad sermon. While its apogee was reached in Cotton Mather's *Magnalia Christi Americana* "a monumental elegy to a defunct corporate idea" in which John Winthrop is set up as Nehemia *revividus,* a hagiography of the founders is present in all the sermons of this genre.[79] In fact, the developing sense of the past as expressed in the jeremiads was an important factor in delineating the collective future. For in their continuing seizing upon the present generation's failures in light of past accomplishments, the ministers effectively posited a new source of collective identity. By using the past as a point of reference for the present, the past thus became an important locus of collective membership as well. By judging the present in light of the past, the present became, in a sense, infused with that past. A sense of continuity emerged as the present generation was called upon to assume the burdens of returning the Church to the proper ways:

> And you who are of the Rising Generation, Adult Youth and Young men, You are many of you, if not most of you a third Generation... You cannot many of you remember the works which God wrought for your forefathers—You have never seen the Churches in their first Beauty and Glory, nor Worship and Ordinances of God in their first Spiritual Power and Purity... O therefore that Youth and Young persons could lay this Consideration unto their hearts; and be moved also to engage in this Work of Reformation, before it is too late, by labouring unto a sound Conversion and a religious Conversion in the dayes of their Youth.[80]

The call to a reformation, to a return to first principles, was *mutus mundi* a call to continue the work of the earlier generation: "The solemn work of this day is Foundation-work; not to lay a new Foundation, but to continue and strengthen and beautifie, and build upon that which hath been laid."[81] Past and present are thus, despite the failures of the latter, brought into "coevall" state. A continuous line joining the one to the other emerges in all the sermons, perhaps most saliently in Danforth's *Brief Recognition of New England's Errand into the Wilderness* (1670), where both past history and present crises are treated as one. Note how, in the following, Danforth addresses his hearers in the first person plural, imputing to his contemporaries participation in the great work of the founding generation:

> In *our* first and best times the kingdom of heaven brake in upon us with a holy violence and every man pressed into it. What mighty efficacy and power had the clear and faithful dispensation of the gospel upon *your* hearts? How affectionately and zealously did *you* entertain the kingdom of God? how careful were *you*, even all sorts, young and old, high and low, to take hold of the opportunities of your spiritual good and edification, ordering *your* secular affairs (which were wreathed and twisted together with great variety) so as not to interfere with *your* general calling, but that *you* might attend upon the Lord without distraction? How diligent and faithful in preparing *your* hearts for the reception of the Word. (Emphasis mine)[82]

Drawing no line between past and present, he joins them in the collective consciousness. The mythical past is, in his address, united with the strife-ridden present.

Analytic Perspectives

It is in this developing sense of the past that the jeremiad intersects with the Half Way Covenant. For what the Half Way Covenant developed in spatial terms, the jeremiad developed in temporal ones. Both were important mechanisms for a redefinition of the terms of communal membership and identity through a restructuring of collective boundaries. As such, they were equally crucial factors in both a relocation and redefinition of the ideal models of communal life.

The Half Way Covenant, as we have seen, broke down the primary ordering and boundary maintaining device of society, that is, the hard and fast division between the visible Church of the regenerate saints and the rest of the community. In so doing, it also broke down the symbolic boundaries of the "ideal community," both concretely and as a symbolic model for ordering social reality. On one level, the jeremiad seems to oppose the progress of the halfway solution through its stress on a return to first principles. The reality, however, was that most of the "jeremiahs" supported the halfway compromise and, with the exception of William Stoughton, James Fitch, Charles Chauncy, and John Davenport, were party to its implementation.[83] Samuel Danforth, Increase Mather (albeit somewhat belatedly), and Jonathan Mitchell were, in fact, active in mobilizing support for the halfway solution.[84] Thus, the jeremiad sermons by the above ministers, as well as those by John Higginson (*The Cause of God,* 1683), John Norton (*Three Choice and Profitable Sermons,* 1664), Thomas Shepard (*Eye-Salve,* 1683), Samuel Wakeman (*Sound Repentance,* 1685), Cotton Mather, and others, did not imply, in their hymns to the past, a return to the form of Church practice upheld in the earlier decades of settlement.[85] Singing the praises of the past, they did not necessarily preach a return to specific past practices. Their use of the past as a referent and measuring rod for the present was, therefore, of a much more labile and amorphous nature. Fidelity to the past and to continuing the holy work of reformation begun by the first generation was, for these ministers, a call to partake in the aura of past purity, holiness, and righteousness.

On a number of levels, this dirge and cry can be interpreted in light of the immediate problems facing ministers and congregants. The waning of the former's authority was, as seen in the jeremiad, met with a call to attend to the godly authority imputed to ministers and magis-

The Half Way Covenant and the Jeremiad Sermon 151

trates with the founding of the colonies. Likewise, the experienced growth of factionalism and social strife was met with a call to return to an idyllic past of brotherly love. Yet the jeremiad was pitched at a level that went beyond the mere offering of a social palliative. The hymn to the past went beyond mere prescriptions for social betterment (which, indeed, took different forms, as evinced in the writings of Cotton Mather, for instance).[86] The past, and again I stress devoid of its concrete Church practice, became an ideal, in fact, a model for the present. In reinterpreting the past, indeed, in its very articulation as a model for the present, the jeremiad worked a subtle but crucial transformation in the fundamental terms of identity and membership in the collective. For, especially against the background of the Half Way Covenant, identification with and in a shared past replaced regenerate sainthood as the focal point of collective identity. No longer participation in the covenanted community of saints, but a sharing of a mythical past became the primary terms of membership in the communities of Massachusetts and Connecticut.

Continuing with this line of inquiry, it may be said that the locus of communal identity moved from a spatial dimension (of the covenanted Church) to a temporal one (of a shared past). In this move, it was concurrently broadened to potentially include all who would share in this past (as opposed to the former definition, limited to those who underwent regeneration). In the broadest possible terms, the jeremiad effected a unification first of new ties of affinity (developed over the course of two generations) with a primordial referent; and secondly with a civil identity, predicated on the potential openness of that referent. In a sense, it thus provided the first precondition for the constitution of a new "tradition."[87] Tradition, as described by one of its foremost students,

> enters into the constitution of meaningful conduct by defining its ends and standards and even its means.... Located at the boundaries of deliberate actions, setting the end or the rules and standards—the traditional stands around the boundaries of the field in which deliberate expediential actions and those which are filled with passion occur. Traditions here are often the "tacit component" of rational, moral and cognitive actions, and of affect, too.[88]

This new tradition was constituted by the sacred character that was imputed to the past. Indeed, the linkage of a past and more precisely, a primordial element with aspects of sacredness, has been, as noted by Edward Shils, a constitutive factor in the making of all traditions. Thus, he queries:

> How does pastness become infused with sacredness? Why does the past sometimes arouse the tremendum numinosum which is aroused by the contemplation of the holy? It probably has to do with origins, with decisive events, with "great moments" which shaped what came later. It has some primordial qualities which are associated with birth, marriage and death and it finds expression in our confrontation with the past.[89]

This confrontation with the past was expressed in precisely that move of the sacred referent of collective life from the existing Church to a mythical past. This move was perhaps the most important innovation in late seventeenth-century communal life, allowing, as it did, for cultural continuity and for the construction of a civil or secular collective identity. Here it is useful to compare this development with the original terms of collectivity construction in 1630. For there, the break with the past and with its primordial referents required the positing of a new sacred or charismatic locus to collective life, which took the form of the Church covenant of saints. The analytic difference between these two modes of maintaining a system of beliefs has been defined by Edward Shils. The first instance can be described, in his terms, as a set of beliefs

> recommended by a concentratedly and intensely charismatic individual [or community, which] has no past. Its authority depends on its immediately present contact with the source of its authority or validity. Its persuasiveness rests on the immediacy of the link to the source of charisma which reception provides.[90]

As opposed to this, the sharing of a belief or idea through a past in a common tradition, involving the creation of a *communis opinio,* works along different lines:

> It works because it entails a perception of the quality resident in other minds, and this perception opens the mind to a "contagious effect.". . . The perception of a certain "state of mind" in others arouses a disposition towards a similar "state of mind" in the perceiver—where the perceived "state of mind" is of sufficiently massive frequency. The anonymous "they,"

"everybody," etc., are authoritative even where they utter no command, give no directives, and indeed do not in any way address themselves to the potential believer, who only perceives their acceptance of the given belief and is not perceived by them. There is something like this at work in the traditional reception of a belief. In traditional transmission and reception, the communis opinio embraces the past as well as the present; it is the acceptance of a belief which has been accepted by others in the past and by living elders who speak for the past in the present. Those who have a quality of pastness about them "count" as do those who are alive and present.[91]

It was precisely around this pastness that a new collective identity began to crystallize in late seventeenth-century New England, an identity that was, moreover, infused with a particularly salient soteriological moment, as evinced in the millennial rhetoric of the jeremiads that maintained the providential role of New England's errand. This unique development allowed for the construction of a "primordial" identity (in the founding moment of settlement) that was, nevertheless, articulated in highly principled ideological terms. The "religious" nature of this "ideology" did not, however, prevent the gradual interweaving of civil and ecclesiastical identities, as we shall analyze in the following.

Indeed, both the Half Way Covenant and the jeremiad sermons can be viewed as crucial mechanisms in the routinization of the original charismatic basis of both authority and identity in seventeenth-century New England. While the one opened the previously existing borders that defined the charismatic model of community, the other rearticulated that locus of community in terms of a sacred and shared past. The hagiography of the founding generation was, in this context, a crucial mechanism in the institutionalization of charisma among the second generation.[92]

However, reverence for past personages notwithstanding, this move affected as well the overriding definition of authority in the colonies. For with the destructuring of the Church as the charismatic focus of social existence, authority lost its legitimation in terms of its direct embedment in a charismatic community. As a result, authority in the colonies underwent a process of dispersion into the discrete institutional realms of Church and State (or, rather, the institutional apparatuses of civil society). The decline in the original theocratic doctrine of unity in Church and commonwealth was the direct result of this process.

The routinization of charisma and the organization of the terms of collective identity and authority around new loci involved changes and transformations in the major institutional spheres of social life. The very constitution of a new collective identity, devoid of its previous boundaries, involved the construction of new institutional structures wherein the previous distinctions between outsiders and insiders were obviated. Likewise, the new loci of identity implied new norms of boundary maintenance and new rituals of demarcating the moral community. Finally, as mentioned above, the changing locus of charisma involved a change in the models of authority; a change measured in both the differentiation of structures of authority and in the changing content of the henceforth discrete spheres of clerical and lay authority. All these changes registered what in more general terms can be seen as the beginnings of a transition from Church to community as a locus of collective life.

This move from Church to community, which was the basis of that transformation in identity that Richard Bushman called the move from Puritan to Yankee, was an ongoing process whose salient moments in the eighteenth century span the Great Awakening of the 1740s to the decades of the Revolution in the 1760s and 1770s.[93] I would maintain that the particular interweaving of religious and secular identities that was expressed in these events was itself predicated on a transformation of the symbolic categories of meaning and organizational frameworks of social action, which developed gradually in the late seventeenth and early eighteenth centuries. The organizational matrixes of this change are to be found in the changing nature of communal boundaries, collective membership, and social authority, to which we shall now turn.

Notes

1. Walker, ed., *Creeds and Platforms*, 246.
2. Ibid., 246–69.
3. On the Half Way Covenant, see Hall, *The Faithful Shepherd*, 201–16; Pope, *The Half Way Covenant*, 1969; Miller, *The New England Mind*, 93–104; Walker, ed., *Creeds and Platforms*, 238–339; Lucas, *Valley of Discord*, 73–86. It is discussed as well by Mather, *Magnalia*, vol. 2, 276–315.
4. Pope, *Half Way Covenant*, 6.
5. Increase Mather, *The First Principles of New England* (Cambridge, 1675), Postscript, p. 5.
6. Pope, *Half Way Covenant*, 14.

7. Although Perry Miller claims that the term *Half-Way Synod* was adopted as a derogatory expression by contemporaries (1953:95), Robert Pope (1969:8) claims to have found the term *Half Way Covenant* in use only from the 1760s, among followers of Jonathan Edwards.
8. Walker, ed., *Creeds and Platforms,* 328.
9. Hall, *The Faithful Shepherd,* 216.
10. Pope, *The Half Way Covenant,* 185.
11. Hall, *The Faithful Shepherd,* 201.
12. Ibid., 216.
13. For this view of the relation of the Half Way Covenant to political privilege, see Pope, *Half Way Covenant,* 39–42.
14. Mather, *First Principles,* a7.
15. Ibid., Postscript, 1.
16. Quoted in Pope, *Half Way Covenant,* 57.
17. A complete list of the pamphlet literature surrounding the Half Way Covenant appears in Walker, *Creeds and Platforms,* 239–40.
18. Quoted in Hall, *Faithful Shepherd,* 223.
19. John Davenport, *A New Essay for the Investigation of the Truth* (Boston, 1663), 15.
20. Quoted in Pope, *Half Way Covenant,* 57.
21. The themes of pollution and defilement and their relation to social ordering have been treated at length by Mary Douglas, *Purity and Danger* (London: Routledge and Kegan Paul, 1979).
22. A concern with boundaries was also present among those defenders of the Half Way Covenant who legitimized the baptism of third-generation children in these terms. See Mather, *First Principles.*
23. Davenport, *A New Essay,* 15.
24. On the progressive implementation of the Half Way Covenant in different churches, see Pope, *Half Way Covenant,* 206–38.
25. An example of this practice is presented by Pope, ibid., 38–39.
26. William Stoughton, *New England's True Interest* (Cambridge, 1670), 10.
27. Ibid., 10.
28. Ibid., 11.
29. Ibid., 13.
30. Ibid., 21.
31. Pope, *Half Way Covenant,* 185.
32. Ibid., 204.
33. On the form of the jeremiad, see Sacvan Bercovitz, *The American Jeremiad* (Madison: University of Wisconsin Press, 1978), 16.
34. On the persistence of the jeremiad as a literary form, see ibid., 11. On its development, see Miller, *The New England Mind,* 27–39; David Minter, "The Puritan Jeremiad as a Literary Form," in *The American Puritan,* ed. S. Bercovitz, 44–55.
35. See, for example, Samuel Danforth, *A Brief Recognition of New England's Errand into the Wilderness* (Boston, 1670); Urian Oakes, *New England Pleaded With* (Cambridge, 1673); William Stoughton, *New England's True Interest* (Cambridge, 1670); Samuel Torrey, *Man's Extremity, God's Opportunity* (Boston, 1675); idem, *A Plea for the Life of a Dying Religion* (Boston, 1683); idem, *Exhortation unto*

Reformation (Cambridge, 1674); John Norton, *The Heart of New England Rent* (Cambridge, 1661); Jonathan Mitchell, *Nehemia upon the Wall* (Cambridge, 1671); John Higginson, *The Cause of God and His People in New England* (Cambridge, 1663); Increase Mather, *The Day of Trouble is Near* (Cambridge, 1674).

36. Bercovitz, *American Jeremiad*, 27.
37. Ibid., 28.
38. Oakes, *New England Pleaded With*, 19.
39. Stoughton, *New England's True Interest*, 17.
40. Higginson, *The Cause of God*, 11.
41. Ibid., 13.
42. Danforth, "A Brief Recognition," in *The Wall and the Garden: Selected Massachusetts Election Sermons*, ed. W. Plumstead (Minneapolis: University of Minnesota Press, 1968), 61.
43. For a discussion of typology in Puritan writings, see Sacvan Bercovitz, *Typology and Early American Literature* (Amherst: University of Massachusetts Press, 1975), 35–40; and in the writings of Samuel Danforth, Sacvan Bercovitz, "New England's Errand Reappraised," in *New Directions in American Intellectual History*, ed. J. Hingham and P. Conkin (Baltimore: Johns Hopkins University Press, 1979), 75–101.
44. Danforth, "A Brief Recognition," 73.
45. Torrey, *Exhortation unto Reformation*, 27.
46. Mather, *The Day of Trouble*, 23.
47. Stoughton, *New England's True Interest*, 10.
48. Mather, *Day of Trouble*, 24.
49. Torrey, *Exhortation unto Reformation*, 13.
50. Oakes, *New England Pleaded With*, 29.
51. Ibid., 33.
52. Bercovitz, *The American Jeremiad*, 5.
53. Torrey, *A Plea for the Life*, 11.
54. Ibid.
55. Ibid.
56. Oakes, *New England Pleaded With*, 34.
57. Michael Wigglesworth, "The Day of Doom," (1662) in *The Puritans: A Source Book*, ed. P. Miller and T. Johnson, 585.
58. Ibid., 599.
59. Ibid., 603.
60. Ibid., 606.
61. Mitchell, *Nehemia upon the Wall*, 33.
62. Stoughton, *New England's True Interest*, 32.
63. Mather, *Day of Trouble*, 26.
64. Oakes, *New England Pleaded With*, 21.
65. Mather, *Magnalia*, frontpiece.
66. Oakes, *New England Pleaded With*, 26.
67. Stoughton, *New England's True Interest*, 31.
68. Torrey, *Exhortation Unto Reformation*, 31.
69. Mitchell, *Nehemia upon the Wall*, 10.

70. Wigglesworth, "The Day of Doom," 613.
71. Ibid., 612.
72. Mather, *Day of Trouble*, 29–30.
73. Torrey, *Exhortation unto Reformation*, 2.
74. Stoughton, *New England's True Interest*, 18–19.
75. Oakes, *New England Pleaded With*, 21.
76. Mather, *Day of Trouble*, 21.
77. Torrey, *Exhortation unto Reformation*, 33.
78. Stoughton, *New England's True Interest*, 26, 7.
79. Bercovitz, *The American Puritan*, 87.
80. Torrey, *Exhortation unto Reformation*, 37.
81. Stoughton, *New England's True Interest*, 16.
82. Danforth, *A Brief Recognition*, 65–66.
83. See Davenport, *A New Essay;* Charles Chauncy, *Anti-Synodalia Scripta Americana* (London, 1662).
84. For a discussion of the proceedings, see Pope, *Half Way Covenant*, 43–74.
85. Ibid., 90, 99, 171.
86. See, for instance, Cotton Mather, *Bonafacious: An Essay upon the Good that is to be Devised and Designed by Those Who Desire . . . to do Good While They Live* (Boston, 1710).
87. By tradition I refer to that compelling and normative element existing in all societies, which, linking past and present generations, "holds society together in a given form over time"; Edward Shils, *Tradition* (Chicago: University of Chicago Press, 1981), 25.
88. Ibid., 33. For a slightly different, but illuminating perspective, see Michael Hill's (1973:85–104) study of "revolution by tradition" in two monastic orders. His study concentrates on how a normative tradition can be used as a fulcrum for change and renewal. Most relevant is his study of the Franciscan order where he analyzes the process of renewal in terms of a return to a diffuse ideal of origins (as opposed to a detailed organizational blueprint for action) containing both normative and charismatic dimensions.
89. Shils, *Center and Periphery*, 198.
90. Ibid., 188.
91. Ibid., 189.
92. Additional and illuminating perspectives on charisma in the generational context are provided by Uri Almagor, "Charisma Fatigue in an East-African Generational Set," *American Ethnologist* 19 (1983): 635–49.
93. See Richard Bushman, *From Puritan to Yankee: Character and the Social Order in Connecticut 1690–1765* (Cambridge: Harvard University Press, 1967).

6

The Institutionalization of Charisma in Society

In the preceding analysis the Half Way Covenant and the jeremiad sermons were presented as crucial mechanisms in the institutionalization of the original religious visions of the Puritan settlers to New England. They were, in fact, only two of a number of different social mechanisms that developed at the end of the seventeenth and the beginning of the eighteenth centuries that permitted Congregational Puritanism to "go beyond" its original "religious" premises and constitute a wider social and civil tradition.[1] These mechanisms, developing, as it were, against the great symbolic canvas of the jeremiad, were in many ways attempts to reformulate the basic concepts of social ordering that had begun to break down with the institutionalization of the Half Way Covenant in the last two decades of the seventeenth century.

In this chapter, we will analyze the growth of Stoddardism, of Cotton Mather's revival societies, of religious toleration, of covenant owning, and of Church ritualism, in E. Brooks Holifield's terms, of *sacramental renaissance,* as attesting to a major change in the principles and practices of social ordering in New England.

These changes, and the novel mechanisms of social ordering and models thereof will be viewed as providing potential venues for the dispersion of charisma beyond its former locus in the covenanted Church. With the establishment of a new locus of collective life in a shared past, the various mechanisms provided institutional channels for a widening of access to and participation in the center of society. Analytically, these developments will be presented in terms of their contribution to the following changes in the terms of collective life:

1. the creation of new organizational and institutional mechanisms that embodied the growing interweaving of ecclesiastical (Church) and civil (communal) identities within the society;
2. the creation of new mechanisms and modalities by which individual and collective boundaries were ordered and maintained;
3. a reorganization of the Church (and of religious life in general) concomitant with its changing role in society—no longer as an ideal model of the community and legitimator of authority, but as a component of a larger tradition; and
4 the emergence of a civil politics, slowly divorcing itself from the religious realm—as an autonomous dimension of social life.

Finally, and perhaps most importantly for an understanding of the role of seventeenth-century Puritanism in the making of modern consciousness, this chapter will explore the ways in which the above changes led to the development of new sets of individual identities. These new forms of identity which saw the individual as possessing "metaphysical and moral value" have become on the central tenets of modern political and ethical life.[2] The concept of an ethic of individual responsibility achieved through the universalization of ethical ideas has in fact become one of the fundamental and unifying doctrines of modern social existence. The idea of the individual as standing at the center of ethical and moral judgments and indeed of moral agency has thus been seen by many scholars, such as Emile Durkheim, Max Weber, Marcel Mauss, and, most recently, Luis Dumont, as both the defining characteristic of modernity as a civilization and (crucially) as rooted in the religious heritage of ascetic-Protestantism.[3] Few works, however, have attempted to trace the concrete dynamics of its development, which is our task here (at least in the relatively circumscribed case of seventeenth-century New England).

Solomon Stoddard, Cotton Mather, and the Merging of Boundaries between the Church and the World

The concrete organization of a new collective and individual identity took place through a number of different social processes, the most salient of which was "Stoddardism."[4] If the progress of the Half Way Covenant broke down the primary distinctions between the churched and the unchurched, its "logical fulfillment" in the practice of Solomon Stoddard brought both groups together within a new symbolic framework. The crux of Stoddard's innovation was opening up the Lord's Supper to all his congregants. Whereas the Half Way Covenant had done away with the test of relation as a condition for entering the Church, it had maintained the need to provide evidence of saving grace to participate in the Lord's Supper and so to attain full membership. In 1677, Stoddard did away with this form of "double bookkeeping" and "closed the account of separate baptisms."[5] Thenceforth, he admitted all adult Church members into the Lord's Supper. In Perry Miller's telling phrase, "He treated the whole congregation and virtually the whole town (there were still some resolute sinners) as the church."[6]

Cutting the Gordian knot presented by the failure of communicants to experience grace, Stoddard in essence brought the whole community into the Church, a move whose ideal was closer to that of the founding generation than is generally admitted, even if the terms of inclusion were different. The first generation, we recall, also hoped for a unity of civil and Church membership—but one based on the experience of saving grace (in our terms, on participation in the same undifferentiated experience of collective belonging). Stoddard, by doing away with an unrealizable condition, attained, in a sense, the founders' ideal.

By investing virtually the whole of the community with full Church membership and bringing them into the (increasingly important) rite of the Lord's Supper, Stoddard provided a new model for people to articulate their social selves. The Half Way Covenant broke down the boundaries between individuals and groups. The practice of Stoddardism reunited all communal members, crucially, within the Church. This reintegration within the Church of the community was a central stage in the later "sacralization of the political," which would be a salient component of the new American civil identity. For the unity of all communal membership within the Church that had been hoped for earlier was predicated on the attainment of grace, on the internal move from unregenerate sinner to regenerate saint, externally symbolized in the rite of passage of the test of relation. Stoddard did away with that requirement admitting the still unregenerate as full members into the center of the religious or sacred domain. This move, while not precisely a "sacralization" and not exactly of the "political," nevertheless brought the latter realm into a new relation with the former. Moreover, the results of this practice were important in redefining the nature of both realms. For, on the one hand, the Church thereby lost its character as the "pure" locus of the sacred dimension and, on the other hand, the world beyond the Church lost its indelible "otherness," its totally tainted and profane nature. Henceforth, the profane world beyond the Church could no longer be entirely without sacrality, and the world defined by the boundaries of the Church could likewise never be totally purged of the profane. This doctrine, refuting the ongoing Puritan concern with the establishment of the purity of the primitive Christian Church, was indeed explicitly advocated by Stoddard in his *Doctrine of the Instituted Churches* (1700).[7]

Finally, the results of this novel interweaving of realms was felt in the experience of the sacred dimension. For the sacred dimension or locus of existence could not, given the redefinition of Church membership and so of the Church as an institution, be given full expression in its daily practice. It had to find different venues for its expression—at once more "immediate" and also in keeping with the reorientation of Church and community posited by Stoddard. This was the dynamic behind the growth of the different mass revivals, or "harvests," which Stoddard presided over in 1679, 1683, 1712, and 1718.[8]

These revivals, which "gained souls for Christ," represented the first of a series of "enthusiastic" moments that were to develop in the 1720s and 1730s and culminate in the Great Awakening of the 1740s.[9] They therefore provide the first examples of a developing social mechanism that expressed the new terms of social identity, an identity that obviated the differences between Church and community by breaking down the borders between them. The symbolization of the sacred or charismatic dimension, no longer bounded spatially by the Church, was henceforth expressed in the more temporally bounded moments of religious revivalism.

Samuel Stoddard, the "pope" of the Connecticut Valley, did not "rule" unopposed. The practice advocated by him was vehemently opposed by some, mostly by Increase Mather and his son, Cotton Mather.[10] The debates and pamphlet wars between the two sides fill the annals of late seventeenth- and early eighteenth-century New England history.[11] This debate was carried out in the early eighteenth century along two prime axes. The first concerned the nature of Church organization and the second concerned Stoddard's doctrine of "converting ordinances." Stoddard was accused by the Mathers of attempting to undermine New England Congregationalism with a Presbyterian system of Church government, meaning in principle: (a) his

The Institutionalization of Charisma in Society 163

attempt to found a system of national churches, instead of the prevailing doctrine of autonomously organized congregational churches; and (b) his repudiation of the "Congregational doctrine that the power of the Keys belong to the entire congregation," that is, his attempt to centralize power in the hands of the ministry.[12]

The second point of contention was his aforementioned doctrine of "converting ordinances," that is, his belief that the sacrament, rather than a "seal" of the covenant, provided a means of grace, an aid to those who would undergo the conversionary experience.[13]

What is important to note is that in Stoddard's conception, all elements were united in what amounted to a totally new doctrine. Rejecting the Congregational doctrine of community of saints standing apart from the world and bound together by the covenant, he envisioned the Instituted Church as simply an institutional means for the "dissemination of grace," oriented to but a single purpose—"the salvation of sinners."[14] While this doctrine, which claimed membership in any one Church as tantamount to membership in all (since all particular churches were but manifestations of "the visible Catholic Church"), struck at the heart of the New England Way (which saw each Church as the autonomous locus of identity), as it brought Church and community together again;[15] it also led to more conversionary experiences than the New England churches had experienced in decades. Perhaps it is this that explains the willingness of the younger members of Stoddard's congregation to accept his innovations and his stress on ministerial prerogatives in admitting new members, taking the "keys," as it were, out of the hands of the "congregation."[16] For, as opposed to developments following the Cambridge Platform of 1648, where increased ministerial authority and privilege were the source of conflict and contention, in this case, the increase in ministerial power did not imply a dissociation of that authority from its roots in community. No longer bound to a particular group, authority in the Church no longer legitimized itself through its immediate links with a particular body of communicants. Moreover, whereas before, the ministers, by presiding over the test of relation, appropriated for themselves the role of "gatekeeper," overseeing the entrance to the salvational collective (of regenerate saints) and thus aroused the ire of their congregants, Stoddard rejected the very idea of the test of relation as a boundary maintaining device, separating sheep from goats and marking the boundaries of the community.

While Stoddard never fully achieved his dream of the Instituted Church system and while he failed to significantly influence Church policy in eastern Massachusetts, his doctrine became common practice throughout the Connecticut Valley in the early years of the eighteenth century. By the time of his death in 1729, only three churches there continued to resist his innovations.[17] And although the debate between the Mathers and Stoddard petered out in the first decades of the eighteenth century into a long, drawn-out polemic on the sacrament of the Lord's Supper, leaving Stoddard much the worse for it, his influence was deeply felt even beyond Connecticut, for he "inaugurated," in Perry Miller's words, that "era of revivalism" that would reach fruition under his grandson Jonathan Edwards in the Great Awakening.[18] The major importance of this novel development was, as we have seen, in a fundamental reordering of the respective realms of Church and community, breaking down the boundaries between them and hence allowing an interpenetration of profane and religious/sacred dimensions of social existence.

Interestingly enough, a similar move toward breaking down the discrete realms of Church and community was undertaken by the Mathers as well, if less successfully. The varied and only partially successful attempts by Cotton Mather to organize religious and reforming societies in the early eighteenth century point to a similar attempt to conflate the Church and the world beyond its boundaries. If, given his loyalty to the original covenant doctrine, Cotton Mather could not break down the boundaries separating regenerate from unregenerate in the ultimate manner advanced by Solomon Stoddard, he nevertheless tried to bring the Church, in however attenuated a manner, into the world. Thus, he established reforming societies to suppress disorders such as "drunkeness, profanity and patronage of bawdy houses."[19] Limited in membership and confined in the main to Boston and its near environs, these were less successful than the religious societies that he also established.[20] These latter societies, which lasted throughout the eighteenth century and were devoted to good works and piety, were oriented to the evangelical goals of spreading the "Maxims of the Everlasting Gospel."

In the organization of these religious societies, Mather, in fact, reproduced in microcosm the original social vision of the founding generation. Directed toward "the Worthy Designs of Reformation," each society was to have both minister and magistrate working together to further the Kingdom of God.[21] Although the original vision of ecclesiastical and civil authority working together in "co-ordinate state" to build the "Cittie Upon the Hill" had failed, Cotton Mather, close to a century later, remained true to the original vision. The one crucial change was that the locus of this work of Reformation was no longer in the covenanted churches of regenerate saints but in a religious society located beyond the borders of the Church. And even as Cotton Mather continued to maintain that the good works of the unconverted were unacceptable to God (i.e., continued to posit a boundary between the unregenerate and those with saving grace), his very organization of religious societies outside the Church, containing all ranks of people, laid the basis for a social identity that united both regenerate and unconverted. It can, in a sense, be said that whereas Stoddard brought the world into the Church, Cotton Mather, in the organization of reforming and religious societies, brought the Church into the world.[22] The bringing of the Church "into the world" was manifest as well in the increasing tendency of early eighteenth-century Congregational ministers to "spiritualize the common actions of life."[23] The increasing concern with "illustrious provinces" and scientific thought in general renewed pietistic interest in New England as "the scientists confirmed the ministers in the confidence that the visible and concrete material order was transparent to an invisible and spiritual realm."[24]

One of the leaders of this new sensationalism was Cotton Mather. Himself a member of the Royal Society, he managed to organize support among Boston divines to instruct their congregations on the spiritual aspects of daily actions, a theme that he pursued in his handbooks on "spiritualizing the most earthly things."[25]

Of further importance in understanding Mather's religious societies as a mechanism for the forging of a new social identity, especially in light of later developments, were their evangelical and, in fact, eschatological meanings. As pointed out by Robert Middlekauff, Mather conceived his religious societies as being formed to advance the eschatological ends of history: "The organizations would take as their purpose the advancing of history to the end of the world."[26] In Mather's diaries, the unitary themes of eschatological hopes, religious societies, and a new social identity are, in fact, given expression.[27]

The vision of forging a community actively engaged in bringing about the work of cosmic redemption was not a new one in New

England. Cotton Mather stood squarely within the earlier New England tradition of eschatological hopes and expectations. His innovation, however, was in the concrete organizational forms he proposed to bring about the great instauration. For he transposed the arena of soteriological activity from the Church to religious societies existing in the world beyond its borders and, in so doing, contributed to the eradication of hitherto existing borders between individuals in society. Finally, here, as with Stoddard's open communion, the innovation was more than simply a blurring of boundaries. It was a move toward the construction of a new social identity, one which, if opposed to Stoddard in principle, was in practice very similar. For, like Stoddard's open communion, Mather, too, instituted a social mechanism that contained the seeds of a new model of collective life. Based on the interweaving of sacred and mundane spheres and the interpenetration of Church and civil identities, this identity, although maintaining the original millennial premises of New England tradition, broadened their referents to society at large and so provided, in a sense, new points of contact between the periphery and the social center.

The opening up of the social center to broader groups in the construction of a new social identity is related to the third element, which registered the changing nature of boundaries and social ordering in late seventeenth-century New England—the establishment of religious toleration. The issue of religious toleration had been one that constantly plagued the colonists in their relation with England.[28] Its long and tortuous history began in the 1640s, with the acceptance by Cromwell in England of the principle of toleration, and lasted throughout the century. Even the promulgation in England of the *Act of Toleration* in 1689 did not immediately bring about its desired effect.[29] Throughout the whole of this period, the colonists constantly attempted to avoid the demands of either the Commonwealth or, after the Restoration, the Crown, to grant greater toleration to Quakers and Baptists and to allow dissenting sects the right of the franchise. The change in this pattern of attempting to conceal from the English authorities the truth of the New England Way, after the Glorious Revolution and the Andros Revolt in New England, was due to more than the new charter granted by William and Mary.

True, the terms of the new charter, which required the granting of liberty of conscience to all except Catholics, was a strong "motive" in favor of toleration. True, too, that the actual progress of religious

The Institutionalization of Charisma in Society 167

toleration (as opposed to the lip service paid it) was slow and staggered. In 1708, for instance, Samuel Sewall refused to sign a warrant for a Quaker meeting house, saying: "I would not have a hand in setting up their Devil Worship."[30] Yet the sense remains that by the end of the seventeenth century and the beginning of the eighteenth century, something fundamental had begun to change in the attitude of Congregational ministers and magistrates toward dissenting sects.[31] Already by the late 1660s, political and entrepreneurial elites successfully protested the expulsion of Baptists from Massachusetts and, in the following decade, the magistrates themselves refused to enforce existing civil laws against Quakers and Baptists. The last whipping of a Quaker occurred in 1677 and in 1682, the Massachusetts General Court testified to the abolition of all laws against Anabaptists from its statute books. More importantly, in 1718, Cotton Mather himself presided over the ordination of a Baptist minister in a Boston church.[32] These facts point to more than a mere acquiescence to laws stemming from England and imposed from without (as had characterized New England for more than fifty years). They point to a changed climate, to a new appreciation by the leaders of the Congregational church of the terms of collective identity and membership. The granting of religious toleration and, more especially, the acceptance of its principle by such foremost religious elites as Increase and Cotton Mather provide further evidence of that restructuring of internal boundaries that began with the Half Way Covenant and was given added saliency with the developments studied above. As with Stoddardism and Mather's religious societies, the principle of religious toleration marked the end of the hitherto existing boundaries between the Church of covenanted saints and the world, and permitted the emergence of a new definition of the collectivity, which would include all members of the society.

The Interiorization of Collective Boundaries

In analyzing the late seventeenth-century innovations of Stoddard and Cotton Mather, we concentrated on their effect in abrogating previously established boundaries between (as well as definitions of) insider and outsider, between Church and community, and between the sacred and profane. The interrelated themes of membership in the ideal collective and sacrality raise, however, at least two salient questions. For if the sacred and profane dimensions of existence were indeed interwoven in late seventeenth-century Puritan culture, what became of the boundaries between these two realms? If Stoddard brought the world into the Church and allowed all Church members admittance to the sacrament, how was the differentiation between sacred and profane nevertheless maintained? This problem, pressing as it is in itself, takes on an added importance when we recall that the boundaries of the sacred were also the boundaries of the collectivity (of regenerate saints) or, at the very least, of its ideal model. If, indeed, the jeremiad provided the basis for a new sense of collective self—including all members of society—we must still ask ourselves what became of that crucial mechanism of boundary maintenance by which all societies define and order their collective existence.

In this context, we submit that together with the breakdown of primary ordering mechanisms occasioned by the Half Way Covenant (and more fully worked out in Stoddardism and in Cotton Mather's organizational activities), there developed an interiorization of boundaries, as well as of individual and collective identities, which was itself a critical development in the emergence of a new sense of collective self.[33] This interiorization of boundaries is one element in the "internalization of symbolic constructs," which Liah Greenfeld, following Edward Shils and Max Weber, argues is essential for the working of a rationalized society.[34] As Shils himself has shown, the construction of a rational, systematized, and coherent normative order rests on the dispersion (and attenuation) of charisma, on the sensitization of broad groups on the periphery to a "routinized" charisma incumbent in the social center.[35] This process of bringing peripheral groups into direct contact with the central value system of society, with its charismatic center, rests ultimately on the "internalization of values and cognitions." Ultimately, of course, this internalization of moral norms is at the heart of Durkheim's concept of a moral community constrained by moral authority. However, the constitution of a moral community, or, in Talcott Parsons's words, of an "internal environment of the system of action," must be understood as a process—part of the institutionalization of charisma in society.[36] It cannot, in the context of any specific social formation, be taken for granted. It provides, in fact, a "prime" moment in the making of any tradition or perduring social order.[37]

In the context of late seventeenth- and early eighteenth-century New England, this development can most easily be seen in the reconstruction of the socially defined arena where the move from profane to sacred dimension was effected. If, in the early decades of settlement, this was effected in the public sphere, in the communal rite of the test of relation, by the end of the century, it was carried out within the private soul of the individual communicant. Similarly, whereas the earlier decades symbolically objectified the boundaries of the community as those running between the regenerate saint and unregenerate sinner, by the early eighteenth century, the broadened (more inclusive) definition of communal boundaries was conceptualized as being within each individual. Integrating all communal members in one collective definition (through an emerging referent of a common past), the boundaries between insider and outsider no longer ran through the community, but rather through each individual member. As a result, the crossing of a boundary in the move from profane to sacred and from outsider to insider—to membership in the collective—became less a public ceremony and more a private rite. This process, in its more analytic moments, has been noted by Roger Caillois, who termed it the "internalization of the sacred" and described it as the state where "any external criterion seems inadequate, from the moment that the sacred becomes less an objective manifestation than a pure attitude of mind, less a ceremony than a profound sensation."[38]

It is to this interiorization of boundaries, as a salient component in the making or remaking of cultural identities, that we can look for the concrete dynamics of the "internalization of symbolic constructs" in seventeenth- and eighteenth-century New England Congregationalism. The actual working out of this social mechanism progressed along a number of related, if analytically different, axes.

To begin on the purely symbolic level, the clearest expression of the transposed locus of boundaries between profane and sacred (from within the community to within the individual) was the growth of "sacramentalism" in late seventeenth-century Puritanism.[39] The "sacramental renaissance" studied by E. Brooks Holifield saw the emergence in late seventeenth-century and early eighteenth-century New England of a mass of meditational manuals instructing the communicant (and the minister) on how to prepare for the Lord's Supper.[40] These sacred meditations, whether published in New England or imported from England, urged the communicant "to purge himself of impurity and to approach the sacrament with humility and sanctity."[41] Nonexistent until the last decade of the seventeenth century, these manuals poured forth from the New England presses in the first decades of the eighteenth century, the period that also witnessed the mass importation of these manuals from England to meet a demand the New England presses could not adequately service.

A most interesting aspect of these meditational manuals (and poems) in terms of our hypothesis was the period of their emergence.[42] The late seventeenth century and early eighteenth century was, we recall, a period dominated by the issue of Stoddardism, both by its practice and by the fierce polemic that the practice engendered. The parallel between both developments is most striking. For Stoddardism, in effect, did away with that boundary that had hitherto kept the sacred apart and inviolable. As the Lord's Supper gained in importance in the religious sensibilities of late seventeenth-century Puritanism, the previously established boundaries around "that Holy Ordinance" were dismantled.[43] For, whereas previously, the test of relation had served as a type of rite of passage, separating the profane (person and world) from the sacred (symbolized in admission to both the body of communicants and the Lord's Supper), Stoddard's policies did away with that rite and opened communion to all. And yet it is clear that in bringing the "World into the Church," he did not thereby deny or negate the essential distinctiveness of the sacred dimension of existence.

The arena of the sacred necessitates, by its very definition, a separation from the world. As anthropologists from Emile Durkheim, Marcel Mauss, and Arnold Van Geneep on have shown, all social formations maintain a distinct set of beliefs and practices designed to set the sacred off from the mundane world.[44] These practices, moreover, always entail some form of transposed state, some symbolic crossing of boundaries from one state to the other (when contact with the sacred is made). And so we must ask ourselves: what became of these boundaries in late seventeenth-century (post-Stoddardian) Puritanism? The answer is, I believe, to be found in the increased stress upon preparationism (a doctrine that had existed, if less centrally, in early decades) and the need for the communicant to bring himself to that inner state in which he could approach the Lord's Supper.[45]

In the doctrine of preparation for salvation, the crossing of boundaries from profane to sacred took place not within the community (thus dividing it in two, those participating in the arena of the sacred and those still excluded), but within the believer himself. What is important to note in this development is what was changed. For it was not that the transformed state (from profane to sacred) was transposed—it was always the individual believer who underwent a transformation—but the arena of transformation itself, which moved from its communal to an individual locus. This was a crucial development for the developing terms of both communal and individual identities. For we noted earlier how the public (or semipublic) rite of the test of relation was also one of communal solidarity, of an assertion of boundaries, maintaining the outer limits of the moral community. In that earlier case, the boundaries of membership, the inclusion or exclusion of members from the ideal community, was asserted through the entrance of each communal member into the charismatic or sacred realm, a move that in a sense symbolized his entrance into the normative order. A hundred years later, with the dispersion of charisma and the addition of a past referent to communal identity, the boundaries of the collectivity were no longer homologous to those between the profane and the sacred. The normative order was seen to reside within each individual, just as each was seen to be a member of the community. It is precisely this deeper significance of the increasing stress on preparationism and sacramental piety that comes to the fore when we place them in their social context (defined, on one the hand, by the Half Way Covenant and the jeremiad, and, on the other, by Stoddardism and Mather's own evangelicalism). It is, moreover, important to explicate that the increasing sacramentalism was not only within the churches that adopted the practice of Solomon Stoddard, but a development affecting all of New England. The inclusiveness of this development points to a generalized shift in sensibilities and a reformulation of the basic terms of New England collective life.

Yet another arena where a developing sense of inwardness and piety was felt in late seventeenth-century New England was in the increasing stress on what has been called the "new Baptismal Piety."[46] Following the Half Way Synod, more and more ministers and congregations devoted themselves to fulfilling the terms and obligations of baptism. It is thus no surprise that the sacrament of baptism gained in importance with the implementation of the decisions of the Synod of 1662. For with the Half Way Covenant, baptism itself became the major symbol of the individual's entrance into the Church (and, as we have seen, in no small measure into the community as a whole). In baptism, the individual was brought into the moral community and expected to live according to its prescriptions and constraints. In a

172   Innerworldly Individualism

sense, it replaced the test of relation as the "gateway" into the collective. What is important is how the inner logic of realizing what was termed the *baptismal covenant* stood in relation to the previous test of relation. Once again, the temporal category of duration replaced a temporal moment circumscribed in time and space as the arena where the "covenant" was implemented. Instead of being objectified in a public rite, the covenant was articulated in terms of the duties and obligations (taken on with baptism) of each individual. Indeed, the baptismal doctrine, as developed by John Davenport and others, stressed obligations as its primary element.[47]

The increasing inward-turning of religion in this period, concomitant with the broadening definition of the collective beyond the boundaries of regenerate sainthood, was manifest as well in a new set of practices that evolved with the baptismal doctrine. One of the more far-reaching developments of eighteenth-century Congregationalism was the principle of private baptism. Originally proposed in 1700 by Stoddard in his *Doctrine of the Instituted Churches,* the first private baptism was administered in 1718, thus breaking with the New England doctrine that a sacrament must be a "visible gospel addressed to a faithful congregation."[48] The recognition inherent in this practice (and doctrine) of the private nature of the sacrament of baptism, devoid of its public function, is of a similar nature with regard to the privatization of the Lord's Supper. Through opening it to all communicants, the latter lost its character as a communal boundary maintaining device. Similarly, even in the case of baptism, the very mechanism of entry into the community had, by the early eighteenth century, lost its public and communal function and become a matter for the individual.

This development was, however, but the final result of a complex redefinition of boundaries that we have been analyzing. Its parallel was to be found in the new rites of community that developed in the last quarter of the seventeenth century.[49] With the boundaries of the sacred and so of the social center no longer strictly homologous with Church membership, a new form of affirmation of community developed. Thus, the growth of the new baptismal piety was not without its public side. The emergence and growth of what has been termed *covenant renewals* from 1675 onwards points to the continuing public nature of the new piety. As we shall see, however, while these covenant renewals of late seventeenth-century New England shared the character of a public ceremony with the earlier practice of the test of relation, their internal logic, meaning, and dynamics were very different. Less a rite of inclusion/exclusion and more a ritual of consensus, the covenant renewals were another mechanism in the remaking of New England Puritan culture.

The new practice of covenant renewals was begun in Norwich, Connecticut in March 1675.[50] The original concept of "owning the covenant" was an outgrowth of the decisions of the Synod of 1662. There, it is recalled, proposition 5 stated that "Church members who were admitted in their minority [and who] Understanding the Doctrine of Faith and publickly professing their assent thereunto ... and solemnly owning the covenant before the Church" were to be considered members of the Church.[51] In practice, this meant that those members of the Church who were baptized into it by virtue of their parents' regenerate experience and not their own, with their now baptized infant children in tow, explicitly and individually assented in public to the *principles* of New England church policy. As Perry Miller pointed out, "this was more than a mere understanding of abstractions, more than a vague desire: it was an explicit assent."[52] Fifteen years later, being "bound unto various duties, and in special unto those solemn personal profession that pertain to adult members, not as then entering into a new membership, but as making a progress in memberly duties," these now adult children, together with their parents, "owned the covenant" and renewed their original pledge.[53] The critical change, as Perry Miller has pointed out, is that the "renewal" of the covenant transformed what had been a "particular and individual recitation" into "a communal chant."[54]

What James Fitch, the pastor of the Norwich church, did then, "with the approval of his congregation," was to call upon the entire Church to "reaffirm the original church covenant."[55] This practice spread rapidly throughout Connecticut, Massachusetts, and the Plymouth Colony. In many churches the practice of mass covenant renewals was part of the implementation of the Half Way Covenant. As described by Robert Pope, the practice ran as follows: "First the church voted to renew the covenant; meetings with the children followed; and the process culminated with the entire congregation confessing its faults and pledging to hew closer to God's word."[56] While, originally, the owning of the covenant was restricted to Church members, by 1690, ministers were inviting those members of the community not connected to any Church to participate in these renewals. By participating in the covenant renewal, these were then eligible for halfway status. As Pope notes: "When this occurred, the church covenant, once restricted to the visible saint and his children, took on an entirely new dimension."[57]

This "new dimension" is precisely that transformation whereby the "covenant" became the basis for a collective identity beyond the confines of the Church of visible saints. This transformation was felt in the specific and defining features of the covenant renewals—traits that, in fact, point to the basic dissimilarity between them and the earlier test of relation, whatever their superficial resemblance. As noted above, the covenant renewals implied a willful and cognitive affirmation of intellectual principles and value premises. Reaffirming their baptismal obligations, the participants in these covenant ownings manifested their consent to a set of abstract doctrines. Moreover, owning the covenant implied more than just an affirmation of principles and practices. For the younger members of the Church, it implied as well a voluntary commitment to prepare for full communion.[58]

With the practice of mass renewals, this affirmation, once an individual practice, became a communal rite. As a mode of expressing communal solidarity, it was, of course, very similar to the earlier test of relation, but its fundamental terms were different. For there, the rite marked a changed spiritual and emotional state; here, a cognitive affirmation of values, principles, and communal obligations. There, the rite marked a passage from one spiritual, moral, and communal state to another, a passage that effectively marked the division of the community into those within the social center and those beyond its ken. Here, the rite marked a unitary affirmation of principles, binding all participants (especially after 1690, when even those beyond the Church participated in the festival and, as a result, were admitted into the Church). It must further be recalled that the "days of humiliation" on which these communal rites occurred were also those on which the jeremiad sermons were preached.[59] These sermons, with their providential meanings, on the one hand, and past locus on the other, provided the symbolic and rhetorical framework uniting all participants in a sense of community.

A critical component in this sense of unity and communal affirmation, beyond its broader and more inclusive nature, was its underlying logic. For while these ceremonies no doubt had a strong emotive and affective aspect, they were nevertheless rooted in a cognitive, willful, and rational notion of affirmation of principles. While this bespoke an increasing Arminian stress (on the efficacy of willful acts for salvation) within Congregational Puritanism (and is thus also interesting in light of the increasing concern with the doctrine of free will among Puritan divines), its major importance lies in the possible light it sheds on the changing terms of community in late seventeenth-century New England.[60] For the earlier definition of membership in the community rested on a highly charged emotional state based on the conversionary experience. It was, moreover, precisely this experience as a manifestation of the workings of grace that was seen as the basis of both authority and communal identity and membership. By the last decades of the seventeenth century, with the affirmation of community rooted not only in (an affective) recognition of a shared past, but also in a cognitive acceptance of a normative order, we thus are witness to a critical change in the very logic of communal identification. In this latter case, social ordering in general, and its manifestation in the definition of community in particular, were based on a cognitive and symbolic acceptance of normative principles.

This affirmation of normative principles as the basis of membership in the community was not confined to the practice of covenant renewal. It was evident as well in what Paul Lucas has termed the "moral evangelicalism" of the last third of the seventeenth century. Paul Lucas, in studying the admittance practices of the churches of Connecticut in the period between 1670 and 1725, found a marked increase in the use of "moral behavior," as opposed to conversionary experience, as the means of judging an applicant's suitability for admittance to the Church.[61] As he succinctly put it, "moral behavior gradually replaced conversion experience as the most important criterion for membership—and moral behavior was determined by the applicant's ability to abide by the standards of the group."[62] Interestingly enough, this new stress on adherence to group-based norms gained expression in the furthering of the ministers from the proceedings of admission to the Church and a return to the collective/group-based interview of applicants (that is, to a practice similar to the one that fell into disuse following the Cambridge Platform). Reminiscent of the early years of settlement, the religious "revival" of the last third of the seventeenth century was, in its underlying logic, essentially different; for, in contrast to the former, it neglected the spirit and concentrated, instead, upon behavior. "The brethren tried to mold the church into a vehicle for moral consensus and proper behavior among members and nonmembers alike."[63] That this adherence to a set of normative principles was seen as providing the integrating force in society by its members marks a critical change in the self-definition of any society.

In this context, it is important to note that the practice of covenant renewal was given active encouragement by both civil and ecclesiastical authority in the Massachusetts and Plymouth colonies. In the midst of King Philip's War, the general court of both colonies encouraged the practice of covenant renewal as a means of mitigating the suffering of the people.[64] Thus, the Plymouth General Court on the day of humiliation it convened during the war "added thereto a solemne motion to all our ch[urch]es to renew a covenant engagement to God for Reformation of all provoking evils."[65] More important was the support given the practice by the Reforming Synod of 1679.[66] In legitimizing the practice of renewal, the Synod's resolution hastened its acceptance among the churches of New England. In so doing it gave institutional support to a practice that was, however implicitly, redefining both the boundaries of the community and its inherent meaning. In the long run, this process resulted in a new concept of the moral order as resting, ultimately, not on grace but on the moral behavior of each and every individual who carried within the possible sources of salvation as well as damnation. Significantly, by the end of the seventeenth century and the early years of the eighteenth century, the criteria for membership in the churches of New England came to rest less and less on the attestation of saving grace and more on the (public or civic) moral rectitude of the individual communicant.[67] Personal morality rather than collective grace had become the defining terms of the normative order and of participation therein.

It is perhaps appropriate at this stage to review briefly the social dynamic we have attempted to trace in the above. Having analyzed the major symbolic and institutional innovations of mid-century (the jeremiad and the Half Way Covenant) as elements in the remaking of collective boundaries and definitions, we went on to see their more concrete organizational derivatives in the doctrine of Stoddard, in Cotton Mather's revival societies, and in the growth of religious toleration. These developments were viewed as crucial mechanisms that led to a new form of social integration by breaking down the hitherto existing boundaries between Church and community. The

The Institutionalization of Charisma in Society 177

new sense of social integration was itself predicated on the "displacement" of the boundaries of the normative moral order from within the community to within each individual. This transference of the loci of boundaries (and so also of boundary maintenance), which we termed the interiorization of boundaries, was analyzed as a major stage in the symbolization, systematization, and internalization of charisma, that is, of its routinization and so of the ascetic-Puritan worldview. For only by transposing the boundaries of nature and grace from the world outside to individuals acting within that world could "world mastery" be effected by ascetically conditioned, innerworldly, and morally conscious individuals. In seventeenth-century New England, this development was manifest in the transformation of both collective and individual identities. Both within each individual (as in the doctrines of preparationism, sacramentalism, and baptismal piety) and in the ritual of community (which established the boundaries of a shared moral order, including the churched and the un- or not yet churched), a new concept of the moral order was constituted.

There remains, however, one crucial and as yet unexplored element of this ongoing dynamic—the connection between the process of interiorization and the development of mass covenant renewals, or later of Stoddard's "harvests," which were forerunners of the awakenings of the 1720s and 1730s and later of the Great Awakening of the 1740s. How, one may well ask, was the process of interiorization of boundaries related to mass ceremonies of collective affirmation? Both were components of a new moral order, of a new definition of individual and collective existence. What, then, was the nature of the relation between them, if any?

Interesting light has been shed on this problem by Boyer and Nussenbaum in their study of the Salem witch trials. Noting the fact that "confessing witches were seldom hanged," Boyer and Nussenbaum develop the notion of the trials as a public mechanism for "self-purgation and self-definition."[68] Viewing the witch trials as a ceremony of public confession, they go on to note that

> By first projecting upon others the unacknowledged impulses which lay within themselves, and then absolving those they had accused, the accusers could bring such impulses into the open, gain at least temporary mastery over them and thereby affirm their commitment to social values in which they very much wanted to believe.[69]

Indeed, stated thus, this form of confession bears a great degree of similarity to the days of humiliation and the rite of covenant owning, except that in the latter case (as in the Great Awakening) the community collectively admitted its iniquity and thus purged itself of sin. Accusing themselves of sin, whether in the covenant ownings or in the enthusiasm of the Awakening, was a vital recognition of precisely that internalized "otherhood" we analyzed above.[70] As a manifestation of interiorized boundaries it worked as a cathartic mechanism, allowing "the communicant who is both participant and observer [to] experience repressed emotion and discharge it."[71] With the boundaries of the moral order no longer running between communicants, but within each individual, the boundary maintaining device changed accordingly into the type of cathectic ceremony manifested in the covenant renewals, "harvests," and, in specific circumstances, witch trials.

The Great Awakening and the New Terms of Collective Identity

The full flowering of these cathectic ceremonies was reached in the third and fourth decades of the eighteenth century. In 1733, 1734, and 1735, Jonathan Edwards, Stoddard's grandson, led a series of revivals in Northhampton, Connecticut. These revivals were characterized by "a great and earnest concern about the great things of religion, and the eternal world," which "became universal in all parts of the town, and among persons of all degrees and ages."[72] Setting the stage for the major flowering of revival in the early 1740s, the revivals in Northhampton saw, "scarcely a single person in the town, young or old, left unconcerned about the great things of the eternal world."[73] For Jonathan Edwards, the "multiplication" of "true saints" resulted in a "glorious alteration in the town; so that in the spring and summer following anno 1735, the town seemed to be full of the presence of God, it was never so full of love, nor of joy, and yet so full of distress as it was then."[74]

The self same sentiments that characterized the revivals of 1735 in Northhampton characterized as well the response to George Whitefield's preaching in the 1740s. The Great Awakening of the 1740s was a mass outpouring of the spirit that fundamentally changed the terms of collective identity in New England. Arising out of the increasing distance between minister and congregation, the changing role of the Church in daily life, and the increased ritualism of religion, it may, in fact, be seen as a response, on the level of community, to the changes that had taken place in the sphere of institutional religion and ecclesiastical authority. The terms of this response effected, however, a reworking not only of religious models of community, but of collective identity, *tout court*.

Following on the implications of the Half Way Covenant, and of Stoddardism, the individual churches increasingly lost their autonomous character as pressure developed among the ministers in Massachusetts and Connecticut for a more Presbyterian, that is, national system of Church organization. In the sphere of Church policy, the early eighteenth century was marked by the growth of a unitary Church framework. Taking the form of ministerial conventions, ministerial meetings, and later associations, all served to strengthen the prerogatives and power of the ministry at the expense of the congregations.[75] And while not particularly successful in Massachusetts, the Connecticut *Saybrook Platform* of 1708 "established a system of country ministerial associations to aid in the settling of disputes and by inference to strengthen the hand of each local pastor."[76] This was accomplished through the transfer of "sovereignty from the congregation where the Cambridge Platform had placed it, to the consociation (that is, the assembly of clergymen), where the lay member had virtually no power."[77] This move, it may be noted, led to the domination of the congregations by the elders in a system that resembled the Presbyterian government of Scotland more than the early Puritan doctrine as enshrined in the Cambridge Platform. As argued by Williston Walker, the Saybrook Proposals (and similar developments in Massachusetts), while the source of much conflict in individual churches, ultimately reformed the state of Congregational policy through the formation of standing councils, or consociations, to which almost all local churches were affiliated.[78]

The break with the concept of the autonomous and local Church of covenanted saints marked a major transformation of Congregational policy. It is to be remembered that the earlier New England Congregationalists, following William Ames, saw each individual church as "possessing the means of its own salvation," that is, as a charismatic center in itself.[79] The move to a broader form of affiliation was, therefore, a logical concomitant to the growth of a collective definition of membership, embracing all churches and members in one social center. This change was expressed as well in the growing attempt to argue ministerial authority in sacerdotal as opposed to covenantal terms. This growing sacerdotalism, while leading some ministers back into the Anglican fold, nevertheless became a feature of New England's Congregational policy.[80] Both developments were thus part of society's changing locus—from the individual churches, to the institutions of the broader collective.

This move had, moreover, possible derivatives on a number of additional and changing aspects of religious life in this period. The changing locus of collective life may well have been felt in those changing practices studied above. For we have seen how the growing ritualism in Church practice—as evinced in the "sacramental renaissance" and the "new baptismal piety"—were developing at the same time as the individual churches were losing their primary social function as a boundary maintaining device, ordering social and individual identities. The increasing ritualism of religious practice was mirrored in other symbolic forms as well. Thus, Allen Ludwig has pointed out the rather enigmatic rise of pictorial representations of death on New England tombstones from the 1690s to 1710.[81] As opposed to their earlier rustic simplicity, New England tombstones began to represent the image of the "winged imps of death" in that very period when the Church as a boundary ordering mechanism was undergoing its most essential revision.[82] Similarly, the different poetic meditations on the Lord's Supper, especially by New England's foremost colonial poet, Edward Taylor, display an imagery and symbolism that had hitherto been lacking in the poetic endeavors of New England's earlier generations. While certainly in need of greater research, this increasing ritualism of late seventeenth-century religious life can arguably be connected to the changing position of the Church and its ministers within the overall context of social life. A response to the relocation of the boundaries of the moral order (to include those beyond the parameters of Church membership), a ritual attitude may well have been the Church's response to the development of new boundary maintaining mechanisms and models of social ordering. In other words, ritualism may well have been one response to a changing conception of the social order, whereby the ministers no longer maintained their symbolic role as primary articulators of collective meaning and the Church no longer served as the sole source of the social ordering.[83]

The Great Awakening was, in more than one way, a response to these changes in the place of the Church and its ministers in collective life. The extreme nature of this response, however, split the churches and congregations of New England and the middle colonies. The split into "Old Lights," those such as Isaac Stiles of Connecticut and Charles Chauncey of Boston, who opposed the new "enthusiastic" preaching of the "New Lights," such as Gilbert Tennet, James Davenport, and, of course, the more staid Jonathan Edwards (as well as his successors in the New Divinity preachers, such as Samuel Hopkins and Joseph Bellamy) spelled the end of any possible ordering of social existence in terms of seventeenth-century Congregational and covenantal theory.

The break with Congregational policy was marked on both the doctrinal and, more importantly, the "sociological" level of the Awakening message. The religious message of the Awakening was a "return" to strict Calvinist principles of predestination, thus repudiating in effect the covenant as a basis for the symbolic ordering of social life. Moreover, the form taken by this message—the manner of its transmission (by itinerant preachers) and reception (by mass audiences in open fields)—was totally different from anything that had presaged it. The message of the Awakening was transmitted by itinerant preachers (sometimes laymen), who had no contact or familiarity with their audience, who preached according to the timetable of their travels and not on set days (Sundays), and so disrupted work and the structured flow of social life.[84] Their sermons were pitched at an emotional level, beyond anything previously experienced by New England congregants. In the words of Harry Stout,

> The revivalists sought to transcend both the rational manner of polite Liberal preaching and the plain style of orthodox preaching in order to speak directly to the people at large. Repudiating both the conventions of the jeremiad and the ecclesiastical formalities, they assaulted the old preaching style no less devastatingly than they attacked the doctrines of covenant theology. Their technique of mass address to a voluntary audience forced a dialogue between speaker and hearer that disregarded social position and local setting.[85]

The Awakening preachers thus attacked the very basis of the Congregational Way, the Covenant Formula, with its highly sophisticated taxonomy of the conversionary experience, replacing it with a direct appeal to the emotions. The itinerant ministers attacked as well the established ministry (often by name) denigrating learning, edification, and doctrinal competence as secondary to the "affections" in the working of the divine spirit.[86] Warning of the *Danger of an Unconverted Ministry* (1740), preachers such as Gilbert Tennet taught people to distinguish between a "dead ministry" and a "faithful ministry" of "Godly Persons" to whom it was "both lawfull and expedient to go" when the properly ordained minister was found to be of "lesser Gifts."[87] Breaking, in such a way, the institutional link between ordained ministers and congregants (articulated through the covenanted Church), as well as the increasingly hierarchical and sacerdotal conception of the ministry that had developed over the seventeenth century, the itinerants posited a new relationship between ministers and congregants. This conception saw the minister as "knit" to his people "in a spiritual and pure love, and as it were, a conjugal tenderness."[88] In many ways, this celebrated union of minister and congregant recalls the original charismatically defined nature of their relation as posited at the start of settlement one hundred years earlier. Devoid of institutional restraints and hierarchical notions, the ministry and congregants shared a similar experience of grace. The important difference between these two models was that, whereas earlier, this union was predicated on the covenanted Church of visible saints as the institutional locus and nexus of the charismatic tie, in the Awakening, Church affiliation was bypassed and the charismatic dimension was seen to rest in the linkage between the minister and the populace at large.

The very possibility, however, of articulating charisma beyond the realm of the covenanted Church rested on those processes of interiorization of moral boundaries and transference of the social locus of charisma from the covenanted saints to the community at large that we have been studying. The Awakening thus completed the process begun in the covenant renewals of defining the charismatic dimension of existence in terms relevant to the whole of the populace and not just Church members. A new basis was laid for the construction of a communal solidarity—without the covenant and in opposition to the ordained ministry, be they Congregationalist or Presbyterian.

In opposing the established ministry, the Awakening preachers laid themselves open to charges of religious "enthusiasm." Certainly, the mass book burning orchestrated by James Davenport (to which he added his vestments) in New London in 1743 did little to mitigate the fears of the Awakening's opponents.[89] Nor were Jonathan Edwards's philosophical defenses of the role of the "affections" and emotion in religion always convincing.[90] And, indeed, the label of enthusiasm was one that supporters of the Awakening had difficulty living down. Jonathan Edwards's sophisticated and worked out defense of Awakening practice was, in fact, the most important and serious attempt to deal with the criticism thrown at the Awakening preachers.[91]

Enthusiasm, that great bugbear of seventeenth- and eighteenth-century religious life, could take many forms. A proper understanding of these forms, especially in the context of eighteenth-century New England social developments, must, however, rest on the prior differentiation between "enthusiasm" as a derogatory term of abuse and as a mode of experience. As a term of abuse, it was, from the sixteenth through the eighteenth century, hurled at different sectarian groups opposing the given, official, and institutional channels of grace (and social order). Often used to deride the sectarian movements of the Reformation articulating a doctrine of inner grace, Anabaptists, Quakers, Fifth Monarchy Men (and, in New England, followers of Anne Hutchinson), and in the eighteenth century, such groups as the "French Prophets" in London, as well as the Parisian "convulsionaries," were a continual reminder of the dangers of enthusiasm.[92] The New Light preachers and their followers were themselves condemned as enthusiasts (notably in Charles Chauncey's *Seasonable Thoughts on the State of Religion* [1743]) and compared not only to Quakers and followers of Anne Hutchinson, but to the French Prophets as well.[93]

If, however, we attempt to go beyond the contemporary labels to an understanding of the phenomenon involved, a new direction of analysis is opened up. For while contemporaries harped on the subversive effects of the Great Awakening, linking it not only with the French Prophets, but to the "Negro Conspiracy" in New York of 1741, as well as to the little liked Moravians, modern historians have been more generous.[94] In the works of Alan Heimart, Harry Stout, and David Lovejoy, as well as in the earlier insights of E. L. Tuveson, the Awakening has in fact been linked to the building of a national entity and to the construction of a new collective ideology through providing an "ethos" and a "fervor" to the developing political vocabulary of natural rights and republican liberties.[95] In slightly different terms, as was recognized by such contemporaries as Lord Shaftesbury, Tom Paine, and John Adams, some elements of what may be called "internalized enthusiasm," or charismatic sources of social action, were necessary to the many different forms of worthwhile activity, including that of political mobilization and the forging of new political commitments in eighteenth-century America.⁹⁶ Thus, the historian Ruth Bloch argues that:

> in the long run, what might be called the implicit political message of the Great Awakening—its call to rebellion, equality and mass participation—laid an ideological groundwork for the American Revolution that was quite independent of the whig confirmation of liberty that occurred during the French and Indian War.⁹⁷

The very terms of revolutionary rhetoric, *liberty* and *tyranny,* were, as she points out, infused, during the Awakening, with a deep admixture of religious and political meanings, politicizing the sacred and sacralizing the political in the making of a new civil identity.⁹⁸

What developed out of the Great Awakening was indeed nothing less than a unique merging of Christian ideas of grace with the civil polity on the one hand, and the later inculcation of these ideas with a belief in progress, natural law, and individual virtue, on the other hand. This symbolic vision became central to the post-eighteenth-century American national character and identity, informing and structuring the unique components of what Robert Bellah would later call the American civil religion.⁹⁹

This new sense of national identity found in the Revolutionary decades of the 1760s and even in the awakenings of the 1730s and 1740s marked a beginning. It represented an emerging synthesis of seventeenth-century Puritan religious culture with a growing eighteenth-century civil one. Benjamin Franklin, that most paradigmatic of all eighteenth-century Americans, could still recall his meeting with Cotton Mather and the influence of the latter's *Bonificious* on his life.¹⁰⁰ Striding into the New World, he still had at least a toehold in the old. But then, of course, this old world had itself changed.¹⁰¹ Cotton Mather presided over the inauguration of a Baptist minister in 1718, evincing a toleration not possible to him or others in the seventeenth century, when the model of the ideal community was that of the covenanted Church of regenerate saints. By the culmination of the Great Awakening in the mid-1740s, this model of communal identity had significantly changed.

End and Beginning

Though the developing political discourse of eighteenth-century New England is the subject for an independent study, its importance for understanding the changing locus of Puritan social life lies in its very emergence.[102] For, in such writings as John Wise's *Vindication of the Churches of New England* (1717) as well as in such publications as James Franklin's *New England Courrant,* there emerged a definition of society and of authority that reflected the changing structures of collective identity and membership that we have been studying.[103] The very decline in the idiom of grace engendered a reemergence of natural law theories as the foundation of the social order. Thus, while in 1645 John Winthrop viewed natural liberties as "corrupt, evil and brutish." By 1671, John Mitchell in his jeremiad *Nehemiah on the Wall,* refers to "the eternal law of god, that Eternal, Immutable Moral Rule, engrave on the forehead of the Law and the Light of Nature." This law "being supreme limits all laws and considerations" and, as we see, begins to unite Puritan ideas of grace with more ancient, classical notions of natural law.

Of even greater significance in this development was John Wise's *Vindication of the Government of New-England Churches.* Intervening in the debate over Church policy, Wise develops the very ideas of Grotius on the confluence of the laws of nature and natural reason. For Wise, man's "Original Liberty [is] Instampt upon his Rational Nature, he that intrudes upon this Liberty, Violates the Law of Nature." Quoting Plutarch to the effect that "Those persons only who live in obedience to Reason, are worthy to be accounted free," Wise posits reason and the law of nature as the sources and goals of human endeavor. Drawing on diverse sources, from Puffendorf to Ulpian (who Wise quotes on man's natural right to be free), Wise was instrumental in inculcating classical natural law theory into the political debates of the early eighteenth century in New England.[104]

Of course Wise was not alone and as the eighteenth century progressed, more and more political arguments were drawn from the classical and early modern corpus of natural law theory. By the 1750s and 1760s preachers such as Jonathan Mayhew, Daniel Shute, Jasson Haven, Samuel Cooke, and others were referring to the "troika" of God, nature, and reason as the foundations of politics and government.[105]

The continuing importance of this confluence of religious and secular themes (of a rhetoric of grace and of law and natural rights) in the construction of new terms of collective identity can be assessed in the writings of John Adams. His *A Dissertation on Cannon and Feudal Law* (1765) can in fact be seen as both a clarion call to the study of natural law as well as an example of that "enthusiasm" (associated earlier with the Awakening preachers) transferred from the religious to the civil realm, and from a term of abuse to a source of (national) pride.[106] This, what David Lovejoy has referred to as "enthusiasm of liberty," that "noble infirmity" that suffused the eighteenth-century discourse of civic virtue, tied the natural law tradition of the civic humanists to the more indigenous Puritan traditions of the seventeenth century.[107] It finds further expression in Adams's *Novanglus or a History of the Dispute with America from its Origins in 1754 to the Present Time* (1775) where he asserts: "I have always considered the settlement of America with reverence and wonder, as the opening of a grand scene and design in Providence for the illumination of the ignorant and the emancipation of the slavish part of mankind all over the earth."[108] Here we find the latter day, secular, and civic manifestation of those (religious) visions of providential history that have been traced (notably by Pocock and Tuveson) to the concept of visible saints, the Puritan commonwealth, and the workings of the Great Awakening.[109] Significantly, however, we find these in a text replete with references to the natural law tradition and to the writings of Aristotle, Plato, Grotius, Puffendorf, Locke, Harrington, and Sydney.[110] It is this unique interweaving of religious and civil traditions that came to characterize the civil society tradition in the United States, setting it off from those of other nation-states and giving to the unity of natural law doctrines and religious themes their particular saliency in eighteenth-century America.

The move from Church to community as locus of membership was thus articulated over the eighteenth century in the shifting political discourse, from visible saints to constitutional subjects. This move, while finding expression in countless pamphlets and political tracts of the period, was also, as we have seen, profoundly ambiguous. For of central importance in understanding the terms of this new collective model is the particular dialectic it contained whereby the very secular concept of citizenship was infused with a sacred dimension. The basis of this notion must itself be sought in the earlier move from Church to community, which was not simply a transfer of the locus and charismatic center of collective life. It involved a very particular redefinition of both realms, a redefinition of spheres that saw a high degree of interpenetration of the sacred and the secular. The politicization of the sacred in the earlier decades of settlement gave way to the sacralization of the political. While this uniquely American phenomenon, in both its religious and political "moments," was most evident in and following the period of the Great Awakening, its preconditions, as we have argued, were already present in such practices as Stoddardism or Mather's religious societies, these being in essence organizational mechanisms that extended and deepened the social implications of the Half Way Covenant. Through these mechanisms, the boundaries of collective identity, in essence of the moral order, were redefined. We recall, moreover, that one critical element in this redefinition was the interiorization of the boundaries separating insider from outsider. The personal interiorization of "otherhood" had its corollary in the collective affirmation of the normative order.

Though difficult to substantiate, there seems moreover to be a direct relation between this development of late seventeenth-century Puritan culture and the emergence in the eighteenth century of rhetoric of national virtue. It is, of course, difficult to extrapolate the use of a particular political idiom, especially one with such a rich and resonant past as virtue, from a given social practice.[111] Yet the concept of a national virtue in colonial America seems to have reflected those transformations we have been studying throughout. These transformations involved, in the first place, the concept of a unitary collective, and in the second, one infused with a special charismatic dimension of grace. The broader, more societal dimensions of this change can be explained through the various practices of the Half Way Covenant, Stoddardism, covenant renewals, and the evolving symbolic mode of the jeremiad. Yet, on the level of the individual—and the concept of national virtue rested ultimately on the integrity of each person—the explanation would seem to lie in that particular privatization of collective grace as conscience, which characterized late seventeenth-century religious and social practice.[112]

In more analytical terms, the whole set of changes studied above bespoke the development of a new framework of cognitive and affective commitments on the part of people to the source of collective membership, identity, and authority. These changes marked, in fact, the institutionalization of the original charismatic dimension of settle-

188   Innerworldly Individualism

ment. The process of institutionalization and routinization involved two prime developments: the first, a dispersion of charisma within the institutional frameworks of social life, and the second, a sensitization of "peripheral" elements to the newly routinized charisma. By dispersion of charisma, I refer to that process designated by Shils as

> spreading the particular charismatic sensitivity to persons who did not share it previously. This means a considerable extension of the circle of charisma: more persons have to become charismatic, existing institutions have to have charisma infused into them, new institutions have to be created.[113]

Recalling our earlier analysis of religious intolerance, we noted how the persecution of dissenting sects was rooted in their articulation of alternate loci of charismatic meaning and identity. Threatening not only the authority of ministers and magistrates (itself rooted in the charismatic community of covenanted saints), the Baptists and Quakers of mid-century threatened as well the very terms of collective identity and cosmic meaning. In these terms, the later acceptance of the principle of toleration (above and beyond the fact of its imposition) itself marks a reformulation of the very terms of collective identity. This change, whose beginning we saw in the jeremiad sermon, with the strong stress on a collective past, carried with it a relocation of the charismatic center, or locus of existence. In fact, given the argument that restructuring of collective boundaries was part of the constitution of a new identity or tradition, such a reformulation and relocation of the charismatic dimension is only to be expected. Relocated beyond the Church, the charismatic dimension was also reformulated. For, in the process of its removal from the confines of the covenanted Church of regenerate saints, it was also "dispersed" among the community at large, which was, in fact, what such diverse developments as Stoddardism and Mather's religious societies signified—the construction of new institutional arrangements. These different developments had the unitary effect of opening the social center and bringing more and more people into some form of relation with it. The very "opening of the center," whether symbolically, in Stoddard's open communion, alternatively, in Mather's efforts to unite people in the doing of good for the greater glory of God, or institutionally, in the broadening definition of the collective with the *Act of Toleration* (1689), all signify new modes of participation in the central orders of society—a participation that rested on some form of inclusion within the arena of an increasingly institutionalized charisma. This transformation, of bringing people into relation with the center of society through somehow sharing in its uniquely charismatic dimension, is, in essence, what the institutionalization, routinization, or in fact, dispersion of charisma necessarily imply.

The other aspect of the dispersion of charisma was, as noted, the sensitization of people to its symbolic expression—a sensitization that took place through that interiorization of collective boundaries and identity studied above. This dynamic, which involved transposing the boundaries of the moral order from "out there" to inside, has important sociological implications, not solely in the development of new individual identities (based on an internalized conscience) but on the terms of collective membership as well. For the source of communal identity and authority no longer rested on a shared experience of grace but, in the first case, on a shared past, and in the second, on a "Lockean" understanding of natural rights based on the moral, what would Kant would later term *transcendental* individual (that is to say, that individual endowed with conscience and moral agency who would become constitutive of the nascent political community).

In a sense, then, we have just about come full circle. From a genuinely charismatic locus of collective identity, membership, and authority, we have studied the concrete process of its institutionalization through the changing organizational and symbolic forms of social life. Moreover, we have been at pains to point out that the process of routinization, while transforming the articulation of the pure or genuine charismatic dimension of social life, did not totally negate its presence, a presence that continued to infuse the "meaning" of America with a sacred dimension, rooted ultimately in the history of the seventeenth-century Puritan communities of visible saints.

In this context we may look to such popular works as Joseph Morgan's *History of the Kingdom of Basaruch* (1715) as well as to the theological writings of Jonathan Edwards and his followers who wove a sacred dimension into the very fabric of American national identity.[114] One of the most moving and instructive examples of this writing is perhaps in the following quote from Samuel Sewall's *Phoenomena quoedam Apocalyptica* (1697):

190   Innerworldly Individualism

As long as Plum Island shall faithfully keep the commanded Post; Notwithstanding all the hectoring Words, and hard Blows of the proud and boisterous Ocean; As long as any Salmon or Sturgeon shall swim in the streams of Merrimack; or any Perch, or Pickeril, in CranePond; As long as the Sea-Fowl shall know the Time of their coming, and not neglect seasonably to visit the Places of their Acquaintance: As long as any Cattel shall be fed with the Gras growing in the Medows, which do humbly bow down themselves before Turkie-Hill; As long as any Sheep shall walk upon Old Town Hills, and shall from thence pleasantly look down upon the river Parker, and the fruitfull Marshes lying beneath; As long as any free and harmless Doves shall find a White Oak or other Tree within the Township, to perch, or feed, or build a careless Nest upon; and shall voluntarily present themselves to perform the office of Gleaners after Barley-Harvest; As long as Nature shall not grow Old and dote; but shall constantly remember to give the row of Indian Corn their education, by Pairs: So long shall Christians be born there; and being first made meet, shall from thence be Translated, to be made partakers of the Inheritance of the Saints of Light.[115]

Here we see a unique interweaving of religious and secular models, of the "inheritance of the saints of light" with the very mundane particularism—I would even say primordial terms of identity—based solely on attachment to a specific place over three generations. Attachment to local culture and a shared past are here tied to a religious tradition out of which the unique terms of American civil identity would be forged.

This interweaving, which was accomplished in and following the Great Awakening, rested, however, as we have seen, on the development of a special set of social practices or mechanisms and symbolic models in the preceding generation. And, while the full flowering of this particular "civil religion" is a subject in and of itself, its very uniqueness invites a few comparative remarks by way of conclusion.

Notes

1. On the importance of going beyond the original premises of the Calvinist religious tradition as necessary to its institutionalization, see S. N. Eisenstadt, *The Protestant Ethic and Modernization: A Comparative Perspective* (New York: Basic Books, 1968), 22–24.
2. Marcell Mauss, "A Category of the Human Mind: The Notion of Person: The Notion of Self," in *The Category of the Person,* ed. M. Carrithers, S. Collins, and S. Lukes (Cambridge: Cambridge University Press, 1985), 20.

3. Emile Durkheim, *Sociology and Philosophy* (New York: The Free Press, 1974), 35–62; Louis Dumont, "A Modified View of Our Origins"; Marcell Mauss, "A Category of the Human Mind."
4. On Stoddardism and the Stoddard-Mather controversy, see E. Brooks Holifield, *The Covenant Sealed: The Development of Puritan Sacramental Theology in Old and New England 1570–1720* (New Haven, CT: Yale University Press, 1974), 192–220; Miller, *The New England Mind,* 227–36, 256–65, 276–87; Lucas, *Valley of Discord,* 169–87.
5. Miller, *New England Mind,* 227.
6. Ibid., 227.
7. Solomon Stoddard, *The Doctrine of the Instituted Churches* (London, 1700). See also Lucas, *Valley of Discord,* 152.
8. On these revivals, see Miller, *New England Mind,* 235, 280.
9. On the development of the Awakening in Connecticut, see Bushman, *Puritan to Yankee,* 183–95.
10. For the views of another major ministerial figure engaged in this conflict, in opposition to Stoddard, see Edward Taylor's *Foundation Day Sermon* of 1690 and his *Revised Foundation Day Sermon* of 1692–93.
11. A detailed list of this pamphlet literature can be found in Walker, ed., *Creeds and Platforms,* 240–41, 280–83.
12. Hall, *Faithful Shepherd,* 210.
13. This debate is analyzed in Lucas, *Valley of Discord,* 152–68.
14. Ibid., 156–57.
15. Ibid., 154.
16. Ibid., 132.
17. P. Miller, 1953:284.
18. Ibid., 182, 183; Miller, *New England Mind,* 283.
19. On these societies, see Robert Middlekauff, *The Mathers: Three Generations of Puritan Intellectuals* (London: Oxford University Press, 1971), 270–78.
20. The methods for the organization of these societies were worked out by Cotton Mather in his *Methods and Motives for Societies to Suppress Disorders* (1703) where he calls on men to "sublimate" their "Natural Affection to Society . . . into a Religious Affection to Associate For the Interests of Religion" (T. Holmes, 1974:679). Other works of this genre include *Religious Societies* (1724) and *Faithful Monitors* (1704) (T. Holmes, 1974:II,898; I,360).
21. Middlekauff, *The Mathers,* 271.
22. This tactic marked the major difference between Mather's doctrine and that of English evangelicals such as Josiah Woodward who envisioned Christian Union "within the Church." On Woodward's influence on Cotton Mather, see ibid., 270; and on the differences between them, ibid., 411.
23. Holifield, *The Covenant Sealed,* 94.
24. Ibid., 94.
25. See, for example, Cotton Mather, *Christianus per Ignem* (Boston, 1702). A brief summary of this, as well as of all of Cotton Mather's voluminous writings, can be found in Thomas Holmes, *Cotton Mather: A Bibliography of His Works,* vol. 1 (Newton, MA: Crofton, 1974), 147–53.

26. Middlekauff, *The Mathers,* 276–77.
27. Cotton Mather, *The Diary of Cotton Mather,* vol. 2 (New York: Ungar Press, n.d.), 202.
28. Discussion of this aspect of the relations between England and the New England colonies can be found in Zakai, *Exile and Kingdom,* (1982), 451–545; Hall, *Faithful Shepherd,* 228–37; Miller, *New England Mind,* 9, 10, 38–50, 119–29.
29. See Watts, *Dissenters,* 259; Miller, *New England Mind,* 127.
30. Miller, *New England Mind,* 167.
31. Hall, *Faithful Shepherd,* 230–31.
32. Middlekauff, *The Mathers,* 216.
33. I have adopted this term from Arnold Momigliano, "Marcell Mauss and the Quest for the Person in Greek Biography and Autobiography" in *The Category of the Person,* 83–92, who uses it in his analysis of the concept of the "person" in early Greek biography.
34. Greenfeld, "Two Charismas," 129.
35. Shils, *Center and Periphery,* 12–16.
36. Parsons, "Durkheim on Religion," 219. For Durkheim's concept of moral community and moral reality, see Durkheim, *Sociology and Philosophy,* 35–79.
37. From a more evolutionary perspective it can be stated that this process of routinization of charisma stands at the root of those integratory processes defining an (ideal) *Gesellschaft* (society) as opposed to the *Gemeinschaft* (community) integrated on the basis of genuine charisma.
38. Roger Caillois, *Man and the Sacred* (New York: The Free Press, 1959), 132.
39. See E. Brooks Holifield, "The Renaissance of Sacramental Piety in Colonial New England," *William and Mary Quarterly* 29 (1972): 33–48; idem, 1974. The following analysis of "sacramentalism," the doctrine of "preparationism," and the "privatization" of public rite stands in contradiction to the interpretation offered by Hambrick-Stowe in his *The Practice of Piety: Puritan Devotional Disciplines in Seventeenth Century New England* (Chapel Hill: University of North Carolina Press, 1982). Hambrick-Stowe, as is well known, argues for the continuity of private devotionalism across the seventeenth century and indeed back to the sixteenth century (pp. 23–52). He also draws parallels between Puritan and Catholic devotionalism (pp. 25–39). Careful attention to his sources will reveal, however, that most of the sources he brings to substantiate his thesis are from the latter half of the seventeenth century. This is especially true of his sections entitled "Preparation for the Sacrament" (pp. 206–18) and "Private Devotion" (pp. 156–93). Furthermore, the section "Heart Religion" (pp. 25–53), which argues the sixteenth- and early seventeenth-century continuity of Catholic with Puritan devotionalism, offers very few Puritan documents (of that time period) to substantiate the argument. Finally, reliance on Samuel Sewall, Edward Taylor, and Cotton Mather serves to root devotional practice in the later part of the seventeenth century. If, indeed, as argued here, the surge in devotionalism in the last third of the seventeenth century is correct, and in this I follow E. Brooks Holifield (as does Hambrick-Stowe who, however, ignores his seminal chapter "Sacramental Renaissance"), there was, from a sociological perspective nothing strange in the increasing similarity of Puritan with Catholic practice. For it was precisely the

crises (or contradiction) of institutionalization that led the "sect" to adopt "Church" type practice. This of course was Weber's own thesis. The argument offered here is that the process of institutionalization—devoid of an office charismatic institution—engendered a different social dynamic than had characterized Catholic civilization. The ultimate result of this development was the emergence of the morally autonomous individual.

40. These are discussed by Holifield, *The Covenant Sealed,* 197–225.
41. Ibid., 201.
42. For examples of the poetry of this "sacramental renaissance," see Edward Taylor (1960). An analysis of Edward Taylor as a "private poet" can be found in Karl Keller, "The Example of Edward Taylor," in *The American Puritan,* ed. S. Bercovitz, 121–38.
43. The growing importance of the Lord's Supper can be seen in Cotton Mather's *A Companion for Communicants* (Boston, 1690).
44. Durkheim, *The Elementary Forms*; Henri Hubert and Marcell Mauss, *Sacrifice: Its Nature and Function* (Chicago: University of Chicago Press, 1964); Arnold Van Geneep, *The Rites of Passage* (Chicago: University of Chicago Press, 1960).
45. See Holifield, *The Covenant Sealed,* 159–68. Further aspects of the doctrine of preparation were studied by Miller, "The Puritan Theory of Sacraments in Seventeenth Century New England," *The Catholic Historical Review* 22 (1937): 409–25; idem, "Preparation for Salvation in Seventeenth Century New England," *Journal of the History of Ideas* 4 (1943): 259–86; Pettite, *The Heart Prepared,* 1966.
46. Holifield, *The Covenant Sealed,* 186–96.
47. Ibid., 189.
48. Ibid., 192.
49. For some theoretical perspectives on communal rituals, see S. F. Moore and B. G. Myerhoff, eds., *Symbol and Politics in Communal Ideology* (Ithaca, NY: Cornell University Press, 1975); idem, *Secular Ritual* (Assen, Netherlands: Van Gorcum, 1977), esp. 3–24.
50. Miller, *The New England Mind,* 116–18; Pope, *The Half Way Covenant,* 224–48.
51. Walker, *Creeds and Platforms,* 328.
52. Miller, *New England Mind,* 115.
53. Walker, *Creeds and Platforms,* 334.
54. Miller, *New England Mind,* 116.
55. Pope, *Half Way Covenant,* 241.
56. Ibid., 243.
57. Ibid., 246.
58. Ibid., 246.
59. Miller, *New England Mind,* 117.
60. For the role of the intellect in Puritan religion see: Norman Fiering, "Will and Intellect in the New England Mind," *William and Mary Quarterly* 19 (1972): 515–58; Robert Middlekauff, "Piety and Intellect in Puritan New England," *William and Mary Quarterly* 22 (1975): 452–70.
61. Lucas, *Valley of Discord,* 242.
62. Ibid., 126.
63. Ibid., 244.

64. This point is discussed by Walker, *Creeds and Platforms*, 412.
65. Pope, *Half Way Covenant*, 241.
66. This Synod was convened by Increase Mather to meet the challenge faced by New England in the aftermath of the Indian Wars, the Boston fires of 1676 and 1679, the smallpox epidemic, and the threats to the charter by the Stuart regime, as well as by the attempt in 1679 to introduce episcopacy into New England.

    Aside from the heavy physical toll taken in the colonies by the above, the last twenty years of the century were those of a decline in piety and religion that the Synod attempted to address. Among its calls for reform and the means to achieve it, it passed a resolution affirming that "Solemn and explicit Renewal of the Covenant is a Scriptural Expedient for Reformation," stating explicitly that "It seems to be most conducive unto Edification and Reformation, that in Renewing Covenants, such things as are clear and indisputable to be expressed, that so all the Churches may agree in Covenanting to promote the interest of holiness and close walking with God."

    On the background to the Reforming Synod of 1679, see W. Walker, 1960:410–22. On the later, eighteenth-century relation between the English church and New England, see Carl Bridenbaugh, *Mitre and Sceptre: Transatlantic Faiths, Ideas, Personalities and Politics 1689–1775* (New York: Oxford University Press, 1962).
67. Lucas, *Valley of Discord*, 126, 242, 244.
68. Paul Boyer and Stephen Nussenbaum, *Salem Possessed: The Social Origins of Witchcraft* (Cambridge: Harvard University Press, 1974), 215. Further perspectives on the Salem witch-trials are explored by John Demos, *Entertaining Satan* (Oxford: Oxford University Press, 1982) and Robert Weisman *Withcraft, Magic and Religion in Seventeenth Century New England* (Amherst: University of Massachussets Press, 1984). Important contemporary accounts are those of Cotton Mather, *The Wonders of the Invisible World* (London, 1862) and his father, Increase Mather, *A Farther Account of the Tryals of the New England Witches* (London, 1862).
69. P. Boyer and S. Nussenbaum, *Salem Possessed*, 215.
70. In this context it would be useful to recall H. M. Llynd's insight that "guilt may be a form of communication" (1958:66). As she reminds us, "condemnation or punishment is itself a form of communication, relation to one's fellows. It fits in; it gives a code to cling to even if one has violated it." With the increasingly attenuated nature of the ties between collective members and the breakdown of the more homogenous communities of earlier decades, guilt, arising from the transgression of internalized boundaries may easily have been a means of articulating ties between people.
71. Thomas Scheff, *Catharsis in Healing, Ritual and Drama* (Berkeley: University of California Press, 1979), 119.
72. Jonathan Edwards, "A Faithful Narrative of the Surprising Work of God" (London, 1743) in *Jonathan Edwards: Basic Writings*, ed. O. Winslow (New York, 1960), 100.
73. Ibid., 101.
74. Ibid.

75. For these developments as they progressed from the *Proposals of 1705* to the *Saybrook Platform* and beyond, see Walker, *Creeds and Platforms,* 463–516.
76. Hall, *Faithful Shepherd,* 274.
77. Bushman, *Puritan to Yankee,* 151.
78. Walker, *Creeds and Platforms,* 516. See Lucas, *Valley of Discord,* 189–202 on the responses of the individual churches to the Saybrook Platform.
79. Quoted in Zakai, *Exile and Kingdom,* (1982), 280.
80. See Hall, *Faithful Shepherd,* 269, 274. For a study of one such minister who found his way to Anglicanism, see Joseph Ellis, *The New England Mind in Transition: Samuel Johnson of Connecticut 1696–1772* (New Haven, CT: Yale University Press, 1973).
81. Allan Ludwig, *Graven Images: New England Stone Carving and its Symbols 1650–1815* (Middletown, CT: Wesleyan University Press, 1966), 107.
82. Further perspectives on early tombstones and their carving can be found in Edwin Dethlfsen and James Deetz, "Death's Heads, Cherubs and Willow Trees: Experimental Archeology in Colonial Cemeteries," *American Antiquity* 31 (1966): 502–10; and in David Stannard, *The Puritan Way of Death* (New York: Oxford University Press, 1977).
83. On ritualism as a response to social change and anomie, see Merton, *Social Theory,* 203–7.
84. On this theme, see Lovejoy, *Religious Enthusiasm,* 196.
85. Harry Stout, "Religion, Communication and the Ideological Origins of the American Revolution," *William and Mary Quarterly* 34 (1977): 526–27.
86. The doctrine of the importance of the "affections" in religion was most clearly worked out by Jonathan Edwards in his *A Treatise Concerning Religious Affections* (Boston, 1746).
87. See Gilbert Tennet, "Danger of an Unconverted Ministry" (Boston, 1740), in *The Great Awakening: Documents On the Revival of Religion 1740–1745,* ed. Richard Bushman (New York: Atheneum, 1970), 93.
88. Jonathan Edwards, *Church Marriage,* p. 26 quoted in Heimart, *Religion,* 162.
89. Lovejoy, *Religion Enthusiasm,* 183.
90. On different aspects of the response to Edwards, see Morgan, *The Gentle Puritan,* 20–41; Perry Miller, *Jonathan Edwards* (Amherst: University of Massachussets Press, 1981), 133–65; Lovejoy, *Religious Enthusiasm,* 190–94.
91. These were elaborated in such works as *Some Thoughts Concerning the Present Revival of Religion in New England* (1742), *A Treatise Concerning Religious Affections* (1746), *Freedom the the Will,* 1754. The most famous of Edwards's revival sermons was his "Sinners in the Hands of an Angry God," preached at Enfield Connecticut on 8 July 1741.
92. On the French Prophets, see Hillel Swartz, *The French Prophets* (Berkeley: University of California Press, 1980). On the convulsionaries of St. Medard, see Robert Kreiser, *Miracles, Convulsions and Ecclesiastical Politics in Early Eighteenth Century Paris* (Princeton: Princeton University Press, 1978).
93. See Lovejoy, *Religious Enthusiasm,* 188. Chauncey's tract was to be a model for polemics against enthusiasm in general for many years.
94. Ibid., 194–214.

196 Innerworldly Individualism

95. Stout, "Religion, and the Origins," 541.
96. See, for instance, Shaftesbury's ideas on "enthusiasm" as developed in his *Characteristicks of Men, Manners, Opinions, Times,* 3 vols. (London, 1737), especially the "Letter Concerning Enthusiasm" in volume 1 and the "Miscellaneous Reflections" in volume 3. Some of these themes are explored in Ernest Tuveson, *The Imagination as a Means of Grace* (Berkeley: University of California Press, 1960).
97. Ruth Bloch, *Visionary Republic—Millennial Themes in American Thought 1756–1899* (London: Cambridge University Press, 1985), 46.
98. Ibid., 63.
99. Robert Bellah, "Civil Religion in America," *Daedalus* (Winter 1967): 1–21.
100. Kenneth Silverman, *The Life and Times of Cotton Mather* (New York: Columbia University Press, 1985), 63.
101. Benjamin Franklin was, for Max Weber, the paradigmatic example of the new "bourgeois" man spawned by ascetic-Protestantism. See Weber, *The Protestant Ethic,* 50–54, 64–65, 124, 151, 180, 263.
102. The literature on this subject is of course immense. Much of the relevant primary material can be found in Bernard Bailyn, *Pamphlets of the American Revolution 1740–1776* (Cambridge: Belknap Press, 1965). See also his study *The Ideological Origins of the American Revolution* (Cambridge: Harvard University Press, 1967).
103. John Wise, *Vindication of the Government of New England Churches* (Boston, 1717).
104. Ibid., 32–47.
105. Carl Becker, *The Declaration of Independence* (New York: Vintage Press, 1958), 78.
106. John Adams, *Dissertation on Cannon and Feudal Law* (Boston, 1765), 126.
107. Lovejoy, *Religious Enthusiasm,* 227.
108. John Adams, *The Papers of John Adams,* vol. 2, edited by Robert Taylor (Cambridge: Belknap Press, 1977).
109. For some perspectives on post-seventeenth-century millennialism (or intimations of providential history) in America, see Christopher Beam, "Millennialism and American Nationalism," *Journal of Presbyterian History* 54 (1976): 182–99; Ira Brown, "Watchers for the Second Coming: The Millenniarian Tradition in America," *Mississipi Valley History Review* 39 (1952): 441–58; Rutherford DeLamage, "The American Idea of Progress," *Proceedings of the American Philosophical Society* 91 (1947): 307–14; Ira Mandelker, *Religion, Society and Utopia in Nineteenth Century America* (Amherst: University of Massachussets Press, 1984); William McLoughlin, "The American Revolution as a Religious Revival: The Millennium in One Country," *New England Quarterly* 40 (1967): 99–110; idem, *Revivals, Awakenings and Reforms* (Chicago: University of Chicago Press, 1978; James Moorhead, *American Apocalypse: Yankee Protestants and the Civil War 1860–1869* (New Haven, CT: Yale University Press, 1978); Reinhold Niebuhr, *The Kingdom of God in America* (New York: Harper and Row, 1937); Stow Persons, "The Cyclical Theory of History in Eighteenth Century America," *American Quarterly* 6 (1954): 147–63; David Smith, "Millennarian Scholarship

in America," *American Quarterly* 17 (1965): 535–39; Harry Strout, *The New Heaven and New Earth: Political Religion in America* (New York: Harper and Row, 1974); Timothy Weber, *Living in the Shadow of the Second Coming: American Premillennialism 1875–1925* (New York: Oxford University Press, 1979). Works by Ernest Tuveson and J. G. A. Pocock have already been referred to.

110. Adams, *Papers,* 230, 291–93, 311–12.
111. For a contextualization of the concept of "virtue" within the history of political thought, see J. G. A. Pocock, "Modes of Historical Time in Early Eighteenth Century England," in his *Virtue, Commerce and History* (Cambridge: Cambridge University Press, 1985), 37–50.
112. For the deep social implications of this privatization of what on a national level was called virtue, see Cotton Mather's works on the doing of "good," but especially in his *Bonifacius.* See also Silverman, *Cotton Mather,* 232–85.
113. Shils, *Center and Periphery,* 133.
114. Note that the title of Morgan's work combines the two Hebrew words *basar* and *ruach* ("flesh" and "spirit") in yet another example of the type of intertwining of nature and grace, of the world and the Church that we have been discussing throughout. Jonathan Edwards, *A History of the Work of Redemption* (Worchester, 1803).
115. Samuel Sewall, *Phaneomena quadem Apocalyptica* (Boston, 1697), 59.

7

Conclusion

This study has attempted to substantiate and trace the development of a particular social process: the emergence and institutionalization of a new charismatic locus of center construction and collectivity formation in one post-Reformation society—New England. The most fundamental and defining characteristic of this attempt was the construction of a polity based on the principles of grace and a new appreciation of the workings of grace within the processes of historical time. As intimated, if not fully developed, in chapter 1 it would appear that the origins of this development, if not its actual trajectory, were not unique to New England. Intimation of this-worldly grace and ultimate transcendence were at the heart of Christian civilization from its inception. Their institutionalization and symbolization in the rite of the Eucharist served, until the Reformation, as the charismatic focus of Western Christian civilization. The breakdown, or destructuring, of the sacraments and their ritual process, both symbolically and physically in the practices of certain Reformation societies, "freed," as it were, the charismatic dimension from its institutional embodiment in and by the Church. This was evident not only among Puritans in New England but among other Reformation communities in Holland, England, and Scotland, as well.

200 Innerworldly Individualism

This change in the overall framework of cultural assumptions or orientations of Western Christendom was, moreover, intimately linked to a changing conceptualization of the sacred in Reformation communities. This change, as we have seen, involved a redefinition of the terms of collective membership and the boundaries thereof. In a less Durkheimian fashion (and more explicitly Weberian one), this change can be viewed as a major restructuring of the soteriological premises of Western Christendom. By this I mean a move within post-Reformation Western civilization as a whole (but more pointedly within certain Reformation states and societies), from a relative dissociation of this-worldly and otherworldly modes of salvation, to a greater interweaving of this-worldly and otherworldly activities as relevant to salvation.[1] In combining Augustinian piety with the practical tasks of "world building," the Puritans of both old and New England present one of the most salient examples of this interweaving, where the "merger of the spiritual with the terrestrial" took the concrete form of constructing a "Holy Commonwealth."

In its own terms and given the exigencies of history and the fractured and imperfect reality of human existence, such an attempt was predestined to failure. Any attempt to posit a perfect social order, over and against the chaos and mutability of human existence is bound to fail. And yet, such attempts are the very stuff of our history, intimately connected to what Max Weber defined as those universal problems of meaning addressed by theodicies; that is, the promise of salvational religions to overcome the inherent finiteness of human existence, the problems posed by the discrepancy between fate and merit and the "perfection of the transcendent order" in contradistinction to the "imperfection of reality."[2] The attempt by Puritans in New and old England to impose the orders of grace into the workings of the world was precisely such a theodic vision of redemption. In England this vision expired with the failure of the Barebones Parliament; in New England it was transformed to become a major component of the modern worldview. This precisely is its interest to us. The idea of the individual as the moral foundation of the social order, of the political realm (not politics per se) as a soteriological arena, the transcendental status accorded to individual rights, the notion of collective identity, and membership based on the acceptance of a set of (abstract) principles (of justice) rather than on ascriptive criteria are, after all, the overarching principles (if not always the practice) of modern states and societies. As we have attempted to argue, the development of these ideas (as well as the particular saliency they have always held in the United States) cannot be understood without reference to seventeenth-century developments and the transformation of ascetic-Protestantism into the secular political creeds of the eighteenth century. In this sense and as noted in the Introduction, seventeenth-century New England Congregationalism has been taken as a "case study" of modernity, in some ways paradigmatic and in some ways illustrative of broader historical trends that took place in different societies at different times.

To be sure, the Reformation in general and Puritan practice in particular served to redraw the cognitive and affective maps of European societies in different ways. We have concentrated here on only one society and on only one aspect of this transformation, that is, its redefinition of the terms of collective membership through a restructuring of the soteriological premises of social existence. To understand this we have chosen to see the new this-worldly articulation of grace among New England Congregational Puritans as a major change and transformation of the charismatic dimension in Christian civilization. This change (and more especially) the subsequent internalization of grace as conscience proved a central aspect of eighteenth-century modernity as it emerged from the religious visions of the seventeenth century. Indeed, the extent that we are all innerworldly individuals is precisely the extent to which we have internalized the religious ethic of seventeenth-century Puritans.

As we have seen, however, statements on the order of generality such as "a redefinition of the terms of collective membership" or "a restructuring of the soteriological premises of existence" are not in themselves sufficient to explain the concrete and complex patterns of social ordering as it developed within seventeenth-century collectivities. Indeed, our study of New England emphasized how the very attempt to institutionalize the new "metahistorical" principles of social order led to their reformulation. It is therefore perhaps appropriate at this point both to review the historical developments we have traced above and, at the same time, place them in a broader framework of analysis, in order to better understand their role in the making of the modern world.

A Summary of Findings

We have concentrated throughout on the spheres of communal identity and membership and social authority as two of the institutional arenas where the new charismatic principles of social ordering were embodied, and have viewed how, over the course of one hundred years, the institutionalization of charisma involved a redefinition of both symbolic and organizational realms within both spheres of social life. As we have further seen, the concrete process of institutionalization was, to a large extent, structured by the activities of different groups of social elites in their attempts to either maintain or assert a hegemonic role as purveyors of cultural meaning and models of social ordering. In this context, we have concentrated on how the ministers, in their attempt first to institutionalize the charismatic premises of the settlement (in the period of the Cambridge Platform) and later to reassert their waning authority (in mid-century), led to a reformulation of the basis of their authority, of the definition of the social order and of the very terms of collective membership.

The social action of these elites was carried out, however, in a constant tension with other groups in society, with, as noted, other groups of religious elites (such as the followers of Anne Hutchinson, the Baptists, and the Quakers), as well as with a growing mercantile elite, articulating different values and collective desiderata. The concrete process of mutual impingement and contention between these different groups took place, as we have been at pains to stress, under the dual constraints of: the initial principles of social ordering, and the very attempt to translate these into institutionalized premises of a perduring normative order.

The particular working out of the latter dynamic—to which we have devoted the major part of this analysis—resulted in what we have termed the "preconditions" for the much-studied latter day growth of the American "civil religion."

Moreover, in analyzing the particular dynamic through which charisma was routinized in seventeenth-century New England, we noted the importance of a number of prime factors that can be summarized as follows:

1. *The break posited by the first generation of Puritan emigrants with the prevailing terms of collective membership and identity in England.* Sharing with their English coreligionists a rejection of the

traditional collective rites of communality, the New England Puritans exacerbated the Puritan break with local culture in their very move to the New World. With their move to the American Strand, they constructed new symbolic models and organization mechanisms for the constitution of a social order. These were based on the "original" or "purely" charismatic locus of their beliefs, linked, as these were, to the Puritan notion of grace. These beliefs formed the overarching framework of cultural meaning and social order in New England, and as such, they informed the concrete structuring of models of social authority and collective identity in the early years of settlement.

2. *The original set of cultural assumptions were founded on an immediately felt connection to the ultimate sources of cosmic order, that is, to the sacred locus of existence.* With the process of institutionalization, begun in the first years of settlement and defined explicitly through the Cambridge Platform, a contradiction developed between the concrete needs of social ordering and the authority (ministers and magistrates) held accountable to such needs and a definition of community that made all members "saints." This contradiction was expressed in the first three decades of settlement as the growing retraction of authority from its roots in a community defined by a shared participation in the experience of grace, a process that led to a questioning not only of the legitimation of authority, but of the very basis of collective existence.

3. *The growth through the Jeremiad sermons of a past referent to communal identity and collective membership.* This addition of what was, in a sense, a primordial element into the highly "ideological" terms of communal identity (membership in the community of covenanted saints) presented the foundation around which a new form of collective identity could crystallize. However, as is crucial to note, the infusion of this primordiality into the overall terms of cultural meaning was itself a highly ambivalent process. For it was done through a reemphasis of nonprimordial categories, that is, through a stress on the soteriological meaning of collective life. Thus, in contrast to Europe, where the primordial elements in the overall definitions of the collective were relatively dissociated from their transcendental locus, in America they were intimately intertwined. As we shall discuss in the following, it was the unique nature of this interrelation that contributed to the specificity of American culture and civilization. In New England, this interrelation took place in the core definition of the

collective. It was embodied in the nascent social center and articulated by the major religious and political elites of society, and not, as was often the case in European societies by marginal groups and elites, protesting the major orders and symbols of the center. This, together with the fact that such a crystallization of primordial and ideological symbols took place preceding political independence, were salient factors determining not only the nature of eighteenth-century social life, but of American nationalism and national identity as well.

4. *The organizational restructuring of external boundaries through the Half Way Covenant.* The breakdown of the original notions of communal membership progressed through a fundamental process of institutional restructuring. By admitting children of unregenerate members into the Church, the Half Way Covenant both guaranteed the continuity of the corporate idea and extended membership in the corporate group to include virtually all members of the society. In a sense, the Half Way Covenant was thus almost an exercise in self-deceit, an Indian rope trick, which maintained the ideal notion of the covenant as the basic terms of collective membership and authority, while denying its practical derivatives (which turned, after all, on the experience of regeneration). In addition to the Half Way Covenant, such practices as Stoddardism and Mather's revival societies were crucial mechanisms in the creation of new organizational frameworks of collective membership. In different ways, they both furthered the crystallization of a new sense of collective identity, which, going beyond the original "theocratic" ideal nevertheless maintained the previous connection of the terms of community to those of salvation.

5. *The interiorization of the terms of membership in the collective —through such mechanisms as the covenant renewals, revival "harvests," growing Pietism, and sacramentalism.* As studied above, the interiorization of the boundaries of the normative order was a crucial aspect of the routinization, dispersion, and symbolization of the charismatic dimension of social life, and as such, of a reintegration of community in terms taken, if transposed, from the first decades of settlement. That is to say, instead of residing solely in the covenanted Church of regenerate saints, the charismatic dimension of collective existence and group identity was broadened to allow all members of society access to it. Through this process, it was also redefined and asserted through the "intellectual" or rational venues of covenant owning, as well as through the more emotive aspects of such rites. Characteris-

tic of both, however, was a new stress on the individual locus of collective affirmation, as part of the changing definitions of the moral order.

Together, these diverse, if related, developments provided crucial organizational mechanisms and symbolic models for the incorporation of a charismatic element into New England and later American collective identity. For, while new collective boundaries were redefined and new modes of legitimacy developed, the particular intermingling of sacred and secular elements, which had characterized the first years of settlement (resting, as it did, on the original or purely charismatically defined group), was maintained.

The very success of the incorporation and institutionalization of charisma into the overall framework of cultural assumptions and value premises and its continual existence as a referent for collective identity raises, however, a number of questions of a comparative nature. For if, as we have argued, the idea of grace was a constitutive component of Western Christian civilization from its inception—the concrete expression of its charismatic locus—and if the Reformation marked a major restructuring of this element, freeing it from its embedment in the more otherworldly aspects of Church ritual, how, then, are we to explain the place of New England in these developments? Was New England, in fact, a unique case or just an example of a broader set of changes? What was the relation of its conception of grace to the wider premises of the Reformation? And how can the specificity of development in different historical collectivities be explained?

Charisma and the Wider Premises of the Reformation

Let us begin by reviewing the wider premises of the Reformation and especially of English Puritan socioreligious thought. As analyzed in chapter 1, Puritan social practice broke down existing solidarities between believers and posited in their stead a new mode of expressing mutual commitments, obligations, and ties, through the covenant contracted between believers to ensure the religiosity of each. This bond of the covenant served as a new basis of solidarity among those who undertook to live a godly life. It represented a new locus of individual and collective identity with its own borders and outer limits of membership. Together with this new bond of communality, Puritanism also projected new notions of authority in the Church. Those in positions of authority were seen to be "called" and so rooted in the community of believers, drawing their ultimate legitimacy from the selfsame covenant bond that united all communal members and not, as in the Roman Catholic church, from a sacramental office handed down from apostolic times.

The new bonds forged under ascetic-Protestantism were, in essence, a recasting of the bonds of "community" as a shared tradition into new bonds of "communality." These bonds of a new "communion," in Herman Schmalenbach's sense, were to be the basis of the new communities forged by Puritans within English society.[3] The social restructuring of the bonds of communality and of authority was, in essence, part of the restructuring effected by the Reformation in general, but specifically in ascetic-Protestantism of the relation between the Church and the world. Within medieval Catholic Europe, the only "life-calling" legitimized in sacred terms was that of the monastic orders. As noted by Weber and others, the importance of the Reformation lay precisely in its "endowment of secular life with a new order of religious life as a sphere of `Christian opportunity.'"[4] It was thus only with the Reformation that secular callings were given a religious legitimation and were perceived as possible paths to salvation.

This orientation toward a greater this-worldliness, toward the "justification" of the whole person and his everyday life in terms of salvation, was, of course, at the center of Weber's famous Protestant ethic thesis. Its implications, however, are broader (as Weber himself realized) than simply the rationalization of economic activity. For with the "demise of the older images of 'Religion' and world, Law and Grace" and with mundane life imbued with soteriological efficacy, the way was opened for rebuilding secular society in the selfsame image of perfection that had characterized monastic life.[5] As pointed out by Benjamin Nelson,

> a fundamental reorientation of the social and cultural patterns of the Western world could not occur until the medieval administration of self and spiritual direction fell before the onslaughts of Luther, Calvin and their followers. So long as a distinction was made between the special calling of monks who lived "outside the world," systematically observing a rule in their pursuit of the status of perfection and everyone else in the world, who lived irregularly, without benefit of a rule, in the midst of continued temptation; so long was there a brake on the incentive of ordinary men and women to forge integrated characters with a full sense of responsibility.

The Protestant notion of disciplined character nourished by a resolute conscience replaced the medieval sense of life as a round of sin and penance.[6]

This new sense of responsibility and moral authority was expressed in a pursuit of the status of perfection within the orders and institutions of the world.[7] Forming the basis of this pursuit was, as Nelson himself has indicated, the particular Protestant form of "illuminism," rooted in the immediacy of grace.[8] No longer mediated by the sacraments (and thus no longer contained within the institutions of the Church), grace became present in an immediacy, one of whose expressions was in the very this-worldly attempt to build the Kingdom of God on earth. This doctrine, a "key conception" of modernity as a civilizational form, was a logical derivative of the significance attached to this-worldly activity by ascetic Protestantism.[9] As such, it was one important element in the new moral order imposed on Europe by the impingement of Calvinist elites. This order, according to Benjamin Nelson,

> developed a new integration of life, both personal and political through the rearrangement of existing boundaries . . . older maps were redrawn, fixing new co-ordinates for all focal points of existence and faith: religion-world, sacred-profane, civil-ecclesiastical, liberty-law, public-private. . . . [In this rearrangement] New scope and authority were given to the Inner Light, sparked by the Holy Spirit. This was the Holy Spirit within each individual and within groups. This inspiration came to serve as the basis for vastly expanded involvement of new participants in a variety of different relations of self and world: charismatic activism, quietistic mysticism, covenanted corporate consensualism, natural rights individualism, a religion of Pure Reason.[10]

Of course, the concrete forms taken in different historical societies by this conception of Inner Light and the immediacy of grace differed greatly. The differences were related to, among other factors, the degree of institutionalization attained by groups carrying these religio-ethical orientations, and thus effected the paths taken by the different modalities of social action summarized by Benjamin Nelson.[11] In our own study, we have indeed concentrated on the relation of inner grace to charismatic activism, as well as to the redefinition of communal existence, stressing the continuities between the covenant and later political philosophy based on the doctrine of natural rights.

These perspectives bring us, then, to the next set of questions, of the comparative aspect of New England's development, a perspective for which we can at present posit only the first indications and possible paths for future research.

The Comparative Perspective

The intimate linkage between the Protestant conception of grace and the wider premises of the Reformation returns us then to the question of the place of New England Puritans within the wider framework of Reformation religion. And, indeed, from the perspective of the prevailing religious orientations of seventeenth-century Puritan thought, New England Puritanism was not altogether unique. What was unique, however, was its very success in the concrete process of center construction and collectivity building. For the New England Puritans combined their beliefs on the course of sacred history (and their own place therein) with the building of concrete institutional orders. Of these, we have concentrated on the construction of new frameworks and definitions of community and authority. While both were originally rooted in the purely charismatic locus of grace, and although the process of institutionalization severely affected and, to an extent, transformed the original definitions of these spheres of social life, they maintained their referents into the eighteenth century and beyond.

Of overwhelming importance in this continuity was, as we have seen, the specific combination of the doctrine of visible saints with other elements of collective identity, which only became relevant with the second and third generations. The elements, not only of generational continuity, but of attachment to local vistas, to a shared past, and thus to more "primordial givens," formed an important variable in the ability of seventeenth-century New Englanders to transcend the original terms of membership and definitions of community and to broaden their charismatic locus. As is made abundantly clear in the opening lines of Samuel Sewall's *Phaenomena quaedam Apocalyptica* (1691), these primordial givens were already, by the end of the century, central referents for collective identity:

> Not to begin to be; and so not to be limited by the concernments of Time and Place; is the Prerogative of God alone. But as it is the Priviledge

of Creatures, that God has given them a beginning; so to deny their actions or them, the respect they bear to Place and successive duration, is under a pretence of Promotion to take away their very Being.[12]

It was, indeed, this sense of a shared beginning, which enabled the construction of a civil identity, that could combine both Lockean notions of natural rights with a soteriological dimension to collective membership. In consequence, by the eighteenth century in New England the concept of "saints" stood not apart, but at one with that of the developing notions of citizen.

One illustrative example of this new identity was in the Great Awakening, which fused together secular notions of collective identity with religious intimations of divine grace. Indeed, the very centrality of these beliefs during the Great Awakening and, similarly, the extent and forceful impingement of the "New Lights" on society during the Awakening sets it off from similar developments in other countries. For example, England, too, in the 1740s, experienced a resurgence of a "politics of grace," among the "French Prophets."[13] Similarly, at the same time, in Paris, the "Convulsionaries of St. Medard" both decried the degeneration of the Church and looked forward to the "imminence of the Last Days."[14] Both European cases, however, were manifestly marginal and sectarian in nature. And although they carried with them political overtones, especially in the case of the Parisian convulsionaries of 1731, they were far from being forces of social restructuring on the scale of the Great Awakening. They arose and faded within a relatively circumscribed circle of devotees and were far from the mass phenomenon that characterized the infusion of grace during the Awakening in New England. Grace had receded from the increasingly rational, Deistic centers of European social and religious life, while in New England, it was wedded to the fundamental structures of collective existence.[15]

Another example of this interweaving of religious and secular dimensions can be felt in the reconstruction of natural law doctrines in eighteenth-century America and the related idea of the individual as constitutive of the political community. This fact was both noted and analyzed by Georg Jellinek (whose work served as an inspiration for Weber's own). Already in 1895, Jellinek compared the U.S. Bill of Rights (from different states), the French *Decleration Des Droits De L'Homme Et Du Citoyen,* and, more significantly, the English Bill of

Rights of 1689, Habeus Corpus Act of 1679, and the 1628 Petition of Right. His conclusions are worth quoting:

> The American bills of rights do not attempt merely to set forth certain principles for the state's organization, but they seek above all to draw the boundary line between state and individual. According to them the individual is not the possessor of rights through the state, but by his own nature he has inalienable and indefeasible rights. The English laws know nothing of this. They do not wish to recognize an eternal, natural right, but one inherited from their fathers, "the old, undoubted rights of the English people."[16]

In English law, there is, for Jellinek no autonomous grounding of individual rights in a set of natural principles but solely in tradition "the laws and statutes of this realm."[17] In attempting to explain how the "inherited rights and liberties, as well as the privileges of organization, which had been granted the colonists by the English kings" became transformed into "rights which spring not from man but from *God and Nature*" (emphasis mine), Jellinek had recourse to the defining traits of Congregational Puritanism that we studied above.[18] While, in analyzing the origins of natural right in New England in terms of religious doctrine, Jellinek emphasized freedom of conscience, we would stress the interweaving of this- and otherworldly realms, natural law doctrine with the idea of the community of saints (that is, of a polity built on grace) as essential background to this aspect of American rights.

The very success of the natural law doctrine—based on self-sufficient individuals endowed with reason—as the foundation of the American political community rested on the synthesis of these ideas with the tradition of the Holy Commonwealth of visible saints, that is, of the transcendent subject of Protestant belief. Not only (transcendental) reason, but (transcendent) grace (that illuminism of sectarian Protestantism noted by Nelson), now redefined in this-worldly terms of individual conscience, continued throughout the eighteenth century to define the terms of individual and social existence in the civil polity. It was, I would maintain, the very continuity of this particular religious heritage that made the positing of a political community of individuals, united by compacts, possible in eighteenth-century America. This, in essence was Jellinek's conclusion as well when he stated that:

> In the closest connection with the great religious political movement out of which the American democracy was born, there arose the conviction that there exists a right not conferred upon the citizen but inherent in man, that acts of conscience and expressions of religious conviction stand inviolable over against the state as the exercise of a higher right. This right so long suppressed is not "inheritance," is nothing handed down from their fathers, as the rights and liberties of Magna Charta and of the other English enactments,—*not the State but the Gospel proclaimed it.*[19] (emphasis mine)

As we can see, Jellinek realized the unique status accorded to "rights" in America. Not derived solely from positive law and not legitimized solely in terms of reason, individual rights had acquired a transcendent justification that is unique in the modern world. This unique status rested ultimately on that "sacralization" of the mundane political sphere (and a somewhat similar valorization of individual social action) that we have studied throughout and that developed as part of the institutionalization and transformation of ascetic-Puritanism over the course of the seventeenth century.

The very fact that salient elements of seventeenth-century Puritanism were incorporated in the traditions of eighteenth-century American thought (and social identity) raise, however, some interesting questions. For the doctrine of a virtuosi religion oriented toward the construction of a community of visible saints would seem—almost by definition—to preclude its institutionalization into a perduring and broader collective set of identities and commitments. What distinguishes a virtuosi religious ethic is, after all, its very particularism and the circumscribed nature of its membership. Indeed, and in at least one crucial aspect, this problem stands at the core of any understanding of Western Christendom, quite beyond the specificities of ascetic-Puritanism. For as was noted long ago by Ernst Troeltsch, there existed within the Christian tradition an abiding dualism between the dictates of an "absolute individualism" and an "absolute universalism."[20] The former, individualist ethic was based on man's "unconditional obedience to the Holy Will of God," while the universalist ethic was rooted in the "fellowship of love among those who are united in God."[21] This distinction has, of course, been a seminal one in the development of sociological thought. On the one hand, it led to the distinction between Church and sect within the sociological analysis of Christianity. On the other, it has led, particularly in the thought of Max Weber and later

212   Innerworldly Individualism

Talcott Parsons, to the study of the conflict between "universalism" and "particularism" as manifest in different civilizations and social settings.[22] Within the thought of the latter, it has indeed become part of a universal matrix for the ordering and categorizing of social formations and the type of solutions they pose to the fundamental problems of human existence.[23] And although this type of broad, comparative sociological inquiry is at present somewhat out of favor, it can, I believe, provide invaluable aid in conceptualizing and resolving our particular problem.

The aforementioned contradictions, between individualism and universalism, between sect and Church, and between particularism and universalism, are all rooted in the conflict within Christian civilization between the "particularism of grace" and the "community of love." This contradiction was not overcome but attenuated in the medieval Church through its sacramental theology. Through the sacraments administered by the priests, the Church effectively institutionalized a universalized grace. "An extension of the Incarnation," the sacraments were "a repetition of the spiritual process through which divine grace enters into human life."[24] The sacraments were the primary mechanism through which the contradictory injunctions of a particularized grace and community of love were united. As such, they were the primary means of the institutionalization of grace and the charismatic locus of the Church as an institution and of Christianity as a civilization. However, as succinctly put by Wolfgang Schluchter,

> The ingenious invention of medieval Catholicism, however, the church as an office-charismatic institution of grace, could not satisfy two demands: the demand of the religious virtuosi to establish an exclusive "community of saints" which visibly separates those religiously qualified from those who are not, and the individual's demand for a direct relationship to God. The first demand was opposed by the church's universalism of grace, the second by the priesthood's sacramentalism.[25]

Both demands were ultimately met only with the Reformation, whose "individualism attacked the core of the office-charismatic institution, its sacramental doctrines and practices."[26] In Louis Dumont's terms,

> Luther and Calvin attack in the first place the Catholic Church as an institution of salvation. In the name of the self-sufficiency of the indi-

vidual-in-relation-to-God they cancel the division of religious labour instituted by the Church. At the same time they accept, or rather Calvin most distinctly accepts the unification obtained by the Church on the political side.[27]

It was, however, only in ascetic-Protestantism, that is, in the Calvinist sects, that the rejection of the medieval synthesis achieved full fruition. For as pointed out by Weber and his followers, these sects "took over the exclusiveness of medieval monasteries," that is, the particularism of grace, "but rejected at the same time belief in the sacraments," those mechanisms that not only mediated between man and God, but also formed the core of the universalist doctrine. As summed up by Schluchter:

> There are two features which unite the various currents of ascetic Protestantism in spite of all differences in dogma and organization—the particularism of grace and the complete devaluation of sacramental grace, more generally of all external means of salvation. Absolute individualism with its subjectivism of grace takes the place of the absolute universalism of the medieval Catholic church with its objectivism of grace.... In ideal-typical terms, the Protestant sect is a particularist association of those religiously qualified members. Members are not born into it; they can be admitted only by virtue of personal religious achievement. It is a visible community of saints, whose domination over the faithful rests ultimately on the belief that it is immediate to God, and on the demand for every member's self-sacrifice and unswerving obedience to God's will. What the Donatists began in the controversy with Augustine's church, ascetic Protestantism carried to its conclusion in the conflict with the post-Gregorian church.[28]

All these, are of course, well-known perspectives within the tradition of Weberian sociology. What has, however, received less treatment within this tradition is the institutionalization of these soteriological premises within different societies. For the abiding question remains—how can a particularism of grace be institutionalized? If there is a Church framework, then it is no longer particular but universal. Every attempt at institutionalization is, by definition, an attenuation of the particularism of grace. As Weber said of the sect (to which he included Calvinism "by virtue of its aristocratic principle of predestination and degrading of office-charisma"),[29] the sect is a group whose very nature and purpose precludes universality and requires the free consensus of its members, since it aims at being an aristocratic group, an association of persons with full religious qualification. The sect does not want to be an institution dispensing grace, like a church, which includes the righteous and the unrighteous and is especially concerned with subjecting the sinner to Divine Law. The sect adheres to the ideal of the ecclesia pura (hence the name "Puritans") the visible community of saints.[30]

While the particular nature of the Church in Calvinism—not as a vehicle for grace but as a "cold divine raison d'etat," "a scourge and not a vehicle for salvation"—allows a solution to this contradiction in the realm of membership in a religious community, there would seem no possibility of institutionalizing these soteriological premises within the larger body of a territorial collective.[31] And yet, the case of New England points to the fact that at least some of these premises were institutionalized within the broader definitions of individual and collective life.

This incorporation and institutionalization in the late seventeenth century took place through identifying the particular community of grace with the whole of the populace. While the Congregational churches themselves became more sacerdotal and sacramental with the development of the Half Way Covenant and Stoddardism, the locus of the community of saints representing the particularism of grace moved from membership in the Church to membership in the community.[32] This "sleight of hand," if you will, was accomplished through two important mechanisms: the interjection of a sense of a shared past into the overall definitions of the sanctified collective; and that particular process of interiorization of boundaries that allowed the interweaving of a sense of shared "pastness" with the criteria of grace and sanctification. By interiorizing the boundaries between the profane and the sacred, this mechanism rooted the community of grace in a shared past. As Weber noted, in the sect of charismatic illuminati, the "community functions as a selection apparatus separating the qualified from the unqualified."[33] The transference of this mechanism from the community to the individual was thus crucial in widening the basis of the qualified, including primal and primordially related kith and kin. In this sense, the intense internalization of the concern with maintaining and demarking the boundaries of membership and inclusion can be seen, in the realm of collective identity and membership, as analogous to the workings of innerworldly asceticism in the realm of economic action, both bringing the individual into the fore as the source of action and moral agency.[34]

Now, to be sure, in some sense this development was not unique to New England but, rather, came to define an important aspect of social action in the modern world in general. For the "privatization of grace" as conscience, an idea inherent to early Christianity was developed throughout the seventeenth century, in the soteriological doctrines of different ascetic-Protestant sects. It continued in the devotional movements of the late seventeenth and early eighteenth centuries and in the privatization of grace beyond the boundaries of a community of saints. Indeed, a similar movement to that noted above in the North American context can be found in the "ethical inwardness" of the Cambridge Platonists. Their stress on moral activity as partaking of a "Universal Righteousness" and on the bifurcation of individual identity by a reasoned virtue (which is "natural") and the vice of excessive appetites marks a similar move toward the interiorization of Puritan beliefs, this time in English Protestantism of the Restoration period. Benjamin Whichcote's dictum that "Hell arises out of a Man's self: And Hell's Fewel is the Guilt of a Man's Conscience" and that Heaven "lies in a refin'd Temper, in an internal reconciliation to the Nature of God, and to the Rule of Righteousness. So that both Hell and Heaven have their foundation within Men" was a fundamental tenet among all the Cambridge Platonists.[35] It resonates with the selfsame interiorization of grace as conscience that we studied above in late seventeenth-century New England and points forward to the ideas of Shaftesbury (who in fact published Whichcote's sermons) and the moral basis of the civil society idea in the Scottish Enlightenment.[36] Ultimately these ideas that stressed the apprehension of God (as the source of our natural goodness) through reason led in the late eighteenth and nineteenth centuries to our more contemporary ideas of the individual as possessing metaphysical and moral value founded on the premise of universal reason.[37] As pointed out by Marcell Mauss,

> It is the Christians who have made a metaphysical entity of the "moral person" (personne morale), after they became aware of its religious power. Our own notion of the human person is still basically the Christian one.... From a simple masquerade to the mask, from a "role" (personnage) to a

"person" (personne), to a name, to an individual; from the latter to a being possessing metaphysical and moral value; from a moral consciousness to a sacred being; from the latter to a fundamental form of thought and action—the course is accomplished.[38]

While one could debate with Mauss just how "accomplished" this course of development is, even (or especially) at the end of the twentieth century, there is little doubt that events in New England both exemplified this development and, in their political derivatives, provided a model (for good or evil as the case may be) for other societies. For while New England may not represent the only society where the soteriological assumptions of ascetic-Protestantism were incorporated into discrete aspects of collective life, it does seem to be the only case where these assumptions provided the basic terms of collective membership and national identity in a nascent political order.

Thus, further comparison of eighteenth-century development in New England, England, and Scotland would show that the selfsame internalization of grace as conscience progressed very differently on either side of the Atlantic. For in New England it was wedded (in the decades of the Awakening) to an ideal of public virtue and civic activism, while in England and Scotland what emerged by the mid-eighteenth century was a valorization of a purely "private" virtue, devoid of public or civic components.[39]

In New England, as we have seen, the development of an internalized conscience, together with the emergent public phenomenon of religious revivals (covenant ownings, "harvests," and later, the Great Awakening itself) served to unite the personal and the political, the private and the public, in novel ways. In this respect and in terms of the developing forms of "modern" political culture (especially its models of collective identity) seventeenth-century New England can be seen to present a rather unique resolution of the tension between Church and sect in Christianity. We have seen that within Christianity, absolute individualism does not permit the founding of the "community of love." Yet the bonds of community are necessary for the constitution of any pervading social order. Traditionally, these bonds were provided in the universalism of the Church through its sacraments—the *ecclesia universalis*. With the growth in the Middle Ages of an autonomous secular realm of the state "in relation to the Church but within a Christian framework," these bonds were also provided by membership in a territorially defined collective (a development that led to the conflict between the two forms of universalism, membership in the *Sacerdotium* and in the *Imperium*).[40]

It was, of course, not until the French Revolution that the forms of political membership and identity effectively replaced religious identity as the broad basis for definition of collective life. The emergence of a modern national consciousness began, however, as noted by Hans Kohn, with the rise of the Tudors and reached its apotheosis in the years of the Puritan Revolution.[41] It is, moreover, with the emergence of this English national consciousness that we can begin to define the uniqueness of New England. For in England, it was the civic tradition of this nationalism, replete with its primordial elements that served as the basic terms of collective solidarity, communal membership, and social identity. To the extent that charismatic elements were part of this civic tradition, they were incorporated into the post-Reformation social center through, among other venues, the scientific idiom.[42] To the extent that they were not so incorporated, that is, to the extent that they represented a specific articulation of the problems of grace in Christian civilization, they were incorporated into the Anglican church in latitudinarian thought. That is to say, they were incorporated in much the same way as the this-worldly orientations of early Christianity were incorporated into the post-Augustinian church.

The course of historical development in New England was radically different. There, a charismatic idiom, rooted in the traditions of the Holy Commonwealth, of a polity based on grace, became part of a very particular collective (and later national) identity. In terms taken from the English context we can state that what was incorporated was the charisma of the Puritan saints and not that of the godly ruler. Although the process of incorporation was effected only through the transformation or attenuation of the enthusiastic (or antinomian) element (i.e., the genuinely charismatic experience), New England remains the only case where such a conception was united with the basic civil, as opposed to ecclesiastic, structures of identity and membership.[43] Again, central to this incorporation of charisma was the merger of grace with a sense of shared past, which was effected through the mechanism of interiorization of boundaries. With the boundaries of "sainthood" no longer maintained by the community, but by the individual's own conscience, the way was opened for a redefinition of the community in broader and more encompassing terms, a dynamic that, indeed, represents a unique resolution to the age-old Christian dialectic of the particularism of grace and the universalism of love.

The above statements are, of course, of a very tentative nature. They are in need of further substantiation and detailed historical research, both horizontally across different societies and vertically, within any one. They are, indeed, intended in the main to provide an analytic framework for just such comparative and historical work.

Thus, for example, comparison with South Africa, where a Calvinist community advancing images of ancient Israel *revividus* also set about building a new culture in a new land, would, one feels, provide a totally different perspective on the resolution of the conflict between the universalism and particularism of grace and the role of primordial criteria of identity within such a resolution.[44] In this context, two elements that would be of central importance in any comparison would be the different connection, in New England and South Africa respectively, between the concept of peoplehood and grace (i.e., of the relation of primordiality to grace) as well as the different types of behavior engendered by a "knowable God" as opposed to the *deus abscondidus* of European Calvinism. Sanctification in South Africa, as pointed out by Sheila Patterson, was not, as in New England, a goal to be achieved, but an already realized state.[45] The reduction of the soteriological tension implied by this conception would seem to be a critical variable in any Weberian informed sociological inquiry.

Similarly, detailed comparison with Calvin's Geneva, and the loss of Calvinism's hegemony there, would aid in understanding the accomplishment of the New England Puritans in incorporating Calvinistic premises beyond a localized framework.

From these few examples the rudiments of a new analytic frame for understanding the role of seventeenth-century religious orientations in the construction of modern collective and individual identities begins to emerge. The break of the Protestant Reformation with the Church as "institution of salvation" and especially the attempt of certain sects to realize the "Holy Community" founded on individual grace (a community of individuals-in-relation-to-God) carried with it a strong potential for the articulation of grace within the workings of history.

In some cases, such as in New England (and to a certain extent in England), a concerted attempt was made to construct a social order based on these assumptions. While a total realization of these soteriological assumptions within the orders of social life was, of course, doomed to failure, they were nevertheless, in different manners and to different extents, institutionalized within the social realm.

In this light, we can again see how the attempt to build a Holy Commonwealth can be treated as a very special articulation of that analytic instance within any social order that Max Weber termed *genuine* or *pure charisma*. The specific nature of this instance of charisma, characterized by the expectation of ultimate transcendence precluded its full or unmediated institutionalization. (And indeed, just as the earlier eschatological orientations of first-century Christendom were incorporated into the Church through their transformation, so the this-worldly articulation of grace by the radical Puritan sects was incorporated in a transformed manner into the major social centers that emerged following the Reformation.) The course of this institutionalization was moreover characterized, in different societies, by the very different modes of incorporation, by the different social, political, and religious realms on which they were brought to bear, by the different social groups and elites who carried these visions and by the manner of their integration into other, existing traditions.

The case of New England, studied here, presents only one example, albeit a most salient one, of the interweaving of earlier religious orientations with the newly emerging civil, secular, and ultimately national entities of the early modern period. The transformation in late seventeenth- and early eighteenth-century New England of the terms of collective identity, of the values and commitments of social actors, indeed transformed and attenuated, but did not negate the earlier premises of social life. The particular mechanisms through which this continuity of symbolic constructs was maintained provides additional insights into the continuity between the seventeenth-century worldview and eighteenth-century notions of social and political praxis. And although the comparative perspective has yet to be fully addressed, a number of general statements can be made, providing both a summary of this work as well as an agenda for future research. In somewhat schematic terms, and in light of the preceding analysis, it can be tentatively stated that:

1. the definition of charisma within Christendom turned on the different interpretations given to grace in different historical periods;
2. a major transformation took place in the organizational frameworks

through which grace was institutionalized following the Reformation;
3. central to the building of modern national as well as individual identities was this institutionalization of grace, which was, however, mediated by other more primordial modes of collective identity; and
4. the particularities of New England and later American national identity rested on the unique process of institutionalization there, relatively devoid of primordial referents.

Within this framework of analysis, the different solutions posited to the problem of institutionalizing charisma are seen as crucial to understanding the course of nation building in different societies. Finally, and perhaps no less speculatively, any attempt to chart the emergence of what Weber has termed the *charisma of reason,* that is, the concrete mechanisms through which there emerged an individual ethic of responsibility, would have to take into account the type of social mechanisms of internalization we have attempted to analyze here. For Weber saw in both ascetic Protestantism and deistic reason the roots of those natural and self-evident rights upon which the modern world order is based.[46] In his own words,

> the consistent sect gives rise to an inalienable personal right of the governed as against any power, whether political, hierocratic or patriarchal. Such freedom of conscience may be the oldest Right of Man—as Jellinek has argued convincingly; at any rate, it is the most basic Right of Man because it comprises all ethically conditioned action and guarantees freedom from compulsion, especially from the power of the State.... All these rights find their ultimate justification in the belief of the Enlightenment in the workings of individual reason, which, if unimpeded, would result in the at least relatively best of all worlds, by virtue of Divine providence and because the individual is best qualified to know his own interest. This charismatic glorification of "Reason" which found a characteristic expression in its apotheosis by Robespierre, is the last form that charisma has adopted in its fateful historical course.[47]

Concrete analysis of the emergence of this last form of charisma in all its historically ambivalent meanings will, I submit, ultimately have to rest on the type of perspective undertaken above, which isolated the making and remaking of both symbolic models and organizational mechanisms through which the social identity of individuals was articulated. (The move to a more "rational" or "willful" articulation of an individual's social identity in the ritual of covenant owning is but one example of this process.) Similarly, such a framework of analysis would aid in isolating the different modes of interweaving of Arminianism and enthusiastic elements in New England and other societies, not only within the sphere of religious beliefs, but in other spheres of social action as well. In New England, the particular interweaving of a "civic-synergism" of Arminian antecedents with an enthusiastic element tied to the indwelling of grace contributed to the specificities of its historical development.[48] As such, it contributed as well to the unique form taken in America by the duality of reason, both liberating and enslaving, opening the way to freedom and at the same time enclosing social action in an iron cage of rational formulas.

Paraphrasing Goethe, Weber has called ascetic-Protestantism a power "which seeks the good but ever creates evil."[49] While originally intended in the context of rationalized economic action, this potential, tied as it is to the very duality of reason, may indeed be evident in other realms of social action as well, specifically in the sphere of social identity, which we have been studying. The very characteristics of American nationalism and its unique merger of universalistic and particularistic premises may, in fact, be rooted in the particular course taken in America by the charisma of reason.

Notes

1. As studies such as those by John Phelan (1970) indicate, the colonization of the Southern American hemisphere, too, had, among such people as the Franciscans, strong providential meanings. Thus, even within the culture of the Counter-Reformation, a change was to be felt in the soteriological efficacy of this-worldly action.
2. Weber, "Religious Rejections of the World and Their Direction," in *From Max Weber*, 358–359; Schluchter, *The Rise of Western*, 44, 51.
3. Schmalenbach, "Category of Communion," 331–47.
4. Talcott Parsons, "Christianity and Modern Industrial Society," in *Sociological Theory, Values and Sociocultural Change*, ed. E. Tiryakian (New York: Harper and Row, 1967), 51.
5. Benjamin Nelson, *The Idea of Usury: From Tribal Brotherhood to Universal Otherhood* (Chicago: University of Chicago Press, 1969), 241. More recent perspectives on Weber's fundamental insight are followed in Miriam Eliav-Feldon, *Realistic Utopias: The Ideal Imaginary Societies of the Renaissance 1516–1630* (Oxford: Clarendon Press, 1982).
6. Benjamin Nelson, "Self Images and Systems of Spiritual Direction in the History of European Civilization," in *The Quest for Self Control: Classical Philosophies*

and Scientific Research, ed. S. Klausner (New York: The Free Press, 1965), 71.
7. The development of a sense of moral responsibility at this time was not restricted to Puritan or even Protestant societies. A similar development characterized the Jansenist religious elites in France. On these, see Bernard Groethuysen, *The Bourgeoise, Catholicism vs. Capitalism in Eighteenth Century France* (London: Cressent Press, 1968); Nigel Abercrombie, *The Origins of Janesnism in France* (Oxford: Oxford University Press, 1936); and in comparison to the Puritans of England, Robin Briggs, "The Catholic Puritans: Jansenists and Rigorists in France," in *Puritans and Revolutionaries, Essay in Seventeenth Century History Presented to Christopher Hill,* ed. D. Pennington and K. Thomas (Oxford: Clarendon Press, 1978), 333–57.
8. Nelson, *The Idea of Usury,* 237; Nelson, "Self Images," 72.
9. Parsons, "Christianity and Industrial Society," 52.
10. Benjamin Nelson, "Conscience and the Making of Early Modern Culture: The Protestant Ethic Beyond Max Weber," *Social Research* 36 (1969): 16–17.
11. See, for example, H. Trevor-Roper, *Religion, the Reformation,* 193–236.
12. Samuel Sewall, *Phaenomena quadem Apocalytica* (Boston, 1697), 1.
13. Hillel Swartz, *The French Prophets* (Berkeley: University of California Press, 1980).
14. Robert Kreiser, *Miracles, Convlusions and Ecclesiastical Politics in Early Eighteenth Century Paris* (Princeton: Princeton University Press, 1978), 248, 243–75.
15. On Deism, see G. Cragg, *From Puritanism to the Age of Reason* (Cambridge: Cambridge University Press, 1950), 136–56; idem, *The Church and the Age of Reason* (New York: Penguin, 1979), 157–67. For additional background, see also Ernst Cassirer, *The Philosophy of the Enlightenment* (Princeton: Princeton University Press, 1951), 160–82; J. H. Randall, *The Making of the Modern Mind* (Boston: Houghton Mifflin, 1926), 282–307; and G. Waring, *Deism and Natural Religion* (New York: F. Ungar, 1967). Further discussion of the relation of the Camisard prophets to English religious thought can be found in Donald Walker (1964:253–63) who also analyzes the changing religious sensibilities of the English Platonists (104–77). For a discussion of Ezra Stiles and his attitude toward Deism, see Edmund Morgan, *The Gentle Puritan: A Life of Ezra Stiles 1729–1795* (New York: Norton, 1962), 64–69, 394, 445.
16. Georg Jellinek, *The Declaration of the Rights of Man and of Citizens: A Contribution to Modern Constitutional History* (Westport, CT: Hyperion Press, 1979), 48.
17. Ibid., 53.
18. Ibid., 80.
19. Ibid., 74–75.
20. Troeltsch, *Social Teachings,* 55–58.
21. Ibid., 55, 56.
22. See, for example, Talcott Parsons, *On Institutions and Social Evolution* (Chicago: University of Chicago Press, 1982), 173–75. Further aspects of Parsons's analysis of Christianity appear in his, "Christianity and Modern Society," and *The Evolution of Societies* (Engelwood Cliffs, NJ: Prentice Hall, 1977), 116–20.
23. See Talcott Parsons, *Towards a General Theory of Social Action* (New York: Harper and Row, 1962), 77, 81–82, 90, 177.

24. Troeltsch, *Social Teachings,* 234.
25. Schluchter, *The Rise of Western,* 168.
26. Ibid., 169.
27. Louis Dumont, "A Modified View of Our Origins: The Christian Beginnings of Modern Individualism," *Religion* 12 (1982): 1–27.
28. Schluchter, *The Rise of Western,* 169.
29. Weber, *Economy and Society,* 1205.
30. Ibid., 1204.
31. Ibid., 1199.
32. It should be noted that Weber himself noted the "loss of the sect character" among Independents in New England through such compromises as the Half Way Covenant, which made of membership a birthright (1978:1208). Our claim here is that the character of this sect or elements of it were not so much lost as transferred from the realm of the Church to that of the civil polity.
33. Ibid., 1204.
34. In this development we actually see the realization in the world of one aspect of that internal value-oriented action that was once the province of monastic life.
35. Benjamin Whichcote, "The Uses of Reason in Matters of Religion," in *The Cambridge Platonists,* ed. C. A. Patrides (Cambridge: Cambridge University Press, 1969), 46, 42–61.
36. Adam B. Seligman, *The Idea of Civil Society* (New York: The Free Press, 1992).
37. Marcell Mauss, "A Category of the Human Mind: The Notion of Person, the Notion of Self," in *The Category of the Person,* ed. M. Carrithers, S. Collins, and S. Lukes (Cambridge: Cambridge University Press, 1985), 1–25 . More sociological aspects of this development have been explored in two recent works by Margaret Jacob, "Private Beliefs in Public Temples: The New Religiosity of the Eighteenth Century," *Social Research* 59 (1992): 59–84 and "The Enlightenment Redefined: The Formation of Modern Civil Society," *Social Research* 58 (1991): 475–95.
38. Mauss, "Notion of the Self," 19, 21, 22.
39. On this privatization of virtue, see John Dwyer, *Virtuous Discourse: Sensibility and Community in Late Eighteenth Century Scotland* (Edinburgh: John Donald, 1987), 95–117; Shelly Burtt, *Virtue Transformed: Political Argument in England 1688–1740* (Cambridge: Cambridge University Press, 1992).
40. Parsons, "Christianity and Modern Society," 50.
41. Hans Kohn, "The Genesis and Character of English Nationalism," *Journal of the History of Ideas* 1 (1940): 69–94; idem, *The Idea of Nationalism* (New York: Collier Books, 1944), 155–83.
42. This has been the subject of numerous studies by J. R. Jacob and M. C. Jacob. Those by the former include "The Ideological Origins of Robert Boyle's Natural Philosophy," *Journal of European Studies* 2 (1971): 1–21; "Robert Boyle and Subversive Religion in the Early Restoration," *Albion* 6 (1974): 275–93; "Boyle's Circle in the Protectorate: Revelation, Politics and the Millennium," *Journal of the History of Ideas* 38 (1977): 131–40. Those by M. C. Jacob include "Millenarianism and Science in the Late Seventeenth Century," *Journal of the History of Ideas* 37 (1976): 335–142; *The Newtonians and the English Revolution* (Ithaca, NY: Cornell

University Press, 1976); *The Radical Enlightenment* (London: George Allen and Unwin, 1981). For a more general perspective on Puritanism and science, see T. K. Rabb, "Puritanism and the Rise of Experimental Science in England," *Journal of World History* 17 (1962): 46–67, as well as Robert Merton's famous *Science, Technology and Society in Seventeenth Century England* (New York: Harper and Row, 1970) and Charles Webster's "The Great Instauration."

43. On American identity, see Robert Bellah, *The Broken Covenant* (New York: Seabury Press, 1975); idem, "Civil Religion in America," *Daedalus* 96 (1967): 1–21. On the postmillennialism of Jonathan Edwards, see C. Goen, "Jonathan Edwards: A New Departure in Eschatology," *Church History* 28 (1959): 25–40.

44. On Afrikaner Calvinism and its role in social development, see William de Klerk, *The Puritans in Afrika* (Harmondsworth: Penguin, 1983); A. Du Toit, "Puritans in Africa? Afrikaaner 'Calvinism' and Kuyperian Neo-Calvinism in Late Nineteenth Century South Africa," *Comparative Studies in Society and History* 27 (1985): 209–40; R. G. Stokes, "Afrikaner Calvinism and Economic Action: The Weberian Thesis in South Africa," *American Journal of Sociology* 81 (1975–76): 62–81.

45. Noted in R. G. Stokes, "Afrikaner Calvinism," 76.

46. On the charisma of reason, especially as carried and articulated by virtuosi or elites, see Gunther Roth, "Socio-historical Model and Development Theory: Charismatic Community, Charisma of Reason and the Counterculture," *American Sociological Review* 40 (1975): 148–57; idem, "Religion and Revolutionary Beliefs: Sociological and Historical Dimensions in Max Weber's Work," *Social Forces* 55 (1976–77): 252–72.

47. Weber, *Economy and Society,* 1209.

48. The *Oxford English Dictionary* defines "synergism" as: "The doctrine that the human will cooperates with Divine grace in the work of regeneration." My only slightly tongue-in-cheek use of the term "civic-synergism" is meant to convey the profoundly political or societal nature of the terms of redemption in eighteenth-century America.

49. Max Weber, *The Protestant Ethic and the Spirit of Capitalism* (New York: Charles Scribner, 1958), 172.

Bibliography

Like any other work in historical sociology, this book owes much to the legions of historians who have worked on and interpreted the period under study. This bibliography does not presume to offer a comprehensive list of works on seventeenth-century New England, but it does hope to offer a fairly complete listing of works dealing with the substantive issues studied above. In the main, the bibliography overlaps but does not coincide exactly with the notes. In a few areas, where the text or notes contain references to issues tangential to the main point being discussed the cited sources are not complete. In these cases, the bibliography provides a more complete listing of those important works that have informed the overall analysis.

Primary Sources

"A Platform of Church Discipline Gathered Out of the Word of God: And Agreed Upon by the Elders: And Messengers of the Churches Assembled in The Synod At Cambridge In New England" (Cambridge, 1649). In *The Creeds and Platforms of Congregationalism,* edited by Williston Walker. Boston: Pilgrim Press, 1960.

"A Confession of Faith Owned and Consented to by the Elders and Messengers of the Churches in the Colony of Connecticut in New England, Assembled by Delegation at Saybrook September, 1708" (Saybrook, 1708). In *The Creeds and Platforms of Congregationalism,* edited by Williston Walker. Boston: Pilgrim Press, 1960.

Proposition Concerning the Subject of Baptism and Consociation of Churches, Collected out of the Word of God, by a Synod of elders and Messengers of the Churches in Massachusets Colony in New England. Assembled at Boston, according to Appointment of the Honoured General Court, in the Year 1663. Cambridge, 1666.

Adams, John. *A Dissertation on the Canon and Feudal Law.* Boston, 1765.

———. *Novanglus* or *A History of the Dispute with America from its Origins in 1754 to the Present Time* (Boston, 1775). In *The Papers of John Adams*, edited by Robert Taylor.

Allin, John. *Defense of the Answer Made unto the Nine Questions on Positions Sent from New England.* London, 1648.

Augustine. *The Confessions of Saint Augustine.* Translated by Edmund Pusey. New York: Modern Library, 1949.

———. *The City of God.* Translated by Henry Bettenson. Harmondsworth: Penguin, 1972.

Bailyn, Bernard. *Pamphlets of the American Revolution 1740–1776.* Cambridge: Harvard University Press, 1965.

Bale, Thomas. *Image of Both Churches.* London, 1553.

Barnes, Thomas, ed. *The Book of General Lauues and Libertyes Concerning the Inhabitants of the Massachusetts* (Cambridge, 1648). San Marino: Huntington Library, 1975.

Bradford, William. *Of Plymouth Plantation.* New York, 1979.

Brightman, Thomas. *The Revelation Illustrated.* Leiden, 1616.

Bulkeley, Peter. *The Gospel Covenant.* London, 1646.

Burr, Aaron. *The Watchman's Answer.* New York, 1757.

Bushman, Richard, ed. *The Great Awakening: Documents on the Revival of Religion 1740–1745.* New York: Atheneum, 1970.

Calvin, John. *Institutes of the Christian Religion,* edited by John McNeill. Philadelphia, 1960.

Chauncey, Charles. *Anti-Synodalia Scripta Americana.* London, 1662.

———. *Enthusiasm Described and Cautioned Against.* Boston, 1742.

———. *Seasonable Thoughts on the State of Religion in New England.* Boston, 1743.

Cotton, John. *A Sermon Delivered at Salem in 1636.*

———. *A Copy of a Letter of Mr. Cotton of Boston in New England . . . With the Questions Propounded to Such as are Admitted to the Church Fellowship and Covenant It Selfe.* London, 1641.

———. *The Pouring Out of the Seven Vials.* London, 1642.

———. *The Keys to the Kingdom of Heaven.* London, 1644.

———. *The Way of the Congregational Churches Cleared.* London, 1648.

———. *An Exposition upon the Thirteenth Chapter of Revelation.* London, 1656.

Danforth, Samuel. *A Brief Recognition of New England's Errand into the Wilderness.* Boston, 1670.

Davenport, John. *A Discourse about Civill Government in a New Plantation whose Design is Religion.* Cambridge, 1663.

———. *A New Essay for the Investigation of the Truth.* Boston, 1663.

Davis, Thomas and Virginia, eds. *Edward Taylor-Church Records and Related Sermons.* Boston: Twayne, 1981.

Edwards, Jonathan. *Sinners in the Hands of an Angry God.* Boston, 1741.

———. *Some Thoughts Concerning the Present Revival of Religion in New England and the Way in Which it Ought to be Acknowledged and Promoted.* Boston, 1742.

———. *A Treatise Concerning Religious Affections.* Boston, 1746.

———. *An Humble Attempt to Promote Explicit Agreement and Visible Union of Gods People in Extraordinary Prayer for the Revival of Religion and the Advancement of Christs Kingdom on Earth.* Boston, 1747.

———. *A Careful and Strict Enquiry into the Modern Prevailing Notions of that Freedom of the Will Which is Supposed to be Essential to Moral Agency, Vertue and Vice.* Boston, 1764.

———. *Two Dissertations I: Concerning the End for Which God Created the World, II: The Nature of True Virtue.* Boston, 1765.

———. *A History of the Work of Redemption.* Worcester, 1803.

Eliot, John. *The Christian Commonwealth.* London, 1659.

Fitch, James. *An Holy Connection.* Cambridge, 1674.

Forbes, A., ed. *Winthrop Papers.* 5 vols. Boston: Massachusetts Historical Society, 1929–47.

Force, Peter, ed. *Tracts and Other Papers Relating Principally to the Origins, Settlement and Progress of the Colonies in North America.* 4 vols. Washington, D.C., 1830–40.

Foxe, John. *Acts and Monuments of These Latter and Perilous Days.* London, 1563

Gardiner, S. R., ed. *The Constitutional Documents of the Puritan Revolution 1625–1660.* Oxford: Clarendon Press, 1968.

Gorton, Samuel. *Simplicities Defence Against Seven-Headed Policy.* London, 1646.

Hall, David. *The Antinomian Controversy: A Documentary History.* Middletown, CT: Wesleyan University Press, 1968.

Heimart, Alan, and Perry Miller, eds. *The Great Awakening: Documents Illustrating the Crises and Its Consequences.* Indianapolis: University of Indiana Press, 1967.

Higginson, John. *The Cause of God and His People in New England.* Cambridge, 1663.

Hooker, Thomas. *A Survey of the Summe of Church Discipline.* London, 1648.

Hutchinson, Thomas. *A Collection of Papers Relative to the History of the Colony of Massachusetts Bay.* 2 vols. Boston, 1865.

———. *The History of the Colony and Province of Massachusetts Bay,* edited by L. S. Mayo. Boston, 1963.

Johnson, Edward. *Wonder-Working Providence of Sions Saviour in New England* (London, 1654), edited by J. F. Jameson. New York: Charles Scribner, 1952.

Jones, Phyllis and Nicholas, eds. *Salvation in New England-Selections from the Sermons of the First Preachers.* Austin: University of Texas Press, 1977.

Jonson, Ben. *Bartholomew Fair.* London, 1964.

Luther, Martin. *Collected Works of Martin Luther,* edited by H. E. Jacobs. Philadelphia, 1943.

Mather, Cotton. *Diary of Cotton Mather.* New York: Ungar Press, n.d.

———. *A Companion for Communicants.* Boston, 1690.

———. *Christianus per Ignem.* Boston, 1702.

———. *Bonafacius: An Essay upon the Good that is to be Devised and Designed by Those Who Desire . . . to do Good While They Live.* Boston, 1710.

———. *The Wonders of the Invisible World, Being an Account of the Tryals of Several Wiches Lately Executed in New England.* London, 1862.

———. *Magnalia Christi Americana.* New York: Russell and Russell (reproduction of the 1852 edition), 1967.

Mather, Increase. *The Mystery of Israel's Salvation.* Cambridge, 1669.

———. *The Day of Trouble is Near.* Cambridge, 1674.

———. *The First Principles of New England.* Cambridge, 1675.

———. *An Earnest Exhortation to the Children of New England.* Boston, 1711.

———. *A Farther Account of the Tryals of the New England Witches.* London, 1862.

Mede, Joseph. *The Key of Revelation Searched and Demonstrated Out of the Naturall and Proper Characters of the Vision.* London, 1643.

Miller, Perry, and Thomas Johnson, eds. *The Puritans, A Sourcebook of Their Writings.* New York: Harper and Row, 1963.

Mitchel, Jonathan. *Nehemia upon the Wall.* Cambridge, 1671.

Morgan, Joseph. *The History of the Kingdome of Basaruch* (Boston, 1715). Cambridge, 1946.

Norton, John. *The Heart of New England Rent.* Cambridge, 1659.

———. *Sion the Outcast Healed of Her Wounds.* Boston, 1664.

Oakes, Urian. *New England Pleaded With.* Cambridge, 1673.

Patrides, C. A., ed. *The Cambridge Platonists.* Cambridge: Cambridge University Press, 1969.

Peek, George, ed. *The Political Writings of John Adams.* New York, 1954.

Plumstead, William, ed. *The Wall and the Garden: Selected Massachusetts Election Sermons.* Minneapolis: University of Minnesota Press, 1958.

Rogers, Richard. *Seven Treatises . . . Called the Practice of Christianitie.* 2d ed. London, 1605.

Sewall, Samuel. *Phaenomena quadem Apocalyptica.* Boston, 1697.

———. *The Diary of Samuel Sewall 1674–1729*, edited by M. Halsey Thomas. New York: Farr, Strauss and Giroux, 1973.
Third Earl of Shaftesbury. *Characteristiks of Men, Manners, Opinions, Times in Three Volumes*. London, 1737.
Shepard, Thomas. *God's Plot-the Paradoxes of Puritan Piety, Being the Autobiography and Journal of Thomas Shepard*, edited by M. McGiffert. Amherst: University of Massachusetts Press, 1972.
Shepard, Thomas, and John Allin. *A Defence of an Answer*. London, 1648.
Stoddard, Solomon. *The Doctrine of Instituted Churches*. London, 1700.
Stoughton, William. *New England's True Interest*. Cambridge, 1670.
Taylor, Robert, ed. *The Papers of John Adams*. Cambridge: Belknap Press, 1977.
Taylor, Edward. *The Poems of Edward Taylor*, edited by D. E. Stanford. New Haven, CT: Yale University Press, 1960.
———. *Foundation Day Sermon*. Boston, 1679.
———. *Revised Foundation Day Sermon*. Boston, 1692–93.
Tennet, Gilbert. *The Dangers of an Unconverted Ministry*. Boston, 1742.
Torrey, Samuel. *Exhortation unto Reformation*. Cambridge, 1674.
———. *A Plea for the Life of a Dying Religion*. Boston, 1683.
———. *Man's Extremity, God's Opportunity*. Boston, 1695.
Wakeman, Samuel. *Sound Repentance*. Hartford, 1685.
Walker, Williston, ed. *The Creeds and Platforms of Congregationalism*. Boston: Pilgrim Press, 1960.
Ward, Nathanial. *The Simple Cobbler of Aggwam in America*. London, 1647.
Whichcote, Benjamin. "The Uses of Reason in Matters of Religion." In *The Cambridge Platonists*, edited by C. Patrides, 42–61.
Wigglesworth, Michael. "The Day of Doom" (Boston 1662). In *The Puritans: A Source Book of Their Writings*, ed. P. Miller and T. Johnson. New York: Harper and Row, 1963.
Winslow, Elizabeth, ed. *Jonathan Edwards: Basic Writings*. New York, 1966.
Winthrop, John. *A Short Story of the Rise, Reign and Ruine of the Antinomians, Familists and Libertines*. London, 1644.
———. *The History of New England from 1630 to 1649*. Edited by John Savage. Boston, 1853.
———. "A Reply to an Answer Made to a Declaration." In *Collection of Papers Relative to the History of the Colony of Massachusetts Bay*, compiled by Thomas Hutchinson, 100–101. Boston, 1865.
———. *General Observations for the Plantation of New England* (1629). Edited by A. Forbes. Boston, 1929.
Wise, John. *Vindication of the Government of New England Churches*. Boston, 1717.

Woodhouse, A. S. P., ed. *Puritanism and Liberty-Being the Army Debates (1647–9) from the Clarke Manuscripts with Supplementry Texts.* London: Oxford University Press, 1966.

Ziff, Lazer, ed. *John Cotton on the Churches of New England.* Cambridge: Harvard University Press, 1968.

Secondary Sources

Abercrombie, Nigel. *The Origins of Jansenism in France.* Oxford: Oxford University Press, 1934.

Almagor, Uri. "Charisma Fatigue in an East-African Generation Set." *American Ethnologist* 10 (1983): 635–49.

Bailyn, Bernard. *The New England Merchants in the Seventeenth Century.* Cambridge: Harvard University Press, 1955.

———. *The Ideological Origins of the American Revolution.* Cambridge: Harvard University Press, 1967.

Ball, Bryan. *A Great Expectation: Eschatological Thought in English Protestantism to 1660.* Leiden: E.J. Brill, 1975.

Baltzer, Klaus. *The Covenant Formulary.* Philadelphia: Fortress Press, 1971.

Battenhouse, Roy, ed. *A Companion to the Study of St. Augustine.* New York: Oxford University Press, 1955.

Battis, Emery. *Saints and Sectaries: Anne Hutchinson and the Antinomian Controversy in the Massachusetts Bay Colony.* Chapel Hill: University of North Carolina Press, 1963.

Beam, Chrisopher. "Millennialism and American Nationalism." *Journal of Presbyterian History* 54 (1976): 182–99.

Becker, Carl. *The Declaration of Independence.* New York: Vintage Press, 1958.

Bellah, Robert. "Religious Evolution." *American Sociological Review* 29 (1964): 358–74.

———. "Civil Religion in America." *Daedalus* 96 (1967): 1–21.

———. *The Broken Covenant.* New York: The Seabury Press, 1975.

Bendix, Reinhard. "Max Weber's Interpretation of Conduct and History." *American Journal of Sociology* 51 (1946–47): 511–26.

———. "Max Weber's Sociology Today." *International Social Science Journal* 17 (1965): 11–22.

———. "The Protestant Ethic Revisited." *Comparative Studies in Society and History* 9 (1966–67): 266–73.

Bercovitz, Sacvan. "Typology in Puritan New England: The Williams-Cotton Controversy Reassessed." *American Quarterly* 19 (1967): 166–91.

———. "The Historiography of Johnson's 'Wonder Working Providence.'" *Essex Institute Historical Collection* 104 (1968): 138–61.

———. *Typology and Early American Literature.* Amherst: University of Massachusetts Press, 1972.

———, ed. *The American Puritan Imagination: Essays in Reevaluation.* New York: Cambridge University Press, 1974.

———. *The Puritan Origins of the American Self.* New Haven, CT: Yale University Press, 1975.

———. *The American Jeremiad.* Madison: University of Wisconsin Press, 1978.

———. "New England's Errand Reapparaised." In *New Directions in American Intellectual History,* edited by John Hingham and Paul Conkin, 85–101. Baltimore: Johns Hopkins University Press, 1979.

Berger, Peter. "Charisma and Religious Innovation: The Social Location of Israelite Prophecy." *American Sociological Review* 28 (1963): 940–50.

Bieler, A. "Calvinism and Capitalism." *Reformed Presbyterian World* 19 (1959): 145–59.

Billias, George, ed. *Selected Essays: Law and Authority in Colonial America.* New York: Dover Publications, 1965.

Birnbaum, N. "The Zwinglian Reformation in Zurich." *Archive Sociologie Religion* 4 (1959): 15–30.

Bloch, Ruth. *Visionary Republic-Millennial Themes in American Thought 1756–1800.* London: Cambridge University Press, 1985.

Bossy, John. "The Mass As A Social Ritual." *Past and Present* 100 (1983): 29–61.

———. *Christianity in the West 1400–1700.* Oxford: Oxford University Press, 1985.

Bourdillon, M. F. C., and M. Fortes, eds. *Sacrifice.* New York: Academic Press, 1980.

Bowersock, George. "Architects of Competing Transcendental Visions in Late Antiquity." In *The Origin and Diversity of Axial Age Civilizations,* edited by S. N. Eisenstadt, 280–287. Albany: SUNY Press, 1986

Boyer, Paul, and Stephen Nissenbaum. *Salem Possessed: The Social Origins of Witchcraft.* Cambridge: Harvard University Press, 1974.

Bozeman, Theodore. *To Live Ancient Lives: The Primitivist Dimension in Puritan Thought.* Chapel Hill: University of North Carolina Press, 1988.

Brandon, S. G. F. *History, Time and Deity: A Historical and Comparative Study of the Conception of Time in Religious Thought and Practice.* Manchester, England: Manchester University Press, 1965.

Brauer, Jerold. "The Nature of English Puritanism: Three Interpretations." *Church History* 23 (1954): 99–108.

———. "Types of Puritan Piety." *William and Mary Quarterly* 56 (1987): 39–58.

Breen, T. H. *The Character of the Good Ruler: Puritan Political Ideals in New England 1630–1730.* New Haven: Yale University Press, 1970.

———. *Puritans and Adventurers Change and Persistence in Early America.* New York: Oxford University Press, 1980.

Breen, T. H., and S. Foster. "Moving to the New World: The Character of Early Massachussets Immigration." *William and Mary Quarterly* 30 (1973): 189–222.

Bridenbaugh, Carl. *Mitre and Sceptre: Transatlantic Faiths, Ideas, Personalities and Politics 1689–1775.* New York: Oxford Univesity Press, 1962.

Briggs, Robin. "The Catholic Puritans: Jansenists and Rigorists in France." In *Puritans and Revolutionaries, Essays in 17th c. History Presented to Christopher Hill,* edited by D. Pennington and K. Thomas, 333–57. Oxford: Clarendon Press, 1978.

Brown, Ira. "Watchers for the Second Coming: The Millenniarian Tradition in America." *Mississipi Valley Historical Review* 39 (1952): 441–58.

Brown, Katherine. "Freemanship in Puritan Massachusetts." *American Historical Review* 59 (1954): 865–83.

———. "Puritan Democracy in Dedham Massachusetts: Another Case Study." *William and Mary Quarterly* 24 (1967): 378–96.

Brown, Peter. "Approaches to the Religious Crises of the Third Century A.D." *English Historical Review* 83 (1968): 542–58.

———. "The Rise and Function of the Holy Man." *Journal of Roman Studies* 61 (1971): 80–101.

———. *The Making of Late Antiquity.* Cambridge: Harvard University Press, 1978.

Bultman, Rudolph. *Primitive Christianity.* Philadelphia: Fortress Press, 1980.

Bumsted, J. H. "A Well-Bounded Toleration; Church and State in The Plymouth Colony." *Journal of Church and State* 10 (1968): 265–79.

Burell, S. A. "The Covenant Idea as a Revolutionary Symbol: Scotland 1596–1635." *Church History* 27 (1958): 13–58.

Burg, Richard. "The Ideology of Richard Mather and Its Relationship to English Puritanism Prior to 1660." *Journal of Church of State* 9 (1967): 364–77.

Burns, Norman. *Christian Mortalism from Tyndale to Milton.* Cambridge: Harvard University Press, 1972.

Burrage, C. *The Church Covenant Idea: Its Origins and Development.* Philadelphia: American Baptist Publication Society, 1904.

Burridge, K. O. L. *New Heaven, New Earth: A Study of Millennial Activity.* Oxford: Basil Blackwell, 1969.

Burtt, Shelly. *Virtue Transformed: Political Argument in England 1688–1740.* Cambridge: Cambridge University Press, 1992.
Bush, Sargent. "Revising What We Have Done Amisse John Cotton and John Wheelwright." *William and Mary Quarterly* 45 (1988): 733–50.
Bushman, Richard. *From Puritan to Yankee: Character and the Social Order in Connecticut 1690–1765.* Cambridge: Harvard University Press, 1967.
Caillois, Roger. *Man and the Sacred.* New York: Free Press, 1959.
Calhoun, Arthur. *A Social History of the American Family from Colonial Times to the Present.* New York: Barnes and Noble, 1945.
Callahan, John. *Four Views of Time in Ancient Philosophy.* Cambridge: Harvard University Press, 1948.
Capp, Bernard. "The Millennium and Eschatology in England." *Past and Present* 57 (1972): 156–63.
———. *The Fifth Monarchy Men: A Study in 17th c. English Millenarianism.* London: Faber and Faber, 1972.
Carrithers, M., S. Collins, and S. Lukes, eds. *The Category of the Person.* Cambridge: Cambridge University Press, 1985.
Carroll, Peter. *Puritanism and the Wilderness.* New York: Columbia University Press, 1969.
Caspary, Gerard. *Politics and Exegesis: Origen and the Two Swords.* Berkeley: University of California Press, 1979.
Cassirer, Ernst. *The Philosophy of the Enlightenment.* Princeton: Princeton University Press, 1951.
Charles, R. H. *Eschatology-the Doctrine of a Future Life.* New York: Schoken Books, 1963.
Christianson, Paul. *Reformers and Babylon: English Apocalyptical Visions from the Reformation to the Eve of the Civil War.* Toronto: University of Toronto Press, 1978.
Chroust, Anton. "The Metaphysics of Time and History in Early Christian Thought." *New Scholasticum* 19 (1945): 322–52.
———. "The Meaning of Time in the Ancient World." *New Scholasticism* 21 (1947): 1–70.
Clark, Francis. *Eucharist Sacrifice and the Reformation.* London: Darton, Longmans and Todd, 1960.
Cochrane, Charles. *Christianity and Classical Culture.* New York: Oxford University Press, 1957.
Cohen, Charles. *God's Caress: The Psychology of Puritan Religious Experience.* Oxford: Oxford University Press, 1986.
Cohen, Erik. "Persistence and Change in the Israeli Kibbutz." In *Community as a Social Idea,* edited by E. Cohen and E. Kamenka, 123–46. London: E. Arnold, 1982.

Cohen, Norman. *The Pursuit of the Millennium.* New York: Oxford University Press, 1972.
Cohen, Ronald. "Church and State in Seventeenth Century Massachusetts." *Journal of Church and State* 12 (1970): 475–94.
Cole, C., and M. Moody, eds. *The Dissenting Tradition.* Athens: Ohio University Press, 1975.
Collinson, Patrick. *The Elizabethan Puritan Movement.* Berkeley: University of California Press, 1967.
———. "Towards a Broader Understanding of the Dissenting Tradition." In *The Dissenting Tradition,* edited by C. Cole and M. Moody, 3–38.
Cragg, Gerold. *From Puritanism to the Age of Reason.* Cambridge: Cambridge University Press, 1950.
———. *The Church and the Age of Reason, 1648–1789.* New York: Penguin, 1979.
Cullman, Oscar. *Christ and Time: The Primitive Christian Conception of Time and History.* London: S.C.M. Press, 1951.
———. *Early Christian Worship.* London: S.C.M. Press, 1953.
Cushman, Robert. "Greek and Christian Views of Time." *Journal of Religion* 33 (1953): 254–63.
Davidson, Edward. *Jonathan Edwards, the Narratrive of a Puritan Mind.* Boston: Houghton Mifflin Co., 1966.
Davis, J. C. *Utopia and the Ideal Society: A Study of English Utopian Writtings 1516–1700.* Cambridge: Cambridge University Press, 1983.
Davis, Natalie Z. "The Sacred and the Body Social in Sixteenth Century Lyon." *Past and Present* 90 (1981): 40–70.
Davison, J. W. *The Logic of Millennial Thought in 18th c. New England.* New Haven, CT: Yale University Press, 1977.
Dawes, Norman. "Titles as Symbols of Prestige in Seventeenth Century New England." *William and Mary Quarterly* 6 (1949): 69–84.
de Klerk, William. *The Puritans in Afrika.* Harmondsworth: Penguin, 1983.
DeLamage, Rutherford. "The American Idea of Progress." *Proceedings of the American Philosophical Society* 91 (1947): 307–14.
DeLoss, William. *The Fast and Thanksgiving Days of New England.* Boston: Houghton Mifflin Co, 1895.
Demos, John. *A Little Commonwealth.* Oxford: Oxford University Press, 1970.
———. *Entertaining Satan.* Oxford: Oxford University Press, 1982.
Dethlefsen, Edwin, and James Deetz. "Death's Heads, Cherubs and Williow Trees: Experimental Archaeology in Colonial Cemetaries." *American Antiquity* 31 (1966): 502–10.
Douglas, Mary. *Natural Symbols: Explorations in Cosmology.* New York: Random House, 1973.
———. *Purity and Danger.* London: Routledge and Kegan Paul, 1979.

Drjivers, H. J. D. "Early Christian Asceticism and Monasticism." Paper presented to the Confererece on Max Weber and the Analysis of Late Antiquity. Bad Homburg, 1982.

Dumont, Louis. "A Modified View of Our Origins: The Christian Beginnings of Modern Individualism." *Religion* 12 (1982): 1–27.

Dunn, Richard. *Puritans and Yankees: The Winthrop Dynasty of New England 1630–1717.* New York: Norton, 1962.

Durkheim, Emile. *The Elementary Forms of Religious Life.* London: George Allen and Unwin, 1968.

———. *Sociology and Philosophy.* New York: The Free Press, 1974.

Du Toit, Andre. "Puritans in Africa? Afrikanner `Calvinism' and Kuyperian Neo-Calvinism in Late Nineteenth Century South Africa." *Comparative Studies in Society and History* 27 (1985): 209–40.

Dwyer, John. *Virtuous Discourse: Sensibility and Community in Late Eighteenth Century Scotland.* Edinburgh: John Donald, 1987.

Eisenstadt, Shmuel Noah, ed. *Max Weber on Charisma and Institution Building.* Chicago: University of Chicago Press, 1968.

———, ed. *The Protestant Ethic and Modernization: A Comparative Perspective.* New York: Basic Books, 1968.

———. "The Axial Age the Emergence of Transcendental Visions and the Rise of the Clerics." *European Journal of Sociology* 23 (1982): 294–314.

———. "Comparative Liminality, Liminality and the Dynamics of Civilizations." *Religion* 15 (1985): 315–38.

———, ed. *The Origins and Diversity of Axial Age Civilizations.* Albany: S.U.N.Y. Press, 1986.

Eliau-Feldon, Miriam. *Realistic Utopias: The Ideal Imaginary Societies of the Renaissance 1516–1630.* Oxford: Clarendon Press, 1982.

Ellemers, J. E. "The Revolt of the Netherlands. The Part Played by Religion in the Process of Nation-Building." *Social Compass* 14 (1967): 93–103.

Elliot, Emory. *Power and Pulpit in Puritan New England.* Princeton: Princeton University Press, 1975.

Ellis, Joseph. *The New England Mind in Transition: Samuel Johnson of Connecticut, 1696–1772.* New Haven, CT: Yale University Press, 1973.

Emerson, Everett. "Calvin and Covenant Theology." *Church History* 25 (1956): 136–44.

Eranos Yearbook. *Man and Time: Papers from the Eranos Yearbook.* Princeton: Princeton University Press, 1973.

Erikson, Kai. *Wayward Puritans.* New York: John Wiley, 1966.

Fanfani, Amintore. *Catholicism, Protestantism and Capitalism.* London: Sheed and Ward, 1939.

Feeley, Hanik. *The Lord's Table: Eucharist and Passover in Early Christianity.* Philadelphia: University of Pennslyvania Press, 1981.

Fiering, Norman. "Will and Intellect in the New England Mind." *William and Mary Quarterly* 19 (1972): 515–58.

Firth, Katherine. *The Apocalyptic Tradition in Reformation Britain 1530–1645.* Oxford: Oxford University Press, 1979.

Flusser, David. *Jewish Sources in Early Christianity, Studies and Essays.* Tel Aviv: Siphriat Hapoalim (Hebrew), 1982.

Foster, Stephen. "New England and the Challenge of Heresy, 1630–1660: The Puritan Crises in Transatlantic Perspective." *William and Mary Quarterly* 38 (1981): 624–60.

Fulbrook, Mary. *Piety and Politics, Religion and Absolutism in England, Wurttenberg and Prussia.* Cambridge: Cambridge University Press, 1983.

Gardner, Alice. *History of Sacrament in Relation to Thought and Progress.* London: Williams and Norgate, 1921.

Garrett, Clark. *Respectable Folly-Millenarianism and the French Revolution in France and England.* Baltimore: Johns Hopkins University Press, 1975.

Gaustad, Edwin. *The Great Awakening in New England.* New York: Harper and Row, 1957.

George, C. H. "Protestantism and Capitalism in Pre-Revolutionary England." *Church History* 27 (1958): 351–71.

George, C. and K. *The Protestant Mind of the English Reformation 1570–1640.* Princeton: Princeton University Press, 1964.

———. "Puritanism as History and Historiography." *Past and Present* 41 (1968): 77–104.

Giddens, Anthony. *Capitalism and Modern Social Theory.* Cambridge: Cambridge University Press, 1971.

Gilpin, Clark. *The Millenarian Piety of Roger Williams.* Chicago: University of Chicago Press, 1979.

Gilsdorf, Aletha. "The Puritan Apocalypse; New England Eschatology in the Seventeenth Century." Ph.D. diss., Yale University, 1965.

Glassman, Ronald, and William Swatos, Jr., eds. *Charisma, History and Social Structure.* New York: Greenwood Press, 1986.

Goen, C. "Jonathan Edwards: A New Departure in Eschatology." *Church History* 28 (1959): 25–40.

Goodenough, Erwin. *The Theology of Justin Martyr.* Amsterdam: Philo Press, 1968.

Greenfeld, Liah. "Reflections on Two Charismas." *British Journal of Sociology* 36 (1985) 117–32.

Greven, Philip. *Four Generations: Population, Land and Family in Colonial Andover, Massachusetts.* Ithaca: Cornell University Press, 1970.

———. *The Protestant Temperament: Patterns of Child Rearing, Religious Experience and the Self in Early America.* New York: New American Library, 1979.

Groethuysen, Bernard. *The Bourgeoise, Catholicism vs. Capitalism in Eighteenth Century France.* London: Cressent Press, 1968.
Gura, Philip. "The Radical Ideology of Samuel Gorton." *William and Mary Quarterly* 36 (1979): 78–100.
———. "The Contagion of Corrupt Opinion in Puritan Massachusetts: The Case of William Pynchon." *William and Mary Quarterly* 39 (1982): 469–91.
———. *A Glimpse of Sion's Glory: Puritan Radicalism in New England 1620–1660.* Middletown, CT: Wesleyan University Press, 1984.
Hall, David. *The Faithful Shepherd: A History of the New England Ministry in the Seventeenth Century.* New York: Norton, 1972.
———. "On Common Ground: The Coherence of American Puritan Studies." *William and Mary Quarterly* 44 (1987): 193–229.
Haller, William. *Foxe's Book of Martyrs and the Elect Nation.* London: Jonathan Cape, 1963.
———. *The Rise of Puritanism.* Philadelphia: University of Pennsylvania Press, 1972.
Hambrick-Stowe, C. *The Practice of Piety: Puritan Devotional Disciplines in Seventeenth Century New England.* Chapel Hill: North Carolina University Press, 1982.
Harnack, Adolf. *History of Dogma.* 7 vols. New York: Dover Books, 1961.
Haroutunian, Joseph. *Piety vs. Moralism: The Passing of New England Theology.* Hamden: Archon Books, 1932.
Harrison, J. F. C. *The Second Coming-Popular Millenarianism 1780–1850.* New Brunswick, NJ: Rutgers University Press, 1979.
Haskins, George. *Law and Authority in Early Massachusetts.* Hamden, CT: Archon Books, 1960.
Hatch, Nathan. *The Sacred Cause of Liberty: Republican Thought and the Millennium in Revolutionary New England.* New Haven, CT: Yale University Press, 1977.
Haushees, Herman. "St. Augustine's Conception of Time." In *Aspects of Time,* edited by C. F. Patrides, 30–37. Manchester, England: Manchester University Press, 1976.
Heimart, Alan. "Puritanism, the Wilderness and the Frontier." *New England Quarterly* 26 (1953): 361–82.
———. *Religion and the American Mind.* Cambridge: Harvard University Press, 1966.
Hepworth, M., and B. Turner, eds. *Confession: Studies in Deviance and Religion.* London: Routledge and Kegan Paul, 1982.
Heyd, Michael. "The Reaction to Enthusiasm in the Seventeenth Century." *Journal of Modern History* 53 (1981): 258–80.

Heywood, Frederick. *John Zizka and the Hussite Revolution.* Princeton: Princeton University Press, 1956.

Hill, Christopher. *Puritanism and Revolution; Studies in Interpretation of the English Revolution of the Seventeenth Century.* London: Mercury Books, 1962.

———. *Anti-Christ in Seventeenth Century England.* London: Oxford University Press, 1971.

———. *The World Turned Upside Down: Radical Ideas During the English Revolution.* Harmondsworth: Penguin, 1975.

———. *Some Intellectual Consequences of Defeat.* London: Weidenfeld and Nicholson, 1980.

———. *The Experience of Defeat: Milton and Some Contemporaries.* Harmondsworth: Penguin, 1984.

Hill, Michael. *The Religious Order.* London: Heinemann Education Book, 1973.

Hingham, John, and Paul Conkin. *New Directions in American Intellectual History.* Baltimore: Johns Hopkins University Press, 1979.

Hoffmann, Ernst. "Platonism in Augustine's Philosophy of History." In *Philosophy and History, the Ernest Cassirer Festschrift,* edited by R. Klibansky and H. Paton, 173–90. New York: Harper and Row, 1963.

Holifield, E. Brooks. "The Renaissance of Sacramental Piety in Colonial New England." *William and Mary Quarterly* 29 (1972): 33–48.

———. *The Covenant Sealed: The Development of Puritan Sacramental Theology in Old and New England 1570–1720.* New Haven, CT: Yale University Press, 1974.

Holmes, Thomas. *Cotton Mather: A Bibliography of His Works.* 3 vols. Newton: Crofton, 1974.

Hopfl, Harvo. *The Christian Polity of John Calvin.* Cambridge: Cambridge University Press, 1982.

Hubert, Henri, and Marcel Mauss. *Sacrifice: Its Nature and Function.* Chicago: University of Chicago Press, 1964.

Hunt, William. *The Puritan Moment: The Coming of Revolution in an English County.* Cambridge: Harvard University Press, 1985.

Isichei, Elizabeth. "From Sect to Church among English Quakers." *British Journal of Sociology* 15 (1964): 207–21.

Jacob, J. R. "The Ideological Origins of Robert Boyle's Natural Philosophy." *Journal of European Studies* 2 (1971): 1–21.

———. "Robert Boyle and Subversive Religion in the Early Restoration." *Albion* 6 (1974): 275–93.

———. "Boyle's Circle in the Protectorate: Revelation, Politics and the Millennium." *Journal of the History of Ideas* 38 (1977): 131–40.

Bibliography 239

Jacob, M. C. "Millenarianism and Science in the Late 17th Century." *Journal of the History of Ideas* 37 (1976): 335–41.

———. *The Newtonians and the English Revolution 1689–1720.* Ithaca: Cornell University Press, 1976.

———. "The Enlightenment Redefined: The Formation of Modern Civil Society." *Social Research* 58 (1991): 475–95.

———. "Private Beliefs in Public Temples: The New Religiosity of the Eighteenth Century." *Social Research* 59 (1992): 59–84.

Jaeger, Werner. *Early Christianity and Greek Paideia.* Cambridge: Harvard University Press, 1961.

James, William. *The Varieties of Religious Experience.* Glasgow: Fontanta, 1960.

Jaspers, Karl. *The Origin and Goal of History.* London: Routledge and Kegal Paul, 1952.

Jellinek, George. *The Declaration of the Rights of Man and of Citizens: A Contribution to Modern Constitutional History.* Westport, CT: Hyperion Press, 1979.

Johnson, Paul. *A Shopkeepers Millennium-Society and Revivals in Rochester New York.* New York: Hill and Wang, 1978.

Jones, James. *The Shattered Synthesis: New England Puritanism Before the Great Awakening.* New Haven, CT: Yale University Press, 1973.

Kaminsky, Howard. "Hussite Radicalism and the Origins of Tabor." *Medievalia et Humanistina* 10 (1956): 102–30.

———. "Chilianism and the Husseite Revolution." *Church History* 26 (1957): 43–71.

———. *The History of the Hussite Revolution.* Berkeley: University of California Press, 1967.

Kammen, Michael. *A Season of Youth. The American Revolution and the Historical Imagination.* New York: Oxford University Press, 1978.

Kapferer, Bruce, ed. *Transaction and Meaning: Directions in the Anthropology of Exchange and Symbolic Behavior.* Philadelphia: Institute for the Study of Human Issues, 1976.

Keller, Karl. "The Example of Edward Taylor." In *The American Puritan Imagination,* edited by S. Bercovitz, 121–38.

Kelley, Donald. *The Beginnings of Ideology.* London: Cambridge University Press, 1981.

Klausner, Yoseph. *The Messianic Idea in Israel.* Tel Aviv: Massada Press (Hebrew), 1950.

Klibansky, R., and M. Paton, eds. *Philosophy and History.* New York: Harper and Row, 1963.

Knappen, M. *Tudor Puritanism: A Chapter in the History of Idealism.* Chicago: Chicago University Press, 1939.

Knox, Ronald. *Enthusiasm: A Chapter in the History of Ideas.* Oxford: Oxford University Press, 1950.

Koenigsberger, H. G. "The Organization of Revolutionary Parties in France and the Netherlands." *Journal of Medieval History* 27 (1955): 224–52.

Kohn, Hans. "The Genesis and Character of English Nationalism." *Journal of the History of Ideas* 1 (1940): 69–94.

———. *The Idea of Nationalism.* New York: Collier Books, 1944.

Kolve, V. A. *The Play Called Corpus Christi.* Stanford: Stanford University Press, 1966.

Krieser, Robert. *Miracles, Convulsions and Ecclesiastical Politics in Early Eighteenth Century Paris.* Princeton: Princeton University Press, 1978.

Jung, Carl. *The Archetypes and the Collective Unconscious.* London: Routledge and Kegal Paul, 1969.

Lambert, Frank. "The Great Awakening as Artifact: George Whitefield and the Construction of Inter Colonial revival 1739–1745." *Church History* 60 (1991): 223–46.

Lambert, Malcolm. *Medieval Heresy: Popular Movements from Bogomil to Hus.* London: E. Arnold. 1977.

Lamont, William. "Puritanism History and Historiography: Some Further Thoughts." *Past and Present* 44 (1969): 133–46.

———. *Godly Rule: Politics and Religion 1600–1660.* London: MacMillan, 1969.

———. *Richard Baxter and the Millennium: Protestant Imperialism and the English Revolution.* London: Helm Books, 1979.

Lang, Amy. "Antinomianism and the Americanization of Doctrine." *New England Quarterly* 54 (1981): 225–42.

Laslett, Peter. *The World We Have Lost: England Before the Industrial Age.* London: Methuen and Co., 1965.

Leach, Edmund. "Two Essays Concerning the Symbolic Representation of Time." In Edmund Leach, *Rethinking Anthropology*, 124–36. London: Athlone Press, 1961.

———. *Culture and Communication: The Logic by which Symbols are Connected.* Cambridge: Cambridge University Press, 1976.

———. "Melchisedech and the Emperor: Icons of Subversion and Orthodoxy." In *Structuralist Interpretations of Biblical Myth,* edited by E. Leach and D. A. Aycock, 67–88, Cambridge: Cambridge University Press, 1983.

Leff, Gordon. "In Search of the Millennium." *Past and Present* 13 (1958): 89–95.

———. "The Pursuit of Holiness in Late Medieval and Renaissance Religion." Papers from the University of Michigan Conference, 1974.

Lerner, Robert. *The Heresy of the Free Spirit in the Late Middle Ages.* Berkeley: University of California Press, 1972.

Leverenz, David. *The Language of Puritan Feeling, an Exploration in Literature, Psychology and Social History.* New Brunswick, NJ: Rutgers University Press, 1980.

Lietzmann, Hans. *Mass and the Lord's Supper: A Study in the History of Liturgy.* Leiden: E.J. Brill, 1979.

Lipset, Seymor. *The First New Nation.* London: Heineman, 1963.

Little, David. "Max Weber Revisited: The Protestant Ethic and the Puritan Experience of Order." *Harvard Theological Review* 59 (1966): 415–28.

———. *Religion, Order and Law: A Study in Pre-Revolutionary England.* Chicago: University of Chicago Press, 1984.

Liu, Tai. *Discord in Zion: The Puritan Divines and the Puritan Revolution.* The Hague: M. Nijihoff, 1973.

Lockridge, Kenneth. "The History of a Puritan Church 1636–1766." *New England Quarterly* 40 (1967): 399–424.

———. *A New England Town, the First Hundred Years.* New York: Norton, 1970.

Lockridge, K., and A. Kreider. "The Evolution of Massachusetts Town Government 1640–1740." William and Mary Quarterly 23 (1966): 549–74.

Logan, A. H. B., and A. J. M. Wedderburn, eds. *The New Testament and Gnosis: Essays in Honor of Robert Mc.L. Wilson.* Edinburgh: T. and T. Clark, 1983.

Lovejoy, David. *Religious Enthusiasm in the New World, Heresy to Revolution.* Cambridge: Harvard University Press, 1985.

Lowith, Karl. *Meaning and History.* Chicago: Chicago University Press, 1949.

Lucas, Paul. *Valley of Discord: Church and Society Along the Connecticut River 1636–1662.* Middletown, CT: Wesleyan University Press, 1968.

Ludwig, Allan. *Graven Images: New England Stone-Carving and Its Symbols 1650–1815.* Middletown, CT: Wesleyan University Press, 1966.

Lynd, Helen M. *On Shame and the Search for Identity.* New York: Harcourt, Brace and World, 1958.

McCarl, Mary. "Thomas Shepard's Record of Relations of Religious Experience 1648–1649." *William and Mary Quarterly* 48 (1991): 433–66.

MacClear, John. "Quakerism at the End of the Interregnum: A Chapter in the Domestication of Radical Puritanism." *Church History* 19 (1950): 240–70.

———. "The Heart of New England Rent: The Mystical Element in New England Puritanism." *Mississipi Valley Historical Review* 42 (1956): 621–52.

———. "The Republic and the Millennium." In *Religion in American History,* edited by J. Millder and J. Wilson, 181–99. Englewood Cliffs, NJ: Prentice Hall, 1978.

———. "Anne Hutchinson and the Mortalist Controversy." *New England Quarterly* 54 (1981): 74–103.

McGiffert, Michael. "American Puritan Studies in the 1960's." *William and Mary Quarterly* 27 (1970): 36–67.

McGinn, Bernard. *Visions of the End, Apocalyptic Traditions in the Middle Ages.* New York: Columbia University Press, 1979.

McLoughlin, William. "The American Revolution as a Religious Revival: The Millennium in One Country." *New England Quarterly* 40 (1967): 99–110.

———. *Revivals, Awakenings and Reforms.* Chicago: University of Chicago Press, 1978.

McNeill, John. "Natural Law and the Teachings of the Reformers." *Journal of Religion* 26 (1946): 168–82.

———. *The History and Character of Calvinism.* New York: Oxford University Press, 1954.

Macy, Gary. *The Theologies of the Eucharist in the Early Scholastic Period.* Oxford: Clarendon Press, 1984.

Mandelker, Ira. *Religion Society and Utopia in Nineteenth Century America.* Amherst: University of Massachusetts Press, 1984.

Mannheim, Karl. *Ideology and Utopia.* New York: Harcourt, Brace and Jonavitz, 1936.

Markus, Robert. *Saeculum: History and Society in the Theology of Saint Augustine.* Cambridge: Cambridge University Press, 1970.

Marshall, Gordon. *Presbyteries and Profits: Calvinism and the Development of Capitalism in Scotland 1560–1707.* Oxford: Clarendon Press, 1980.

Mascall, E. R. *Corpus Christi: The Church and the Eucharist.* London: Longmans, 1953.

Mauss, Marcel. "A Category of the Human Mind: The Notion of Person; The Notion of Self." In *The Category of the Person,* edited by M. Carrithers et al., 1–25.

Merton, Robert. *Social Theory and Social Structure.* New York: The Free Press, 1968.

———. *Science, Technology and Society in Seventeenth Century England.* New York: Harper and Row, 1970.

Mervyn, James. "Ritual Drama and Social Body in the Late Medieval English Town." *Past and Present* 98 (1983): 3–29.

Middlekauff, Robert. *The Mathers: Three Generations of Puritan Intellectuals.* London: Oxford University Press, 1971.

———. "Piety and Intellect in Puritan New England." *William and Mary Quarterly* 22 (1975): 457–70.

Milburn, R. L. P. *Early Christian Interpretations of History.* London: A. and C. Black, 1954.

Miller, Perry. "The Puritan Theory of Sacraments in Seventeenth Century New England." *The Catholic Historical Review* 22 (1937): 409–25.

———. "Preparation for Salvation in Seventeenth Century New England." *Journal of the History of Ideas* 4 (1943): 259–86.
———. *The New England Mind: From Colony to Province.* Cambridge: The Belknap Press, 1953.
———. *The New England Mind: The Seventeenth Century.* Cambridge: Belknap Press, 1953.
———. *Orthodoxy in Massachusetts.* Boston: Beacon Press, 1959.
———. *Errand into the Wilderness.* New York: Harper and Row, 1964.
———. *Jonathan Edwards.* Amherst: University of Massachusetts Press, 1981.
Minter, David. "The Puritan Jeremiad as a Literary Form." In *The American Puritan,* edited by S. Bercovitz, 45–55.
Moller, J. "The Beginnings of Puritan Covenant Theology." *The Journal of Ecclesiastical History* 14 (1963): 46–67.
Momigliano, Arnold. "The Pagan and Christian Historiography in the Fourth Century A.D." In Arnold Momigliano, *The Conflict between Paganism and Christianity in the Fourth Century.* Oxford: The Clarendon Press, 1963.
———. "Time in Ancient Historiography." *History and Theory* Beiheft 6 (1966): 1–23.
———. "Marcell Mauss and the Quest for the Person in Greek Biography and Autobiography." In *The Category of the Person,* edited by Carrithers et al., 83–92.
Mommsen, Theodor. "St. Augustine and the Christian Idea of Progress: The Background of The City of God." In Theodor Mommsen *Medieval and Renaissance Studies,* 265–89. Ithaca: Cornell University Press, 1959.
Moore, Sally F., and Barbara Myerhoff. *Symbol and Politics in Communal Ideology.* Ithaca: Cornell University Press, 1974.
———. *Secular Ritual.* Assen/Amsterdam: Van Gorcum, 1977.
Moorhead, James. *American Apocalypse: Yankee Protestants and the Civil War 1860–1869.* New Haven, CT: Yale University Press, 1978.
Moran, G., and M. Vinouskis. "Puritan Family and Religion." *William and Mary Quarterly* 39 (1982): 29–63.
Morgan, Edmund. *The Puritan Dilemma: The Story of John Winthrop.* Boston: Little, Brown and Co., 1958.
———. *The Gentle Puritan: A Life of Ezra Stiles 1729–1795.* New York: Norton, 1962.
———. *The Puritan Family, Religion and Domestic Relations in Seventeenth Century New England.* New York: Harper and Row, 1966.
———. *Roger Williams: The Church and the State.* New York: Harcourt, Brace and World, 1967.
———. *Visible Saints: The History of A Puritan Idea.* Ithaca: Cornell University Press, 1975.

Morrison, Samuel. *The Founding of Harvard College.* Cambridge: Harvard University Press, 1935.
Morton, A. L. *The World of the Ranters.* London: Lawrence and Wishart, 1970.
Mosse, George. "Puritanism and Reasons of State in Old and New England." *William and Mary Quarterly* 9 (1952): 67–80.
———. "Puritan Political Thought and the Case of Conscience." *Church History* 23 (1954): 109–25.
———. *The Holy Pretense: Christianity and Reasons of State from William Perkins to John Winthrop.* Oxford: Basil Blackwell, 1957.
Mullett, Michael. *Radical Religious Movements in Early Modern Europe.* London: George Allen and Unwin, 1980.
Nelson, Benjamin. "Self-Images and Systems of Spiritual Direction in the History of European Civilization." In *The Quest for Self-Control: Classical Philosophies and Scientific Research,* edited by S. Klausner, 49–103. New York: The Free Press, 1965.
———. *The Idea of Usury: From Tribal Brotherhood to Universal Otherhood.* Chicago: Chicago University Press, 1969.
———. "Conscience and the Making of Early Modern Culture: The Protestant Ethic beyond Max Weber." *Social Research* 36 (1969): 5–21.
New, J. F. H. *Anglican and Puritan: The Basis of Their Opposition 1558–1648.* Stanford: Stanford University Press, 1964.
Niebuhr, Reinhold. *The Kingdom of God in America.* New York: Harper and Row, 1937.
Nisbet, Robert. *Social Change and History.* New York: Oxford University Press, 1969.
Nuttal, Geoffrey. *The Holy Spirit in Puritan Faith and Experience.* Oxford: Basil Blackwell, 1946.
Obelholzer, Emil. *Delinquent Saints: Disciplinary Action in the Early Congregational Churches of Massachusetts.* New York: Columbia University Press, 1956.
O'Dea, Thomas. "Sociological Dilemmas: Five Paradoxes of Institutionalization." In *Sociological Theory, Values and Socio-cultural Change,* edited by E. Tiryakian, 71–91. New York: Harper and Row, 1963.
Otto, Rudolph. *The Idea of the Holy.* Oxford: Oxford University Press, 1950.
Ozment, Steven. *The Reformation in the Cities.* New Haven, CT: Yale University Press, 1975.
———. *The Age of Reform 1250–1550. An Intellectual and Religious History of Late Medieval and Reformation Europe.* New Haven, CT: Yale University Press, 1980.
Pagels, Elaine. *The Gnostic Gospels.* New York: Vintage Books, 1981.
Parsons, Talcott. *Towards a General Theory of Social Action.* New York: Harper and Row, 1962.

———. "Christianity and Modern Industrial Society." In *Sociological Theory,* edited by E. Tiryakian, 33–70.
———. *The Structure of Social Action.* New York: Free Press, 1968.
———. *The Evolution of Societies.* Engelwood Cliffs, NJ: Prentice Hall, 1977.
———. "Durkheim on Religion Revisited: Another Look at the Elementary Forms of Religious Life." In *Action Theory and the Human Condition,* edited by Talcott Parsons, 213–32. New York: Free Press, 1978.
———. *On Institutions and Social Evolution.* Chicago: Chicago University Press, 1982.
Patrides, C. F. *The Phoenix and the Ladder: The Rise and Decline of the Christian View of Time.* Berkeley: University of California Press, 1964.
———, ed. *Aspects of Time.* Manchester, England: Manchester University Press, 1976.
Pelikan, Jaroslav. *The Christian Tradition: A History of the Development of Doctrine.* 4 vols. Chicago: University of Chicago Press, 1971–84.
Pennington, Donald, and Keith Thomas, eds. *Puritans and Revolutionaries, Essays in Seventeenth Century History Presented to Chritopher Hill.* Oxford: Clarendon Press, 1978.
Persons, Stow. "The Cyclical Theory of History in Eighteenth Century America." *American Quarterly* 6 (1954): 147–63.
Pettit, Norman. *The Heart Prepared: Grace and Conversion in Puritan Spiritual Life.* New Haven, CT: Yale University Press, 1966.
Phelan, John. *The Millennial Kingdom of the Franciscans in the New World.* Berkeley: University of California Press, 1970.
Piepe, A. "Charisma and the Sacred: A Re-evaluation." *Pacific Sociological Review* 14 (1971): 147–61.
Pocock, J. G. A. *The Machiavellian Moment.* Princeton: Princeton University Press, 1975.
———. "Modes of Political and Historical Time in Early Eighteenth Century England." In J. G. A. Pocock, *Virtue Commerce and History,* 98–117. Cambridge: Cambridge University Press, 1975.
Poggi, Gianfranco. *Calvinism and the Capitalist Spirit Max Weber's Protestant Ethic.* London: Macmillan Press, 1983.
Pope, Robert. *The Half-Way Covenant: Church Membership in Puritan New England.* Princeton: Princeton University Press, 1969.
Pope, W. "On the Divergence of Weber and Durkheim: A Critique of Parson's Convergence Thesis." *American Sociological Review* 40 (1975): 417–27.
Puech, Henri-Charles. "Gnosis and Time." In *Man and Time Papers from the Eranos Yearbook,* 38–84. Princeton: Bollingten Series, 1973.
Quispel, Gilles. "Time and History in Patristic Christianity." In *Man and Time Papers from the Eranos Yearbook,* 85–107. Princeton: Bollingten Series, 1973.

Rabb, T. K. "Puritanism and the Rise of Experimental Science in England." *Journal of World History* 17 (1962): 46–67.

Randall, John. *The Making of the Modern Mind.* Boston: Houghton Mifflin Co, 1926.

Reeves, Marjorie. *The Influence of Prophecy in the Late Middle Ages: A Study of Joachinism.* Oxford: The Clarendon Press, 1969.

Rosenmeier, Jesper. "With My Owne Eyes: William Bradford's of Plymouth Plantation." In *The American Puritan,* edited by S. Bercovitz, 77–104.

———. "New England's Perfection: The Image of Adam and the Image of Christ in the Antinomian Crise 1634–1635." *William and Mary Quarterly* 27 (1970): 435–59.

Rossiter, Clinton. "Thomas Hooker." *New England Quarterly* 25 (1952): 409–88.

Roth, Gunther. "Socio-historical Model and Developmental Theory. Charismatic Community, Charisma of Reason and the Counterculture." *American Sociological Review* 40 (1975): 148–57.

———. "Religion and Revolutionary Beliefs: Sociological and Historical Dimensions in Max Weber's Work." *Social Forces* 55 (1976–77): 257–72.

Rutman, Darrett. *Winthrop's Boston.* New York: Norton, 1965.

———. "The Mirror of Puritan Authority." In *Law and Authority,* edited by G. Billias, 149–67.

Rousseau, Philip. *Ascetics, Authority and the Church in the Age of Jerome and Cassio.* Oxford: Oxford University Press, 1978.

Scheff, Thomas. *Catharsis in Healing Ritual and Drama.* Berkeley: University of California Press, 1979.

Schluchter, Wolfgang. *The Rise of Western Rationalism, Max Weber's Developmental History.* Berkeley: University of California Press, 1985.

Schmalenbach, Herman. "The Sociological Category of Communion." In *Theories of Society,* vol. 1, edited by T. Parsons et al. New York: The Free Press, 1961.

Scholem, Gersom. *The Messianic Idea in Judaism.* New York: Schocken Books, 1971.

Scott, Donald. *From Office to Profession: The New England Ministry 1750–1850.* Philadelphia: University of Pennsylvania Press, 1970.

Seyfarth, C., and G. Schmidt, eds. *Max Weber Bibliographie: Eine Dokumentation der Sekundarliteratur.* Stuttgart: Enke, 1982.

Shils, Edward. "Charisma, Order and Status." In *Center and Periphery Essays in MacroSociology,* edited by Edward Shils, 256–75. Chicago: University of Chicago Press, 1975.

———, ed. *Center and Periphery: Essays in MacroSociology.* Chicago: University of Chicago Press, 1975.

———. *Tradition.* Chicago: University of Chicago Press, 1981.

Silverman, Kenneth. *The Life and Times of Cotton Mather.* New York: Columbia University Press, 1985.
Simmons, Richard. "Freemanship in Early Massachusetts: Some Suggestions and a Case Study." *William and Mary Quarterly* 19 (1961): 422–28.
———. "Godliness, Property and the Francise in Puritan Massachusetts: An Interpretation." *Journal of American History* 55 (1968): 495–511.
Skinner, Quinten. *The Foundations of Modern Political Thought.* Cambridge: Cambridge University Press, 1979.
Smith, Daniel. "The Study of the Family in Early America-Trends, Problems and Perspectives." *William and Mary Quarterly* 39 (1981): 3–28.
Smith, David. "Millenarian Scholarship in America." *American Quarterly* 17 (1965): 535–49.
Solt, Leo. "The Fifth Monarchy Men: Politics and the Millennium." *Church History* 30 (1961): 314–24.
Sommerville, J. C. "Conversion vs. the Early Puritan Covenant of Grace." *Journal of the Presbyterian Historical Society* 44 (1966): 178–89.
Spencer, M. E. "Weber on Legitimate Norms and Authority." *British Journal of Sociology* 21 (1970): 123–34.
———. "What is Charisma." *British Journal of Sociology* 24 (1973): 341–54.
Sprunger, Keith. "William Ames and the Settlement of Massachusetts Bay." *New England Quarterly* 39 (1966): 66–79.
Stannard, David. *The Puritan Way of Death.* New York: Oxford University Press, 1977.
Stein, Stephen. "A Notebook on the Apocalypse by Jonathan Edwards." *William and Mary Quarterly* 29 (1972): 623–34.
Stoever, William. *A Faire and Easie Way to Heaven: Covenant Theology and Antinomianism in Early Massachusetts.* Middletown, CT: Weslyan University Press, 1978.
Stokes, R. G. "Afrikaner Calvinism and Economic Action: The Weberian Thesis in South Africa." *American Journal of Sociology* 81 (1975–76): 62–81.
Stout, Harry. *The New Heaven and New Earth: Political Religion in America.* New York: Harper Row, 1974.
———. "Religion, Communication and the Ideological Origins of the American Revolution." *William and Mary Quarterly* 34 (1977): 519–41.
Swartz, Benjamin, ed. "Wisdom, Revelation and Doubt: Perspectives on the First Millennium B.C." *Daedelus* (Spring 1975).
Swartz, Hillel. "The End of the Beginning: Millenarian Studies." *Religious Studies Review* 2/3 (1976): 1–15.
———. *The French Prophets.* Berkeley: University of California Press, 1980.
Swanson, Guy. *Religion and Regime: A Sociological Account of the Reformation.* Ann Arbor: University of Michigan Press, 1967.

Swatos, William, Jr. "Charismatic Calvinism: Forging a Mission Link." In *Charisma, History and Social Structure,* edited by R. Glassman and W. Swatos, 73–82.
Sykes, S. W. "Sacrifice in the New Testament and Christian Theology." In *Sacrifice,* edited by M. F. C. Bourdillon and M. Fortes, 61–83.
Talmon, Yonnina. "Millenarian Movements." *European Journal of Sociology* 7 (1960): 159–200.
———. "Pursuit of the Millennium: The Relation between Religion and Social Change." *European Journal of Sociology* 3 (1962): 125–48.
Tellenbach, Gerd. *Church, State and Christian Society at the Time of the Investiture Contest.* Oxford: Basil Blackwell, 1962.
Tiryakian, Edward, ed. *Sociological Theory, Values and Sociocultural Change-Essays in Honor of Pitrim Sorokin.* New York: Harper and Row, 1963.
Tolmie, Michael. *The Triumph of the Saints: The Separate Churches of London 1616–1649.* Cambridge: Cambridge University Press, 1977.
Toon, Peter, ed. *Puritans, the Millennium and the Future of Israel.* Cambridge: J. Clarke, 1970.
Trevor-Roper, H. *Religion, the Reformation and Social Change.* London: Macmillan Press, 1967.
Troeltsch, Ernst. *The Social Teachings of the Christian Churches.* 2 vols. New York: Harper and Row, 1960.
Turner, C. H. "Apostolic Succession." In *Essays on the Early History of the Church and Ministry,* edited by H. Swete, 92–214. London: Macmillan, 1921.
Turner, Victor. *The Ritual Process.* Harmondsworth: Penguin, 1974.
———. *Dramas Fields and Metaphors.* Ithaca: Cornell University Press, 1974.
Tuveson, Ernest. *The Imagination as a Means of Grace, Locke and the Aesthetics of Romanticism.* Berkeley: University of California Press, 1960.
———. *Redeemer Nation: The Idea of America's Millennial Role.* Chicago: University of Chicago Press, 1968.
Van der Leeuw, G. "Primordial Time and Final Time." In *Man and Time Papers from the Eranos Yearbook,* 324–50. Princeton: Bollingen Series, 1973.
Van Gelder, Enno. *The Two Reformations of the Sixteenth Century.* The Hague: Nijhoff, 1961.
Van Gennep, Arnold. *The Rites of Passage.* Chicago: University of Chicago Press, 1960.
Vann, Richard. *The Social Development of English Quakerism 1655–1755.* Cambridge: Harvard University Press, 1969.
Voeglin, Eric. *Order and History.* 4 vols. Baton Rouge: Lousiana State University Press, 1976.

Wainwright, Geoffrey. *Eucharist and Eschatology.* New York: Oxford University Press, 1981.
Walker, Donald. *The Decline of Hell-Seventeenth Century Discussions of Eternal Torment.* London: Routledge and Kegan Paul, 1964.
Waltzer, Michael. "Puritanism as a Revolutionary Ideology." *History and Theory* 3 (1963): 59–90.
———. *The Revolution of the Saints.* Cambridge: Harvard University Press, 1965.
Waring, E. G., ed. *Deism and Natural Religion.* New York: F. Ungar Publishers, 1967.
Waters, John. "Family, Inheritance and Migration in Colonial New England: The Evidence From Guilford Connecticut." *William and Mary Quarterly* 39 (1982): 64–86.
Watts, Michael. *The Dissenters.* Oxford: Clarendon Press, 1972.
Weber, Max. "The Sociology of Charismatic Authority." In *From Max Weber,* edited by H. Gerth and C. W. Mills, 245–64. New York: Oxford University Press, 1946.
———. "The Social Psychology of World Religions." In *From Max Weber,* edited by Gerth and Mills, 267–301.
———. "Religious Rejections of the World and Their Directions." In *From Max Weber,* edited by Gerth and Mills, 323–62.
———. *Ancient Judaism.* New York: The Free Press, 1952.
———. *The Protestant Ethic and the Spirit of Capitalism.* New York: C. Scribner and Sons, 1958.
———. *Economy and Society.* Berkeley: University of California Press, 1978.
Weber, Timothy. *Living in the Shadow of the Second Coming: American Premillennialism, 1875–1925.* New York: Oxford University Press, 1979.
Webster, Charles. *The Great Instauration: Science, Medicine and Reform 1626–1660.* London: Duckworth, 1975.
Weisman, Richard. *Witchcraft, Magic and Religion in Seventeenth Century Massachusetts.* Amherst: University of Massachusetts Press, 1984.
Westerkamp, Marilyn. "Anne Hutchinson, Sectarian Mysticism and the Puritan Order." *Church History* 59 (1990): 482–96.
White, Lynn. "Christian Myth and Christian History." *Journal of the History of Ideas* 3 (1942): 145–58.
Williams, Ann, ed. *Prophecy and Millenarianism, Essays in Honor of Marjorie Reeves.* Harlow, Essex: Longman, 1980.
Williams, George. *The Radical Reformation.* Philadelphia: Westminster Press, 1962.
Wilson, R. *The Gnostic Problem: A Study of the Relation between Hellenistic Judaism and the Gnostic Heresy.* New York: AMS Press, 1979.

Winslow, Elizabeth. *Jonathan Edwards 1703–1758.* New York: Collier Books, 1961.

———. *Meetinghouse Hill 1630–1783.* New York: Norton, 1972.

Wolin, Sheldon. "Calvin and Reformation: The Political Education of Protestantism." *American Political Science Review* 51 (1957): 428–54.

———. *Politics and Vision.* Boston: Little Brown and Co., 1960.

Wood, Gordon. *The Creation of the American Republic.* New York: Norton, 1972.

Zakai, Avihu. "Exile and Kingdom: Reformation, Separation and the Millennial Quest in the Formation of Massachusetts and Its Relation with England 1628–1660." Ph.D. diss., Johns Hopkins University, 1982.

———. "The Gospel of Reformation: The Origins of the Great Puritan Migration." *Journal of Ecclesiastical History* 37 (1986): 584–600.

———. *Exile and Kingdom.* Cambridge: Cambridge University Press, 1992.

Zaret, David. *The Heavenly Contract, Ideology and Organization in Pre-Revolutionary Puritanism.* Chicago: University of Chicago Press, 1985.

Ziff, Lazer. "The Social Bond of the Church Covenant." *American Quarterly* 10 (1958): 455–62.

———. *The Career of John Cotton: Puritanism and the American Experience.* Princeton: Princeton University Press, 1962.

———. *Puritanism in America: New Culture in a New World.* New York: Vintage Books, 1973.

———. "The Literary Consequences of Puritanism." In *The American Puritan,* edited by S. Bercovitz, 34–44.

Zuckerman, Michael. "The Social Context of Democracy in Massachusetts." *William and Mary Quarterly* 25 (1968): 521–54.

———. "The Fabrication of Identity in Early America." *William and Mary Quarterly* 34 (1977): 183–214.

Index

A
Act of Toleration, 166, 188
Adams, John, 186
Allin, John, 106, 116–17, 133
American Strand, 32, 47, 53, 203
Ames, William, 179
Anabaptists, 50, 108, 167, 183
Animadversions upon the Antisynodalia Americana (Allin), 133
Answers of the Dissenting Ministers of the Synod, 133–34
Antinomian crisis, 73, 89–96, 121
    protest and contradictions in social order, 77–79
    symbolic and structural context, 86–89
    theological terms of, 79–86
Aquinas, Thomas, 19, 22
Arbella, 28, 64
Augustine, Saint, 15, 20–21
Axial civilizations, 11–14

B
Bale, John, 61
Baptism, 20, 171–72
    of unregenerate offspring, 128–32
Baptists, 79, 112, 166–67, 188
Barebones Parliament, 107, 200
Battis, Emory, 78
Bellah, Robert, 184
Bellamy, Joseph, 181
Bendix, Reinhard, 118
Berangar of Tours, 21
Bercovitz, Sacvan, 138–39
Bloch, Ruth, 184
Body of Liberties, 102
Bonificious (Mather), 184
Book of General Lawes and Liberties, The, 76, 102, 115

Book of Revelation, 15, 61–62
Bossy, John, 79
Boyer, Paul, 177
Brief Recognition of New England's Errand into the Wilderness (Danforth), 140, 149
Brightman, Thomas, 61–62
Bulkeley, Peter, 51, 80–81
Bushman, Richard, 154

C
Caillois, Roger, 169
Calvin, John, 24–27, 64
Calvinism, 24–27, 49, 213–14, 218
Cambridge Platform of Church Discipline, The, 76, 102, 105–6, 109, 111, 163, 179, 203
Cambridge Platonists, 215
Cartwright, Thomas, 29–30
Cause of God and His People in New England (Higginson), 139–40
Charisma, 1–9
    definition of, 4
    institutionalization of, 11, 159–90
    pure, 219
    of reason, 220–21
    routinization of, 119–20
    transformation in early Christianity, 14–18
Chauncy, Charles, 133, 150, 181
Child, Robert, 76
Christianity
    early, 11–18
    and the sacraments, 18–24
Church of England, 30, 54, 56–57
Church of the Visible Saints, 48, 51, 54, 89–90
City of God, The (Augustine), 15, 20–21
Civil magistrate, 115

251

252   Innerworldly Individualism

Communion, 106
Communitas, 95
Confessions (Augustine), 20–21
Constantine, 20
Convulsionaries of St. Medard, 209
Corpus Christi, 16, 21
Cotton, John, 53, 57–58, 62–63, 81–82, 86, 109
Covenanted communities, 63–64
Covenant of grace, 80–86, 117
Covenant of works, 80–86, 117
Covenant renewals, 172–76, 204
Cranmer, Thomas, 26
Cyril, Saint, 20

D
Danforth, Samuel, 140, 149–50
Danger of an Unconverted Ministry (Tennet), 182
Davenport, James, 181–82
Davenport, John, 57, 114, 133–35, 150, 172
Dell, William, 111
Discourse about Civil Government (Davenport), 114
Dissertation on Cannon and Feudal Law, A (Adams), 186
Doctrine of the Instituted Churches (Stoddard), 162, 172
Douglas, Mary, 75
Dumont, Louis, 212–13
Durkheim, Emile, 32, 168

E
Edwards, Jonathan, 164, 178, 182–83, 189
Eisenstadt, S.N., 4–5, 12, 34
Eliot, John, 104
Elliot, Emory, 110
English Civil War, 102, 107
English Protestants, 1–2, 27–28, 50, 58, 63, 215
   providential history, 60–63
Erikson, Kai, 78
Eucharist, 16, 20–24, 31–32, 199

F
Fifth Monarchy Men, 183
First Principles of New England, The (Mather), 133

Fitch, James, 150, 173
Forster, Stephen, 111
Fox, John, 61
Franklin, Benjamin, 184
Franklin, James, 185
French Prophets, 183, 209
French Revolution, 217

G
God's Controversy with New England (Wigglesworth), 145
Gorton, Samuel, 73, 112
Gospel Covenant, The (Bulkeley), 80–81
Grace, 14, 80–86, 117, 199, 207–9
Great Awakening, 162, 164, 177–84, 209
Greenfeld, Liah, 119, 168
Greven, Philip, 110
Grotonists, 121
Gura, Philip, 111

H
Half Way Covenant, 110, 121, 127, 150–54, 159–61, 171, 187, 204, 214
   and collective boundaries, 132–38
   historical background, 128–32
Hall, David, 53, 132
Harvest revivals, 162, 164, 178–84, 204
Higginson, John, 139–40, 150
History of New England (Winthrop), 87
History of the Kingdom of Basaruch (Morgan), 189
Holifield, E. Brooks, 159, 169
Holy Commonwealth, 27, 200, 210, 217
Hooker, Thomas, 61, 63, 102
Hopkins, Samuel, 181
Hutchinson, Anne, 73, 77–89, 91–96, 128

J
Jellinek, Georg, 209–11
Jeremiad sermons, 127, 138–54, 174, 188, 203–4
John of Patmos, 61
Johnson, Edward, 60–62, 64–66
Justification, 84

K
Kelley, Donald, 26
King Philip's Wars, 137, 146, 176
Kohn, Hans, 217

L

Laud, Archbishop William, 48
Lay ordination, 57–58, 105
Lay prophecy, 112–13
Lipset, Seymor Martin, 51
Lord's Supper, 161, 164, 169–72, 180
Lovejoy, David, 186
Lucas, Paul, 175
Ludwig, Allen, 180

M

MacClear, Fulton, 85
Magnalia Christi Americana (Mather), 88, 144, 148
Martin, Ambrose, 111
Massachusetts Bay Colony, 77, 86
Mather, Cotton, 88, 106, 127, 144, 148, 150, 162, 164–68, 184, 187–88, 204
Mather, Increase, 130, 133, 140–41, 143–44, 146–47, 150, 162
Mather, Richard, 57, 109
Mauss, Marcell, 215–16
Middle Ages, 216
Middlekauff, Robert, 165
Millenial movements, 15, 50, 60
Miller, Perry, 53, 87, 138–39, 161, 164, 173
Ministry
    contractual v. sacerdotal, 58–59
    loss of connection with congregations, 109–10
Mitchell, Jonathan, 130, 143, 150, 185
Montanists, 15
Moravians, 183
Morgan, Joseph, 189

N

Nakedness, 113
National virtue, 187
Native Americans, 86
Negro Conspiracy, 183
Nehemiah on the Wall (Mitchell), 185
Nelson, Benjamin, 206–7
New England, 1
New England Courrant (Franklin), 185
New England Puritans, 6–7, 11, 27–35, 201
    break with England, 202–3
    codification of rules of conduct, 102–7
    collective organization of, 59–67, 208–21
    eighteenth century changes in social order, 159–90
    foundations of authority, 56–59
    legitimation of authority, 110–13
    origins of settlement, 47–56
    structural changes in communal life, 107–10
    tensions among, 74–77
    terms of community, 117–21
    and the world, 113–17
New England's True Interest Not to Lie (Stoughton), 136
New England Way, 53, 56, 58–59, 78, 88, 116, 163
New Light, 183
New Model Army, 107
Norton, John, 58, 116, 150
Novanglus or a History of the Dispute with America (Adams), 186
Nussenbaum, Stephen, 177

O

Oakes, Urian, 139, 142, 144, 147

P

Paedobaptism, 112
Parsons, Talcott, 4, 118, 168, 212
Patterson, Sheila, 218
Paul, Saint, 16–17
Pequot War, 86
Perkins, William, 29
Phillips, George, 57
Phoenomena quoedam Apocalyptica (Sewall), 189–90, 208–9
Pocock, J.G.A., 21
Pope, Robert, 131–32, 173–74
Predestination, 181
Presbyterians, 103, 162–63, 179
Principles (Hooker), 102
Protestant ethic, 206
Providential history, 60–63
Puritans. *See* New England Puritans

Q

Quakers, 73, 79, 112–13, 121, 166–67, 183, 188
Quispel, Gilles, 22

R

Reformation, 1–2, 63, 199–201
  change in, 24–27
  New England Puritanism compared with other Reformation religions, 208–21
  wider premises of and charisma, 205–8
Reforming Synod of 1662, 121, 129–31, 133
Reforming Synod of 1679, 176
Reordination, 57
Revivals, 162, 164, 178–84, 204
Rogers, Richard, 32
Roman Catholic church, 206
Rosenmeier, Jesper, 86

S

Sacraments, 16, 18–24, 199
Salem witch trials, 177
Sanctification, 84–85
Saybrook Platform, 179
Schluchter, Wolfgang, 212–13
Schmalenbach, Herman, 108, 206
Scottish Enlightenment, 215
Sermon, 104. *See also* Jeremiad sermons
Sewall, Samuel, 167, 189–90, 208–9
Shepard, Thomas, 86, 88–89, 105–6, 116–17, 150
Shils, Edward, 4–5, 33, 119–20, 152, 168, 188
Short History of the Rise, Reign and Ruine of the Antinomians, A (Winthrop), 94
Sion the Outcast Healed of Her Wounds (Norton), 116
South Africa, 218
Stiles, Isaac, 181
Stoddard, Solomon, 127, 160–72
Stoddardism, 160, 170, 179, 187–88, 204, 214
Stoever, William, 82
Stone, Samuel, 115
Stoughton, William, 136, 139, 143, 148, 150
Stout, Harry, 181
Survey of the Summe of Church Discipline, 63

T

Taylor, Edward, 180
Tennet, Gilbert, 181–82
Tertullian, 90
Theocratic ideal, 64–67
Theodore, 20
Theodosius I, 20
Thomas, Keith, 54
Torrey, Samuel, 140–42, 145, 147
Transcendental, 189
Treatise of the Covenant of Grace (Cotton), 81–82
Troeltsch, Ernst, 24, 50, 211
Tryal of Spirits, The (Dell), 111
Tudors, 217
Turner, Victor, 95, 113

U

Underhill, Captain, 111

V

Van der Leeuw, G., 13
Vindication of the Churches of New England (Wise), 185
Vindication of the Government of New-England Churches (Wise), 185
Voeglin, Eric, 12

W

Wakeman, Samuel, 150
Walker, Williston, 179
Ward, Nathanial, 78, 111
Weber, Max, 3, 6, 9, 17, 32–34, 56, 119–20, 168, 206, 211, 213–14, 219–21
Weld, Thomas, 94
Wheelwright, John, 92–93
Whichcote, Benjamin, 215
Whitefield, George, 178
Whitehead, A.N., 118
Wigglesworth, Michael, 142–43, 145
Williams, John, 57
Williams, Roger, 86
Winthrop, John, 28, 64–66, 87, 94, 148, 185
Wise, John, 185
Wonder Working Providence of Sions Saviour in New England (Johnson), 61–62

Z

Zakai, Avihu, 32
Ziff, Lazer, 88